THE POWER TO PERSUADE

Strategic Arguing at the World Trade Organization

ANGELA GECK

The Power to Persuade

Strategic Arguing at the World Trade Organization

UNIVERSITY OF TORONTO PRESS
Toronto Buffalo London

© University of Toronto Press 2024
Toronto Buffalo London
utorontopress.com
Printed in the USA

ISBN 978-1-4875-4069-2 (cloth)   ISBN 978-1-4875-4071-5 (EPUB)
                                        ISBN 978-1-4875-4070-8 (PDF)

Library and Archives Canada Cataloguing in Publication

Title: The power to persuade: strategic arguing at the World Trade
    Organization / Angela Geck.
Names: Geck, Angela, author.
Description: Includes bibliographical references and index.
Identifiers: Canadiana (print) 20240281330 | Canadiana (ebook) 20240281527 |
    ISBN 9781487540692 (cloth) | ISBN 9781487540715 (EPUB) |
    ISBN 9781487540708 (PDF)
Subjects: LCSH: Persuasion (Rhetoric) – Case studies. | LCSH: World Trade
    Organization – Decision making – Case studies. | LCSH: Debates and
    debating – Case studies. | LCSH: Power (Social sciences) – Case studies. |
    LCSH: International trade – Political aspects – Case studies.
Classification: LCC P301.5.P47 G43 2024 | DDC 168–dc23

Cover design: Michel Vrana

We wish to acknowledge the land on which the University of Toronto Press
operates. This land is the traditional territory of the Wendat, the Anishnaabeg,
the Haudenosaunee, the Métis, and the Mississaugas of the Credit First Nation.

University of Toronto Press acknowledges the financial support of the
Government of Canada, the Canada Council for the Arts, and the Ontario Arts
Council, an agency of the Government of Ontario, for its publishing activities.

Canada Council   Conseil des Arts
for the Arts   du Canada

ONTARIO ARTS COUNCIL
CONSEIL DES ARTS DE L'ONTARIO
an Ontario government agency
un organisme du gouvernement de l'Ontario

Funded by the   Financé par le
Government   gouvernement
of Canada   du Canada

For my parents, who have always been there for me and kindly refrained from asking too often how the book was coming along.

Contents

Illustrations and Tables

Tables

Acknowledgments

I am deeply grateful to my superior of many years and mentor, Jürgen Rüland, who has provided me with very valuable advice, support, and encouragement throughout the whole process of writing this book. He gave me the freedom I needed to work on it in my own time and never lost his confidence in me. I have also greatly profited from the feedback of Ulrich Eith and Gregor Dobler and am much obliged to the State Graduate Funding of Baden-Württemberg, which provided me with a PhD scholarship, without which I would not have been able to embark on the journey of an academic career.

Another group of people this book would not have been possible without is my interviewees, diplomats working at various WTO missions in Geneva, who were so generous to take the time to talk to a young scholar and share their insights into the process of WTO negotiations with her. I am highly indebted to them. The WTO secretariat has been very helpful in providing information. I also greatly profited from informal exchanges with numerous trade experts from civil society as well as academia, whom I met at the WTO ministerial conferences 2009 and 2011 in Geneva, 2013 in Bali, and 2015 in Nairobi as well as the WTO Public Forums 2010, 2012, and 2015 in Geneva. Erin Hannah, James Scott, and Rorden Wilkinson, in particular, have always been very inspiring conversation partners as well as great company.

I received very valuable input on this project from colleagues at the University of Freiburg in Germany, both within the framework of the colloquium at the Chair of International Relations and in personal conversations. I am especially thankful to Anna Meine, who discussed Habermas' theory of communicative action with me. Beyond the circle of colleagues in Freiburg, I profited from stimulating academic exchanges with participants of the Conference of Young International Political Economy (IPE) Scholars 2013 in Heidelberg, the workshop

"Competition Between Conflict and Cooperation" 2013 in Freiburg, the Conference of the International Relations Section of the German Political Science Association (GPSA) 2014 in Magdeburg, the workshop "Norms, Ideas, Heuristics: Cognitive Approaches to World Trade Politics" 2015 in St. Gallen, and the International Studies Association (ISA) Annual Convention 2016 in Atlanta, where I presented papers on parts of the argument made in this book. In particular, I have enjoyed my recurrent conversations about trade politics with Clara Weinhardt, who organized the workshop in St. Gallen together with Klaus Dingwerth, another inspiring acquaintance. Much appreciated financial support for the trip to the ISA Annual Convention in Atlanta came from the Academic Society Freiburg.

At University of Toronto Press, I had the joy of working with Daniel Quinlan. His enthusiasm for the project, his marvellous support throughout the process, and the patient way in which he answered all my questions and waited for me to complete the revisions have made writing this book a wonderful experience. I greatly profited from the thorough reviews provided by two anonymous readers, who made very insightful comments and valuable suggestions. Barb Porter and Stephanie Mazza guided me through the production process and marketing questions with great clarity and kindness. Matthew Kudelka provided highly appreciated support in correcting language errors, smoothing out stylistic quirks, and improving the readability of the book. Michel Vrana designed the fetching cover. I am very grateful to all of them and the whole team at University of Toronto Press. My current superior at the University of Freiburg, Sandra Destradi, has been very supporting and given me the time and space I needed to work on the revisions. Kim Patricia Resech, student assistant at the University of Freiburg, was a tremendous support in the creation of the index. My deep gratitude also goes to the Academic Society Freiburg, which provided financial support for the publication of this book.

The people I am most grateful for, however, are my family and friends, who have supported and encouraged me throughout the whole project. My parents, Wolf Geck and Astrid Belz, have always believed in me and given me all the support I needed on the winding road to writing this book. My children, Zora and Rasmus Geck, have grown up with this project and gracefully endured a mother always working on "this book of hers." Spending time with them has sometimes distracted me from my work, but every minute has been worth it. Their father, Till Westermayer, has shared with me the chores of parenting and the challenges of raising two kids while trying to build a career. He has always been a reliable co-parent, a supporting friend, and a wise discussion partner. Many other friends have provided intellectual and emotional support along the way, cheering me up when I was struggling with the project. Finally, I would not be where I am now without the unwavering support of my partner, Stefan Rother. He has tirelessly read and commented on numerous texts I have produced as part of this project and discussed my ideas with me. More importantly still, he has always encouraged me to pursue my academic goals but also reminded me that there is more to life than work and challenges are tackled more easily with a pinch of humour.

Abbreviations

ACP	African, Caribbean, and Pacific (countries)
AMS	aggregate measurement of support
AoA	Agreement on Agriculture
ATC	(Uruguay Round) Agreement on Textiles and Clothing
BRIC	Brazil, Russia, India, and China (important emerging economies identified by Goldman Sachs economist O'Neill)
C4	Cotton Four (Burkina Faso, Benin, Mali, Chad)
CAP	Common Agricultural Policy (of the EU)
CMA/WCA	Conference of Ministers of Agriculture of West and Central Africa
DDA	Doha Development Agenda
DFQF	duty-free-quota-free (market access for LDCs)
DG	Director-General
DSB	Dispute Settlement Body
ENDA-TM	Environnement, Développement et Action dans le Tiers Monde
FAO	Food and Agriculture Organization (of the UN)
FIPs	five interested parties (in the Doha Agriculture Negotiations, informal WTO decision-making circle consisting of the US, the EU, Brazil, India, and Australia)
FTA	free trade agreement
G4	Group of Four (informal WTO decision-making circle consisting of the US, the EU, Brazil, and India)
G6	Group of Six (G4 plus Australia and Japan)
G7	Group of Seven (G6 plus China)
G20	Group of 20 (coalition of emerging and developing countries in favour of liberalization and special and differential treatment in agricultural trade)
GATS	General Agreement on Trade in Services

GATT	General Agreement on Tariffs and Trade
GDP	gross domestic product
GSP	General System of Preferences (by UNCTAD)
HoD	Heads of Delegations (meeting format)
ICAC	International Cotton Advisory Committee
ICTSD	International Centre for Trade and Sustainable Development
IGO	international governmental organization
IMF	International Monetary Fund
ITC	International Trade Centre
ITO	International Trade Organization
LDC	least developed country
LMG	Like-Minded Group (a coalition of developing countries that initially formed around the goal of preventing new issues like labour standards from being included into the first WTO negotiation round)
MFN	most-favoured-nation treatment
NAMA	non-agricultural market access
NAMA-11	group of developing countries seeking flexibilities to limit market opening in industrial goods trade
NGMA	Negotiating Group on Market Access
NGO	non-governmental organization
Quad	informal decision-making circle in the WTO negotiations consisting of the US, the EU, Japan, and Canada
RCEP	Regional Comprehensive Economic Partnership
ROPPA	Réseau des Organisations Paysannes et des Producteurs de l'Afrique de l'Ouest
RTA	regional trade agreement
SCC	Sub-Committee on Cotton
SSM	special safeguard mechanism
STAX	Stacked Income Protection Plan for Upland Cotton
SVE	(Group of) Small and Vulnerable Economies
TNC	Trade Negotiations Committee
TRIPS	Trade-Related Aspects of Intellectual Property Rights
UEMOA	West African Economic and Monetary Union
UN	United Nations
UNCTAD	United Nations Conference on Trade and Development
USAID	US Agency for International Development
USTR	US Trade Representative
WCA	West and Central Africa
WTO	World Trade Organization
ZIB	*Zeitschrift für Internationale Beziehungen* (German-language *Journal for International Relations*)

THE POWER TO PERSUADE

1 Strategic Arguing as a Means to Power

World trade politics is a complex matter. This is demonstrated, for instance, by the recent megaregional trade agreement, the Regional Comprehensive Economic Partnership (RCEP) concluded between fifteen nations in the Asia-Pacific region in November 2020. The negotiations lasted eight years. The main text of the agreement is 510 pages long; the annexes specifying each contracting party's schedule of commitments and reservations add another several thousand pages.

Negotiations in the World Trade Organization (WTO), which counts 164 members, are no less complicated. The WTO, which superseded the General Agreement on Tariffs and Trade (GATT) in 1995, launched its first negotiating round, the Doha Development Round, in 2001. The only tangible results so far have been the Trade Facilitation Agreement (TFA) adopted at the 2013 ministerial conference in Bali and the Agreement on Fisheries Subsidies adopted at the 2022 ministerial conference in Geneva. Members still struggle to arrive at a consensus on key topics like agriculture, and the future of the round is unclear.

What makes trade politics so complicated these days, besides the diversity of interests countries bring to the table, is the increasing focus on regulatory issues such as intellectual property rights, product standards, and investor–state relations (Chauffour & Maur, 2010; Maur, 2013; Winslett, 2016). These reach far beyond borders and encroach on domestic politics (Shaffer, 2015); they are also much more difficult to understand than classic trade measures like tariffs. When the WTO members meet for their biannual ministerial conference, the ministers of affluent countries bring with them large contingents of staff, experts, and advisers. They need these people in order to take part in several strands of talks running in parallel and often around the clock, but also to understand the technical details and legal fine print of the regulations being negotiated.

At the numerous encounters during the ministerial conference, ranging from plenary sessions to the infamous Green Room gatherings to bilateral meetings over cocktails in a hotel lobby, what trade negotiators do is talk, talk, talk. At the WTO's headquarters in Geneva, most countries maintain permanent missions to the WTO, some of them with staff numbers in the two-digit range. All year round these diplomats argue and try to convince one another. Bargaining instruments like threats and promises certainly play an important role in world trade politics (Jawara & Kwa, 2004). However, they are a measure of last resort rather than normal conduct. The Geneva diplomats I interviewed for this book recount that their day-to-day work revolves around building coalitions and, more generally, generating understanding for their countries' interests:

> One important part of the work basically is to explain to people what our views are and explain basically how the points that we are defending are of interest also to other delegations, why we are defending them, why they are reasonable, and how they are important for other delegations.[1]

> You feel like a salesman sometimes and trying to talk for your ideas and you have to find new angles on it, even if you are not changing the substance of it, you have to find ways, new ways of looking at it or presenting it. So, it's much about, you know, communication.[2]

What can reasonably be called "arguing" thus constitutes a central means for trade diplomats to influence the course of WTO negotiations. Different from the Habermasian concept of communicative action (Habermas, 1984, 1987), which underlies most research on arguing in International Relations (Deitelhoff, 2006, 2009; Deitelhoff & Müller, 2005; Holzscheiter, 2017; Müller, 2004; Niesen & Herborth, 2007; Risse, 2000; Ulbert, Risse, & Müller, 2004), however, this kind of arguing is strategic. By way of arguments, diplomats try to advance the given interests of their countries.

Where arguments are used in such a strategic way, the ability to argue effectively becomes a means of power. Those who possess the power to persuade will often be able to assert their definitions of problems and their preferred solutions. There are other means of power, of course, which come into play. Sometimes, great powers do not yield to arguments – however persuasive they are – but prefer to enforce their interests with threats of economic sanctions or even brute force. At its best, however, persuasive power is subtle. The actors upon whom power is exerted may not even notice that they are being overpowered. It is therefore all the more important for International Relations research – and the social sciences in general – to be able to detect and explain this kind of power.

Through an empirical study of strategic arguing in WTO negotiations, this book asks: Who has the power to persuade? This question, so far, has received no systematic treatment in the literature on International Relations. The research on arguing that is based on the Habermasian concept of communicative action assumes that arguing is a mode of interaction in which the only force that counts is the force of the better argument (Risse, 2000, p. 9). The ability to bring forward good arguments is not seen as linked to (material) power, and arguing situations are thus expected to "disproportionately empower the weaker actors who have less material resources at their disposal" (Risse, 2000, pp. 18–19). "Persuasion" is conceptualized as the opposite of "coercion" (Hanrieder, 2011, p. 404) and thus the normatively superior form of interaction (Holzinger, 2001a, p. 263).

Habermas scholars acknowledge that real world processes of arguing do not conform to an ideal speech situation (Habermas, 1983, pp. 99–102) in which all actors have equal opportunity to participate in deliberation and relations of power are suspended. Yet they uphold communicative action and its institutionalization in the form of deliberative governance (Dryzek & Niemeyer, 2012) as ideals against which political processes at all levels can be criticized and which we should aspire to approximate. Recent publications by German International Relations scholars in the tradition of the Habermas-inspired research on arguing call for a refocusing on normative aspects. Deitelhoff (2017) worries that the normalization of arguing research and its increasing focus on the effectiveness of arguments has deprived researchers of the ability to differentiate between cheap talk and forms of deliberation that have the potential to generate legitimate norms. Wiener (2007, 2014) departs from the research on arguing in stressing the essential contestedness of norms and the importance of their validation in different cultural communities of practice. Her theory of contestation, however, does not contradict but rather expands the Habermas-inspired normative research agenda. Wiener argues that the legitimacy gap in global governance ought to be filled by inclusive procedures for regular contestation of organizing principles and emphasizes that "the theory of contestation carries a turn towards normative theorizing in international relations" (Wiener, 2014, p. 83).

The value of such normative research is without question. This book, however, is not concerned with refining normative ideals of deliberative governance or comparing the negotiating procedures of the WTO to such an ideal. The latter has been done by others, with the hardly surprising result that WTO procedures do not score well (Kapoor, 2004).

Rather, this book is concerned with an empirical analysis of practices of strategic arguing at the WTO and with this question: Which actors have the power to persuade?

There is widespread acknowledgment that research on arguing and deliberative governance needs to pay greater attention to questions of power and inequality. Within political theory, there has been an elaborate discussion about how attempts at realizing deliberative democracy suffer from inequalities among different groups of citizens in terms of access, resources, and capabilities as well as from a constriction of the debate through hegemonic discourses and predetermined policy frameworks. Both of these factors foster the preservation of the status quo and limit possibilities for redressing structural inequalities (Fraser, 1990; Fung, 2016; Kohn, 2000; Mansbridge, 1994; Sanders, 1997; Williams, 2000; Young, 1996, 2001, 2002). This debate has also inspired a number of empirical studies on inequality in deliberative settings (Barnes, 2002; Hendriks, 2009; Mendelberg & Oleske, 2000), but research has so far focused on inequalities among citizens in local or national contexts.

In International Relations, authors called for addressing issues of inequality and power in arguing as early as the initial German debate in the *Zeitschrift für Internationale Beziehungen* (*ZIB*) (Jaeger, 1996, p. 327; Müller, 1996, p. 375). Crawford (2002, 2011) points out that "political argument does not usually occur on a level playing field; persuasive power, like military and economic forms of power, is unevenly distributed and is often correlated with other forms of power" (Crawford, 2011, p. 25). She refers to factors such as media access, positions of political and social visibility and authority, recognized expertise, and the fact that prevailing beliefs and norms usually reflect the positions of the dominant actors (Crawford, 2002, p. 31). Schimmelfennig argues that standards of legitimacy enhance the power of those actors whose preferences are "in line with, though not necessarily inspired by" (Schimmelfennig, 2001, p. 63) societal norms. Since "international regimes in particular bear witness to the fact that the power of norms and the norms of the powerful interact" (Jaeger, 1996, pp. 326–7), the discursive contexts of international negotiations can be expected to favour dominant nations. Jörke (2013a) holds that many processes of persuasion are actually better conceptualized as the socialization of subaltern actors into hegemonic Western norms. These arguments stand in contrast to Risse's assumption that arguing situations empower materially weaker actors. Empirical studies on the distribution of persuasive power in international relations, which could shed light on its relationship to other forms of power, however, are lacking.

This book begins to fill this void. It builds on a strand of arguing research in Political Science and International Relations that addresses strategic forms of arguing. Jon Elster (1991, 1999–2000, p. 406), the originator of the arguing/bargaining dichotomy, considers the "strategic use of purportedly non-strategic arguments." Schimmelfennig (1997, 2001, 2003) complements the concept of communicative action with his concept of rhetorical action. Katharina Holzinger (2001b) discusses bargaining through arguing. Ronald Krebs and Patrick Jackson (2007) analyse rhetorical coercion. I build on these contributions when defining strategic arguing as well as when theoretically substantiating the different practices of strategic arguing that I observe in the WTO context.

The analysis of practices of strategic arguing is based on a practice-theoretic view of arguing. I assume that the interactions of trade negotiators are structured by certain practices, the effective performance of which gives actors the power to persuade. The ability to perform these practices effectively, however, depends on the possession of certain material and immaterial resources, including favourable discursive contexts and regime norms as well as human resources. The distribution of these resources, finally, explains the distribution of persuasive power among WTO members.

The point of this book is not merely to demonstrate that power is involved in processes of arguing; it is also to investigate how this power works and how it is distributed among state actors. It disputes the Habermas scholars' claim that arguing processes generally empower the materially powerless more than bargaining processes. But neither do I claim that "the outcomes of deliberative processes simply replicate the power structures in the world" (Risse, 2013, p. 344), which – as Risse points out – would make it pointless to study them. Rather, I claim that persuasive power follows its own rules, sometimes offsetting the greater endowment of materially powerful actors with bargaining power, but often also adding an additional dimension of inequality to it. Not only in the former but also in the latter case, the distribution of persuasive power makes a difference for international relations and any attempt to make them fairer.

Before delving into the empirical analysis, in the remainder of this chapter I provide a theoretical foundation for the concept of strategic arguing and explain in some more detail the book's practice-theoretic approach as well as its conceptualization of persuasive power in relation to other forms of power. I further explain the methodological approach and empirical data the book is based on and present the structure of the book and its overall argument.

The Concept of Strategic Arguing

The term strategic arguing (Niesen, 2007, p. 14) refers to a specific mode of social interaction in negotiations. The concept is derived from crossing Elster's typology of arguing versus bargaining (Elster, 1991, 1999–2000) with Habermas's distinction between communicative and strategic action (Habermas, 1984, 1987).

In his theory of communicative action, Habermas (1984, 1987) distinguishes two types of social action: "strategic" and "communicative." In strategic action, actors in the pursuit of their egoistically defined interests try to affect the decisions of other actors. In the process, the other actors are treated as objects, which are to be manipulated. In communicative action, actors are not motivated by egoistically defined interests but rather by the goal of finding truth and understanding. The other actors are seen as subjects to debate with. Actors open themselves to being convinced of others' positions if those can bring forward the better arguments (Habermas, 1984, pp. 285–6). In Habermas's theory of communicative action it is thus the truth-seeking or understanding-oriented interaction orientation that distinguishes communicative action from strategic action (Müller, 1995, pp. 374–5; Risse, 2000, 9, 18–19).

For actors to adopt an understanding-oriented interaction orientation, they need to suppose that all have equal access to the discourse, that relations of power are suspended, and that only the better argument counts. Habermas emphasizes that such an "ideal speech situation" is a counterfactual assumption, but he argues that actors have to make this assumption in order to be able to engage in communicative action (Habermas, 1983, pp. 99–102). In interactions beyond the personal level, institutions that ensure conditions that approximate the ideal speech situation are necessary in order to enable deliberative democracy (Habermas, 1996).

Further developing the concept of communicative action, Habermas posits that in this mode of social interaction, the speaker with every speech act raises three validity claims: the claim of propositional truth (what I say is a correct representation of the world of facts), the claim of normative rightness (it is legitimate for me in this situation to say what I say), and the claim of truthfulness (what I say is an authentic utterance of my feelings and motives). Every speech act in communicative action can be challenged in terms of all three validity claims, and the speaker has to be prepared to give reasons for their statement with respect to all three (Habermas, 1984, 307). As they probe the validity of each other's initial positions, the actors reach a shared understanding (Habermas, 1984, pp. 279–86).

This conceptualization of communicative action as an act of raising three validity claims is taken up by Elster (1991, 1999–2000), who, based on his research on debates in constitutional assemblies, identifies two fundamental types of speech acts in political negotiations: bargaining and arguing. For the definition of bargaining, Elster refers to the game-theoretic work of Schelling (1960) on international conflict. According to Schelling (1960, p. 21), bargaining is concerned with the distributional aspect of mixed motive games. It is about inducing other actors to accept a smaller share of the pie by convincing them that one will otherwise call off the entire deal, by threatening negative sanctions, or by promising other benefits of some kind (Schelling, 1960, pp. 22–46).[3] All of these strategies depend on the credibility of one's commitment to act in a specific way – carry out threats or deliver on promises – in response to the others' actions (Schelling, 1960, p. 13). In defining arguing, Elster applies Habermas's concept of communicative action and his three validity claims. Elster proposes that the success of bargaining depends on the credibility of the threats and promises made, whereas the success of arguing depends on the validity of the arguments put forward (Elster, 1999–2000). Elaborating on Elster, Saretzki (1996, 23–4, 33) conceptually distinguishes arguing and bargaining in terms of the claims raised in each speech act type and the criteria used for evaluating these claims. In arguing, actors make empirical statements for which they claim validity in terms of empirical verifiability and consistency as well as normative statements for which they claim validity in terms of impartiality and consistency. In bargaining, actors make demands for which they claim credibility in terms of the seriousness or flexibility of the demands as well as in terms of the ability and readiness of actors to follow through with the threats and promises made.

Elster's definition of arguing, however, does not include an orientation on understanding as is central to Habermas's concept of communicative action. Saretzki holds that Elster conceptualizes both arguing and bargaining from a rational choice perspective, in that he defines arguing in terms of changes that one actor wants to induce in another actor: "To argue is to engage in communication for the purpose of persuading an opponent, i.e. to make the other change beliefs about factual or normative matters" (Elster, 1991, p. 3, cited in Saretzki, 2007, p. 114). Saretzki criticizes this as a one-sided infusion of the concept of arguing with a rational choice logic, because actors by definition are oriented towards pre-defined goals, not towards reaching understanding as in Habermas's concept of communicative action. But Saretzki (1996) also disapproves of the opposite conceptual connection of arguing with a cooperative interaction orientation, which he claims has often been

Table 1.1. Strategic arguing compared to other modes of social interaction

		Speech act type:	
		Bargaining	**Arguing**
Interaction orientation:	Goal-orientation	Bargaining	Strategic arguing
	Understanding-orientation	________	Communicative action

assumed. Saretzki argues that modes of interaction (arguing and bargaining) should be analytically separated from actors' interaction orientations and that possible connections should be explored in empirical research.

Elster's concept of arguing as interpreted by Saretzki can be described as "the less demanding brother of the rational discourse of the theory of communicative action" (Zangl & Zürn, 1996, p. 352n16, my translation), or, to put it differently, as the broader concept: We can speak of arguing as soon as actors perform speech acts in which they raise empirical or normative claims that can be challenged in the light of their propositional truth, normative rightness, and truthfulness. Communicative action, by contrast, is tied to an understanding-oriented interaction orientation and implies the assumption that power relations are suspended. Müller conceptualizes arguing and bargaining as two types of speech acts and communicative and strategic action as two modes of interaction "that include the wider orientation of the speakers and comprise many speech acts" (Müller, 2004, p. 397). He points out that while bargaining is compatible solely with strategic action, arguing is part of communicative as well as strategic action. Based on this, one can distinguish three modes of interaction in political negotiations: bargaining, communicative action (understanding-oriented arguing), and strategic arguing (goal-oriented arguing) (see table 1.1).

This book is concerned with the interaction mode of strategic arguing. While it is difficult to empirically ascertain interaction orientations, because they are intra-psychical phenomena (Deitelhoff & Müller, 2005, pp. 171–7; Ulbert, Risse, & Müller, 2004, p. 2), it is in my opinion safe to assume that trade negotiators are usually oriented towards reaching predefined goals, not understanding. There might be instances when uncertainty about the nature of a new issue and their countries' interests leads them to seek an understanding with fellow diplomats. Certainly, the search for such "islands of persuasion"

(Deitelhoff, 2007, 2009) in terms of a Habermasian reasoned consensus would be a worthwhile topic to research. This book, however, is concerned not with exceptional processes of communicative action, but with the day-to-day strategic arguing of trade negotiators, which constitutes an important but so far underresearched aspect of international trade negotiations.

Most existing analyses of international trade negotiations focus on bargaining. Authors like Odell (2000, 2006) and Steinberg (2002) provide very valuable theoretical conceptualizations of bargaining strategies and bargaining power. The role bargaining plays is indisputable, but this book argues that analyses that focus on bargaining miss important aspects of international trade negotiations or at least cannot account for them in a systematic and theoretically grounded manner.

Through arguing strategies, actors configure the negotiating agenda and manipulate other actors' understanding of the situation, their own interests, and possible solutions, which then form the basis of the latter's bargaining strategies. If we simply take these things as givens, we miss important ways in which actors manipulate negotiation situations and secure gains. Moreover, negotiations always take place in the context of social norms. Actors in international trade negotiations act in a self-interested manner, but they still need their positions to be perceived as legitimate and consistent. State representatives seek to uphold an image of conforming with international norms, even if they do not truly believe in them, because they care about their countries' reputation. In addition, they want to project specific identities, such as that of a responsible great power or that of a developing country in need of special treatment. How successful actors are in constructing specific identities and legitimizing their claims depends on their arguing strategies, and this, in turn, affects their negotiating success. Skilful negotiators are able to manipulate others' perspectives on the normative aspects of a situation or rhetorically trap them into making concessions in order to protect their social image.

While social norms have always underpinned international negotiations, these norms have changed over time. Today more than ever, widespread democratic norms of inclusiveness, transparency, and political correctness require negotiators to explain and legitimize their positions. Decolonialization and increasing multipolarity since the end of the Cold War, the proliferation of international organizations, the politicization of international politics, and the entrance of new actors like non-governmental organizations (NGOs) have led to a multiplication of negotiation forums and a diversification of interlocutors. In this complex environment, state representatives need to devise arguing strategies that conform to the general diplomatic code of conduct as well as the norms of specific international regimes, are mindful of intercultural differences, and appeal to different international partners as well as domestic audiences. The topics negotiators are concerned with have likewise become ever more complex, which gives skilful rhetoricians many possibilities to manipulate others' perceptions of the situation, its problematic aspects, and possible solutions. This is true for trade politics as for other issue areas. Strategic arguing has thus become an ever more challenging and important part of international negotiations. The analysis of arguing strategies greatly enhances our ability to explain negotiating processes and their outcomes. By proposing a framework for such an analysis, this book seeks to complement existing approaches that focus on bargaining.

A Practice-Theoretical View

This book takes a practice-theoretical perspective, as has been suggested by Hanrieder (2011, pp. 408–10) as a way forward for a non-normative research agenda on arguing. It conceptualizes strategic arguing as structured by a bundle of context-specific practices. Following the practice-theoretical approach, practices can be defined as "embodied, materially mediated arrays of human activity centrally organized around shared practical understanding" (Schatzki, 2001, p. 11). That is, practices are patterns of human action that are based on shared cultural understandings of "how to do things." In terms of the analysis of strategic arguing at the WTO, this means that in order to argue successfully trade negotiators have to follow a specific, interactively (re)produced script for how to make a rational, legitimate, and persuasive argument in the context of international trade negotiations. As it marginalizes other forms of expression, the continuous (re)production of this script in the social interactions of the diplomats involves the forcible subjection of actors (Doty, 1997, pp. 378–9).

Practices, however, do not completely determine human actions. Different from structuralist theories, "accounts of order and agreement that refer to practice presume not passive actors but active members, members who reconstitute the system of shared practices by drawing upon it as a set of resources in the course of living their lives" (Barnes, 2001, pp. 25–6). Practices are supra-individual patterns of action, but they exist only in their enactment in the actions of individuals (Schatzki, 2001, pp. 13–14), and they contain a "dimension of indeterminacy or play" (Doty, 1997, p. 377), which leaves room for agency:

What becomes sayable, doable, imaginable within a society results from a process of discursive repetition and dissemination. However, because discourses are inherently unstable, open and often contradictory, as are the subject-positions that are made available within them, there exists the possibility for variation in this process of repetition and dissemination. Herein lays the possibility for agency. (Doty, 1997, p. 385)

Every enactment of a practice involves an interpretation of the intersubjective scripts and an element of agency. What is more, the interactive (re)production of practices involves continuous struggles about their legitimation and meaning:

The politics of practice can be grasped in the ways in which agents struggle to endow certain practices with political validity and legitimacy. New practices emerge out of authoritative definitions of truth and morality as promoted by certain segments of society; but this is a hard work of reification and power struggle. (Adler & Pouliot, 2011b, p. 27)

Practices thus constitute the locus where social order is reproduced as well as contested and changed. In order to make comprehensible the way in which strategic arguing in the WTO-context is structured by practices, this book describes these practices as they are (re)produced at present as if their meaning was fixed. In addition, it analyses discursive challenges to prevailing practices, where these are observable. This is not meant to suggest that the meaning of other practices is not subject to contestation and change. Some practices are relatively stable for the moment, but this is nothing but a temporary picture.

What is important for the question of persuasive power is that practices are influenced by material as well as discursive structures, which enable their enactment and which they (re)produce at the same time (Adler & Pouliot, 2011b, p. 7). Actors can perform practices more or less competently (Adler & Pouliot, 2011b, p. 4). Practices constitute a "power to" carry out certain actions (Barnes, 2001, pp. 28–9). This power, however, depends on certain resources. One, of course, is cultural knowledge about how to do things. Yet there are other resources that actors draw on in their performance of practices. With regard to strategic arguing, these include established ideas and norms, to which actors can link their arguments, as well as statistics and other scientific data used to prove facts. Neither of these resources are available to all actors to the same extent. There are groups of states whose demands are better aligned with the institutional norms and prevailing discourses of the world trade regime than those of others. In addition, some states have better access to scientific analyses and more human resources to review them.

The Power to Persuade and Other Forms of Power

The power to persuade, in the first instance, is the "power to" effectively perform practices of strategic arguing. In the second instance, however, it is also a "power over" those who are persuaded. In the typology of Barnett and Duvall (2005b), persuasive power – just like bargaining power – can be categorized as a form of compulsory power. For the power to persuade constitutes an ability to get other actors to do what they would not otherwise do (Dahl, 1957, pp. 202–3). Power is exerted by one actor over another in a direct interaction.

Persuasive power, however, is related to the three other forms of power identified by Barnett and Duvall. First, it is closely related to the productive power of discourses. For arguing always takes place against a background of at least partly shared assumptions about how the world works, what are legitimate issues to discuss, and what are rational and normatively acceptable options for action. Otherwise, communication would hardly be possible. Habermas acknowledges this by counting a "shared lifeworld" among the preconditions for communicative action. While he emphasizes that basically all elements of this shared lifeworld can be challenged within communicative action, he also points out that they cannot all be challenged at the same time and that they constitute a background of normally unquestioned assumptions, thus enabling actors to act and communicate (Habermas, 1987, 119ff). In his analysis of discourses, Foucault (1971, 1972) has shown how such unquestioned assumptions exercise power by regulating what can be said by whom. The power of discourses is productive power, for it produces subject positions that enable subjects to speak and communicate (Holzscheiter, 2005, p. 735). But it enables them to do so only in specific ways and excludes other ways of speaking as illegitimate, mad, or untrue. Discursive power further regulates the contexts in which certain statements can be made and delimits the range of legitimate speakers (Foucault, 1972, pp. 216–27). Because discursive power shapes the very belief systems and identities of actors, it is always present in arguing processes (Jörke, 2013b), whether actors argue strategically or engage in communicative action.

By conceptualizing the productive power of discourses as one of the factors determining the distribution of the compulsory power of persuasion, this book connects the literature on (strategic) arguing to discourse analysis. To date, these two central strands of research on discourse – one concerned with the power *of* discourse and the other with the power *in* discourse (Holzscheiter, 2010, p. 3) – have hardly been brought into conversation (Holzscheiter, 2017, p. 148). With regard to the typology of Holzscheiter (2014), this book can be categorized as being concerned with micro-interaction on the productive discourse-power relationship. That is, it follows Foucault in conceptualizing discourse and arguing as interlaced with relationships of power, but it focuses on the micro-interactions of actors in a specific institutional environment, not on broad historical structures of meaning. The structures are mostly treated as context for micro-interactions. At some points, I also consider how micro-interactions challenge broader structures and might change them in the long term. Mostly, however, I demonstrate how actors draw on broader structures of meaning and other resources in order to make effective arguments, persuade their counterparts, and reach their negotiation objectives.

The second type of power to which persuasive power is linked is institutional power. Two features of institutions are important for the distribution of persuasive power. First, institutions like the world trade regime contain substantive norms, which delimit the space of institutional framings that actors can draw on and of regime-conforming solutions they can propose. Such institutional norms reflect the discourses prevailing at the time of their establishment. As discourses change, institutional norms, too, become reinterpreted or abolished altogether and complemented or replaced by new norms. But this depends on the initiative of a sufficiently large coalition of reformist powers and usually happens only with a time lag (Goldstein & Keohane, 1993, pp. 20–4). In the medium term, institutional norms thus consolidate and legalize the rules of discourses. Second, institutional procedures mediate the influence of persuasive power by regulating participation in deliberations, stipulating decision-making rules, and shaping how negotiation processes are organized.

Finally, this book claims that persuasive power is also linked to the structural power inherent in the unequal global economic relations. Effective arguing requires human resources for information gathering, analysis, and strategy building. In complex policy fields like international trade politics, the required level of human effort and expertise surpasses the human resource capacities of smaller developing countries. Their ability to make effective arguments is thus circumscribed by resource constraints, which ultimately are based on a relative lack of economic power and their inferior position in global economic relations.

By introducing the concept of persuasive power, this book seeks to widen the concept of compulsory power in international negotiations beyond its equation with bargaining power. The book's focus on persuasive power, however, is not meant to call into question the importance of bargaining power, but only to complement respective analyses.

In exploring persuasive power in the WTO and its linkages to the productive power of discourses, the institutional power of the trade regime's norms and procedures, and the structural power of unequal global economic relations, this book draws on a broad range of publications on trade politics. While classical accounts of power in WTO negotiations focus on market size as a source of bargaining power (Steinberg, 2002, p. 347), overview articles point to other factors that have an impact on power, including unequal negotiating capacities (Shaffer, 2005, p. 134), "discursive tools" (Shaffer, 2005, p. 136), and "ideational power" (Elsig, 2006, p. 13). Capacity constraints have been discussed in depth in the literature on developing countries and small states in the WTO (Apecu Laker, 2014; Barton et al., 2006, p. 172; Blackhurst, Lyakurwa, & Oyejide, 2000; Hoekman & Kostecki, 2009; Jawara & Kwa, 2004, pp. 21–2; Jones, Deere Birkbeck, & Woods, 2010; Michalopoulos, 2001, 2014). A growing constructivist research agenda on global trade governance (Dingwerth & Weinhardt, 2019, pp. 9–11), to which this book also seeks to contribute, addresses the normative background of WTO negotiations, institutional and productive power, and processes of arguing and persuasion within trade politics. Ruggie (1982) described the post-war international economic order as based on a compromise of embedded liberalism that combines open international markets and domestic welfare state interventionism. In Ruggie's constructivist perspective on international regimes, this constituted an intersubjective framework of meaning, one that implied a specific idea of state–market relations and imbued the regimes related to money and trade with a collective social purpose (Lang, 2006). Subsequent publications have discussed whether the embedded liberalism compromise of the post-war years took into account development concerns (Helleiner, 2014a) or marginalized the interests of the Global South (Steffek, 2006).

Other authors have analysed how the principles and norms underlying the trade regime have evolved over time. Lang (2011) holds that neoliberalism has infused international trade law with a minimalist understanding of global economic governance and deprived the trade regime of any collective social purpose. Ford (2003), by contrast, argues that the disembedding of liberalism and the legalization of the trade regime have provided that regime with a truly collective social purpose, shared by countries from the Global North and the Global South. Similarly, Cho (2015, 2018) claims that the GATT/WTO has evolved from a contractual exchange of market conditions to a community with shared norms, which reflect the collective interests of states in a world of integrated global value chains and a common vision of sustainable development. Detailed accounts of the properties and evolution of the development discourse within world trade politics are provided by Alessandrini (2010), Lamp (2017), Weinhardt and Geck (2019), and Weinhardt and Schöfer (2022).

In a related effort, scholars have examined how institutional norms and procedures as well as wider discursive contexts configure power relations between actors in the world trade regime. Taking a historical-institutionalist approach, Chorev (2005) argues that the WTO's strengthened dispute settlement mechanism has redistributed authority to the international level and curtailed states' ability to deviate from the principles of the neoliberal globalization project. In a sociolegal analysis, Conti (2010) shows how the legalization of world trade governance has provided developing countries with new opportunities to assert their interests against the dominant powers, but also with new challenges like the need to muster legal capacity and expertise. Lee (2012) suggests that there has been a general discursive turn at the beginning of the 2000s, one that has placed development at the top of the agenda of various global governance institutions, including the WTO, and provided developing countries with new discursive power. Her work on the subject is interesting also because much of her argumentation is based on her observations on the Doha Round Cotton Initiative (Lee, 2007), which constitutes one of this book's case studies.

The Cotton Initiative also serves as a case study in Eagleton-Pierce's (2013) analyses of symbolic power in the WTO. Bourdieu's concept of symbolic power refers to a veiled type of power based on prestige or status and (re)produced in systems of knowledge and language. In the typology of Barnett and Duvall, symbolic power is most closely related to structural and productive power. With the conceptual tools derived from Bourdieu, Eagleton-Pierce describes doxic beliefs within trade politics and maps out the properties of the linguistic market for the legitimation of power in world trade politics, including the role of classifications, the organization of arguments into orthodox and heterodox opinions, and the social valuation of particular contexts and speakers. In two case studies, he observes how actors navigate this linguistic market and describes what I would call the arguing strategies of the central actors. However, he distances his work not only from a Habermasian approach to arguing as communicative action but also from contributions like Schimmelfennig's (2001, 2003) that theorize strategic forms of arguing. Bourdieu's theory, he argues, is better able to uncover not only intentional but also unintentional exercises of power within speech acts. The drawback is that his approach lacks the conceptual tools for a theoretically founded analysis of arguing strategies. He enlists the "conceptual support" (Eagleton-Pierce, 2013, p. 76) of the concepts of framing and mimicry, but the strength of his theoretical approach lies in the analysis of the linguistic market and its properties rather than in the analysis of the practices of strategic arguing and the distribution of persuasive ability among actors, which this book focuses on.

A number of other constructivist contributions, while not necessarily using the theoretical concept, de facto describe empirical processes of (strategic) arguing in trade politics. Drake and Nicolaides (1992) examine the influence of the trade and services epistemic community on the conceptualization of the General Agreement on Trade in Services (GATS). Crystal (2003) focuses on the way the US convinced developing countries to join the WTO agreements on trade in basic telecommunications and financial services. Sell and Prakash (2004) analyse the competing normative framings of the business and NGO communities with regard to the Agreement on Trade-Related Aspects of Intellectual Property Rights (TRIPS). Odell and Sell (2006) look at the WTO coalition on TRIPS and public health. Morin and Gold (2010) argue that actors in the negotiations on TRIPS and public health became trapped between the logics of communicative and strategic action, with the result that they produced an agreement with symbolic merit but little practical benefit. Wilkinson (2006, 2009, 2012) analyses how the major trade powers have repeatedly employed a discourse of crises and collapse in order to push through asymmetric bargains in GATT and WTO negotiations. Weinhardt (2020) examines the intensifying discursive contestation over the boundaries of the WTO's developing country category. Finally, some authors have explored the influence that civil society actors (Strange, 2014) and experts (Hannah, Scott, & Trommer, 2016) exert on the trade discourse.

Methodological approach and empirical data

The analysis presented in this book is the outcome of a Grounded Theory research project, which focused at first not on strategic arguing but rather, more generally, on the exertion of compulsory power in WTO negotiations. While institutional, structural, and productive forms of power influence actors' chances of realizing their goals without any intentional action in the specific situation being necessary, not only persuasive power but also compulsory power in general depends to a great extent on its active and skilful employment by actors. The initial research question was how diplomats perform practices of exerting power in their interactions in the WTO context.

The purpose of the Grounded Theory approach as introduced by Glaser and Strauss (1967) and further developed by Strauss (1987) and Corbin (Strauss & Corbin, 1990, 1998; Corbin & Strauss, 2008) is to generate theory that is grounded in empirical data. That is, first, the focus is on generating theory or hypotheses as opposed to verifying existing theories. Secondly, hypotheses are derived from the analysis of empirical data. The theory that is generated will usually take the form of "substantive theory" – that is, a "theory" for a very specific subject, such as the practices of exerting power in WTO negotiations. Further studies might then lead to the generation of a "formal theory" that explains a more general and abstract phenomenon such as practices of exerting power in international negotiations (Glaser & Strauss, 1967, pp. 32–5).

The project started with fourteen semi-structured, in-depth interviews with diplomats working at member countries' permanent missions to the WTO in Geneva, conducted in 2010. For these interviews I approached diplomats involved at the "technical level" of the WTO negotiations as opposed to the "political level" at which ambassadors, senior capital-based officials, and ministers meet. While final decisions are made at the political level, the bulk of the negotiations take place at the technical level. The diplomats at the technical level are involved in constant meetings in Geneva and elsewhere and can thus be expected to develop routinized practices for the negotiations. The interviews focused on the "operational knowledge" (Meuser & Nagel, 2009, pp. 470–2, my translation) of the diplomats regarding the logics and institutional rules of their professional interactions. Central questions were which kinds of strategies and tactics the diplomats used to further their countries' goals in the negotiations and which kinds of strategies and tactics on the part of other member-states they were confronted with. The interviews were recorded and transcribed in full, except for two interviews, where the interviewees objected to my recording them. In these cases, I prepared detailed interview protocols right after the interviews.

Following the Grounded Theory principle of "theoretical sampling" (Glaser & Strauss, 1967, pp. 45–77; Strauss & Corbin, 1998, pp. 201–15), I started analysing right after the first interviews and selected further interview partners on the basis of relevant country characteristics such as level of development and level of engagement in the negotiations, which arose from the analysis. My final sample, which is not meant to be representative of the overall population of WTO member-states but only to cover theoretically relevant differences, includes three interviews with diplomats from least developed countries (LDCs), six from developing countries, including three from BRICs countries,[4] four from developed countries, and one from a post–Soviet transition country. All of the LDC countries in the sample were among the most highly engaged in their group. The developing countries selected included highly to medially engaged countries as well as one country with relatively low engagement. The developed countries were highly to medially engaged. The engagement of the post–Soviet transition country was very low. Coding and memo writing were performed according to the "constant comparative method" (Glaser & Strauss, 1967, p. 105) of the Grounded Theory approach and with the help of MAXQDA software.

The substantive theory that started to evolve from my analysis pointed to two major categories of practices diplomats employ to exert power in the WTO negotiations: One involves the setting of positive or negative incentives, which corresponds to the theoretical concept of bargaining; the other includes references to facts and figures as well as normative claims, which can be categorized as arguing. The latter is clearly dominant in the reports of the interviewees. This finding is interesting because trade negotiations are usually viewed as being dominated by distributive problems, and in such situations bargaining, not arguing, is expected to prevail (Saretzki, 1996, pp. 34–5).

Of course, the dominance of arguing strategies in the interviewees' accounts of the WTO negotiations might be due to the fact that all interviewees were diplomats below the ambassadorial level and their experience pertains to the technical level of the WTO negotiations. As Holzinger (2001a, pp. 270–5; 2004, pp. 199–200) as well as Risse and collaborators (Ulbert & Risse, 2005, pp. 364–5; Ulbert, Risse, & Müller, 2004, pp. 27–8) argue, real world negotiations almost always encompass both distributive and cognitive problems, and accordingly both arguing and bargaining play a role. Within the negotiations, however, episodes can usually be distinguished during which distributive issues are discussed and bargaining prevails, as well as other episodes during which cognitive issues are discussed and arguing dominates. It could thus be assumed that the technical level of the WTO negotiations is the forum for discussing cognitive issues and thus arguing prevails, whereas bargaining assumes a dominant role at the political level.

This interpretation creates the impression that the distributive and cognitive aspects of an issue can be separated and dealt with in distinct modes of interaction. In reality, the choice of a specific solution to a cognitive problem will most often also have implications for the distributive dimension of the issue, and vice versa. These interconnections are not hidden to actors, who will certainly keep in mind the distributive consequences when debating alternative solutions to cognitive problems. The diplomats I interviewed clearly portrayed arguing as a strategic exercise in the pursuit of their countries' negotiation objectives. While it might be true that arguing dominates only at the technical level of WTO negotiations, it is nevertheless a very important finding that, at this level, practices of strategic arguing are used as a means to exert power. Even if bargaining power determines the final balancing of interests at the political level, the persuasive power exerted at earlier stages will shape what state representatives see as their interests and which alternatives they bargain about.

Furthermore, the analysis of the interviews clearly showed that the practice of arguing depends on certain resources that smaller developing countries generally complain they do not possess in sufficient amounts. This does not fit well with the assumption of some authors in the debate on modes of interaction that arguing is a weapon of the weak (Risse, 2000, pp. 18–19). Contrary to the conclusions reached in much of the literature on modes of interaction, arguing at the technical level of the WTO negotiations thus proved to be a practice of power, dominated by strategic thinking and dependent on specific resources. To me, this was the most interesting finding emerging from the interviews, and I decided to focus my further research on strategic arguing. In Grounded Theory terms, I developed my substantive theory around the central category (Strauss & Corbin, 1998, p. 146) of making an effective argument.

In order to triangulate (Denzin, 1970; Flick, 2011) the interview material and observe strategic arguing in action, I conducted a qualitative content analysis (Mayring, 1983, 2000) of negotiation documents on two specific Doha Round issues: the sectoral initiative on cotton in the agriculture negotiations, and the debate on sectoral tariff elimination agreements in the negotiations on non-agricultural market access (NAMA). The analysis of these two issues enables a synchronic within-case comparison (Gerring, 2007, p. 28), which increases the robustness of the overall results and allows me to explore the influence different power constellations have on arguing practices. Unlike many other topics currently discussed in the trade realm, both the selected negotiations are concerned with traditional trade-in-goods issues such as tariffs and subsidies, not with new regulatory issues. They are characterized by distributive rather than cognitive problems as well as by low uncertainty about the nature of problems. Within the universe of WTO negotiation issues, these factors make them least-likely cases (Eckstein, 1975) for arguing to dominate the interactions of members (Checkel, 2001, pp. 562–3; Saretzki, 1996, pp. 34–5; Ulbert, Risse, & Müller, 2004, pp. 14–15).

At the same time, these two are diverse cases (Gerring, 2008, pp. 650–2) with regard to the dimension of power relations. In the case of cotton, developing countries have offensive interests. The Cotton Initiative was proposed in 2003 by four small LDCs (WTO, 2003i). The central target and thus the central opponent of their initiative was the US. In the debate on sectoral tariff elimination in NAMA, to the contrary, it was mainly developed countries that were in favour of including sectoral tariff elimination in the modalities. While some developing countries also proposed specific sectoral tariff elimination initiatives, many of them made it clear that they did not want sectoral tariff elimination to be a mandatory part of NAMA modalities, and some even expressed concern about voluntary initiatives. In 2009, the US demanded that emerging countries participate in sectoral tariff elimination, a proposition that met the firm resistance of the emerging countries and constituted one of the central controversies of the Doha Round over the following years. This variance in the actors with offensive interests between the two cases was chosen so as to enable an analysis of differences in the practices of strategic arguing used by developing and developed countries as proponents and opponents of liberalization initiatives.

For each of the two issues, more than ninety official WTO documents – including speeches and written communications by WTO members, minutes of meetings, chairpersons' progress reports on the negotiations, (draft) decisions, and other types of documents – were analysed using MAXQDA. The qualitative content analysis includes deductive as well as inductive elements. Before starting to code the documents, I drew on the literature on strategic arguing in international relations to identify a number of practices of strategic arguing already described in the literature. Some additional strategies were inductively discovered in the empirical material and subcategories were developed according to the constant comparative method of the Grounded Theory approach.[5]

Structure of the Book and the Argument

Based on the interviews and the document analysis on the negotiations around the Cotton Initiative and sectoral tariff elimination in NAMA, I developed a substantive theory about strategic arguing in WTO negotiations. Following the general organizational "paradigm" suggested by Strauss and Corbin (1998, pp. 127–36), the theory built around the central category of "making an effective argument" (see figure 1.1) includes three sets of subcategories: conditions (questions: when, where, why, or how come), actions/interactions (questions: who, how), and consequences (question: with what consequences).

Figure 1.1 A substantive theory about strategic arguing in WTO negotiations

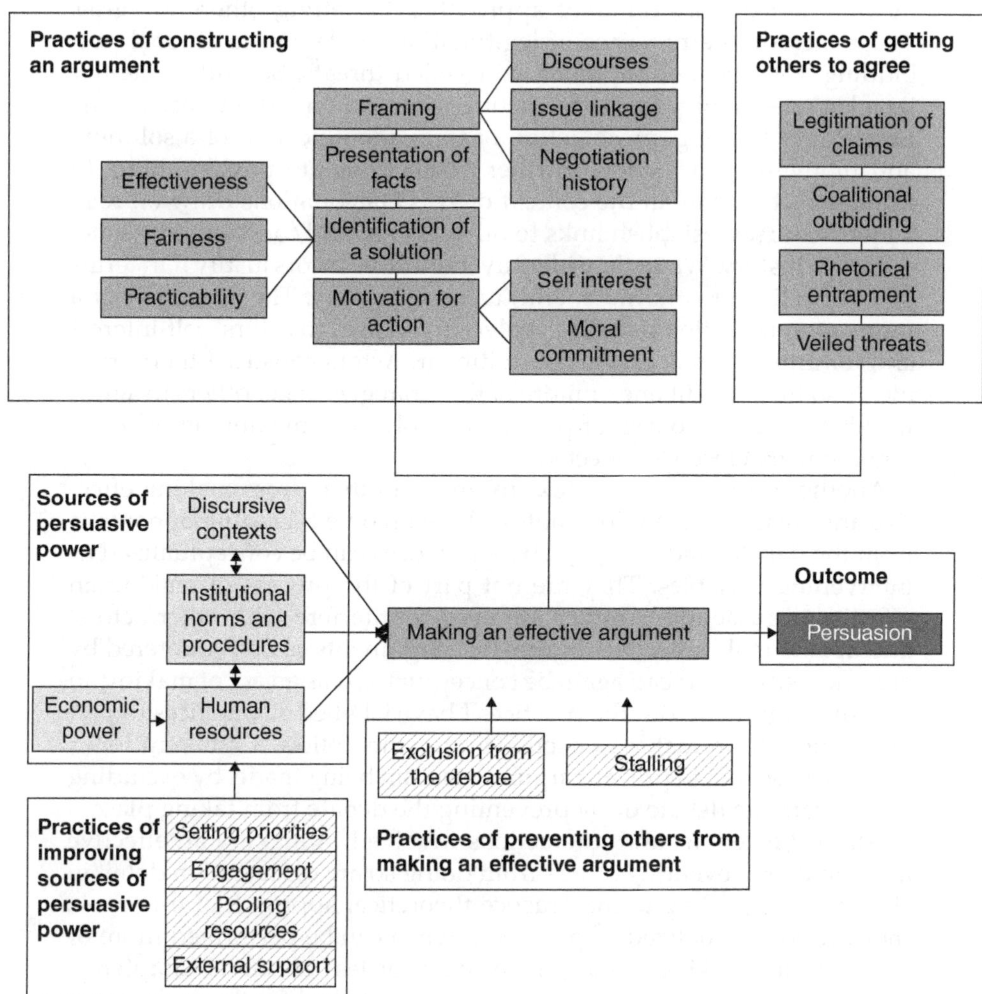

I begin my argument with the subcategory of actions/interactions. There are two sets of practices involved in making an effective argument. I first discuss different approaches to getting others to agree. These include the practices of legitimation of claims, coalitional outbidding, rhetorical entrapment, and veiled threats. Second, I identify the elements involved in constructing an argument. These include the practices of framing, presentation of facts, identification of a solution, and motivation for action. Further distinctions are possible here: In framing, actors may in the context of WTO negotiations draw on relevant discourses, establish links to other issues, and/or relate to the negotiation history. When they identify a solution, actors justify it in terms of its effectiveness, fairness, and/or practicability. The provision of a motivation for action usually involves references to actors' self-interest and/or arguments of moral commitment. Actors construct their arguments so that they fit one or more of the strategies to get others to agree. In this way, the two sets of practices involved in making an effective argument are closely connected.

Another set of practices seeks to prevent others from making effective arguments. In the WTO context these involve excluding opponents from the debate, and stalling. These practices can be conceptualized as intervening variables. They are not part of the process of making an effective argument but rather are used to interfere with other actors' attempts to make effective arguments. Arguments can be countered by arguments, and this can again be conceptualized as an act of making an effective argument. But the practices I have labelled as practices to prevent others from making effective arguments follow a different logic: they are practices to prevent arguments from being made, by excluding actors from the debate or by preventing the debate from taking place.

All of the actions and interactions involved in making an effective argument or preventing others from doing so are discussed in detail in chapter 2. According to the practice-theoretical approach of this book, they are conceptualized as practices, which can be performed more or less skilfully, making the argument more or less effective. Chapters 3 and 4 focus on the two Doha Round issues selected for the within-case comparison, the sectoral initiative for cotton and the debate about sectoral tariff elimination in NAMA. I examine how diplomats from countries with different levels of economic power perform practices of strategic arguing in their argumentations for and against liberalization initiatives.

In chapter 5, I move on to the subcategory of consequences. When actors skilfully perform practices of strategic arguing and manage to make an effective argument, the outcome is persuasion. The chapter discusses how persuasion can be observed empirically and compares the extent to which persuasion has taken place in the sectoral initiative for cotton and the debate about sectoral tariff elimination in NAMA.

The subcategory of conditions, which is of central importance for the distribution of persuasive power, is discussed in chapters 6 and 7. Three general sources of persuasive power determine actors' ability to make effective arguments in the WTO context: Discursive contexts, institutional norms and procedures, and human resources. Because they are closely linked, I combine the analysis of discursive contexts with that of substantive regime norms. Procedural regime norms and more specific institutional procedures are discussed together with differences in human resources.

Chapter 6 examines how discursive contexts and related norms of the world trade regime empower actors to make certain statements but not others. The discursive contexts most relevant for the negotiations over cotton and the debate about sectoral tariff elimination in NAMA are the discourse of liberal economics, the development discourse, and the discourse of sovereign equality. Respective substantive norms of the world trade regime include the liberalization norm, the development norm, and the reciprocity norm. I show how the discursive contexts of world trade politics create different subject positions and empower some actors more than others to make effective arguments, but also how actors contest prevailing discourses and norm interpretations.

Chapter 7 analyses the question who can speak in WTO negotiations. First, it discusses the two conflicting procedural norms of the world trade regime – multilateralism and major interest – and how they allow some actors to exclude others from the debate. Second, it analyses how the unequal distribution of human resources among WTO members advantages or disadvantages different members. A country's economic power strongly influences its ability to adequately staff a permanent mission in Geneva and its ministries at home as well as its access to effective input from domestic stakeholders and research institutions. WTO members who are less well endowed with human resources have come up with various practices for improving their sources of persuasive power: they resort to setting priorities, heightening their engagement, pooling resources with other members, and seeking external support from the WTO secretariat, other international governmental organizations (IGOs), NGOs, and think tanks. These practices are also discussed in chapter 7.

Building on the previous analysis, chapter 8 provides a conclusion regarding the central question of the book: Who has the power to persuade? Generally, it can be said that the ability of country representatives to argue effectively in WTO negotiations, persuade their counterparts, and thereby influence negotiating outcomes depends on the given country's population size, level of development, and number of competitive industries, as well as the liberal nature of their trade policy. This implies that it is the incumbent great powers that are likely to carry the day, not only in bargaining but also in arguing processes. As sobering as this is, there are nuances and dynamics to the picture that give some hope. First, the power of discourses is complex. The development discourse, for instance, does have some advantages for those it labels developing countries. Second, WTO members do not fall neatly into the categories of powerful and powerless. A country can be advantaged by its size, for example, but disadvantaged by its trade policy outlook. Third, human agency can make a difference. This applies to the design of negotiation strategies and the challenging of prevailing discourses, as well as institutional reform.

2 Practices of Strategic Arguing at the WTO

According to practice theory, shared practical understandings about "how to do things" structure all human interaction and constitute social order. "The social is a field of embodied, materially interwoven practices centrally organized around shared practical understandings" (Schatzki, 2001, p. 12). Following this perspective, this chapter reconstructs the practices that structure processes of strategic arguing – defined as the exchange of factual and/or normative arguments among goal-oriented actors – in WTO negotiations.

As the diplomats at member countries' permanent missions to the WTO in Geneva I interviewed for this book recounted, their work is organized around certain practices, which they share with their fellow diplomats. "Everyone kind of more or less follows the same process,"[1] one interviewee observed. Other interviewees spoke about the "way WTO works."[2] Asked about how they could influence the negotiations, they reported about practices of power and strategic arguing, using the second person point of view and thus implying a shared practical understanding among actors: "you argue your point,"[3] "trying to talk for your ideas,"[4] "you have to have factual information,"[5] "you find other people who support you or you become part of groups."[6]

Practices constitute social structures not only because they are iterated but because "communities of practice" (Wenger, 1998) – like diplomats at the WTO – possess shared standards for evaluating whether actors perform them competently or not. The competent performance of a practice does not necessarily result in the achievement of the envisaged goal. A diplomat can argue skilfully and yet not convince his or her counterparts. While it is not a sufficient condition, however, the competent performance of arguing practices is usually a necessary condition for making an effective argument. Adler and Pouliot (2011b, p. 7) remark that "incompetent" performances might in some contexts be more successful in achieving results than conservative strategies. Certainly, innovative and surprising alterations to established practices can sometimes be very successful. More often, however, performances that do not conform to the standards of the community are dismissed as inadequate, illegitimate, or even incomprehensible. What is more, as Adler-Nissen and Pouliot (2014) show in a later article, recognition as a competent or even skilful player endows states with influence in international negotiations. State representatives thus usually seek to enact practices competently.

Beyond practical know-how, whether actors are able to make effective arguments and persuade their counterparts depends on their access to discursive and material resources necessary for the successful performance of practices of strategic arguing. This observation is of great importance to the central question of this book: Who has the power to persuade? In this chapter, I begin my analysis by describing the practices of strategic arguing prevalent in the WTO. Later, the empirical negotiation cases presented in chapters 3 and 4 will fill the abstract categories with life, and chapter 5 will address the question of how to measure the effectiveness of arguments. In chapters 6 and 7, I will discuss the two central resources that enable actors to make effective arguments in WTO negotiations: discursive contexts and human resources.

The practices described in this chapter are divided into three groups: First, actors get others to agree using the practices of legitimation of claims, coalitional outbidding, rhetorical entrapment, and veiled threats. Second, the construction of the arguments they design for these purposes involves the practices of framing, presentation of facts, identification of a solution, and motivation for action. Third, actors who want to rebut arguments made by others have two options: either they make a counterargument (using the same practices as in making original arguments) or they try to prevent others from making effective arguments (using the practices of excluding opponents from the debate and stalling).

As with any other social phenomenon, practices are subject to constant change (Adler & Pouliot, 2011b, p. 18). Such changes can be incremental and unintentional, stemming from variations in the day-to-day performance of practices, or more fundamental, induced intentionally as a result of reflection (Hopf, 2018). When some actors question existing practices and seek to establish new ones while others resist such changes, practices become the object of power struggles (Adler & Pouliot, 2011b, p. 27).

Figure 2.1 Practices of getting others to agree

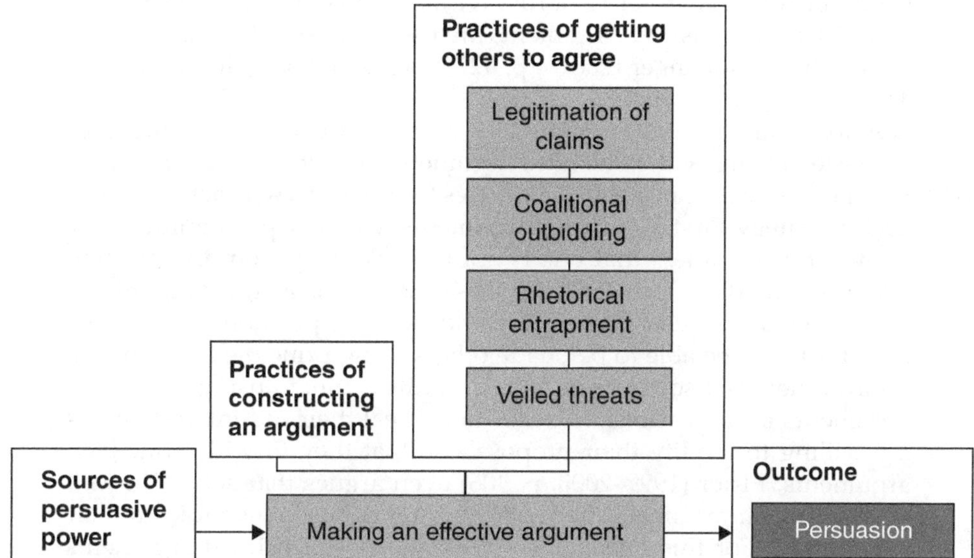

How to Get Others to Agree

There are several ways in which actors can make strategic use of arguments. Building on the existing literature, I distinguish four practices of getting others to agree: through the legitimation of claims, coalitional outbidding, rhetorical entrapment, and veiled threats (see figure 2.1). Together with the practices of constructing an argument, these are the actions involved in making an effective argument.

The practice of legitimizing claims is connected to a fundamental aim of strategic arguing, that is, to get others to consider one's demands. Self-interested claims *per se* are not arguments, but bargaining moves. As Holzinger (2001a, 2001b, 2004) points out, however, in real-life negotiations actors do not simply accept others' claims as given, as bargaining models assume; those others are expected to justify their demands. "Unlike in the economic models, which accept the legitimacy of the mere will, in conflicts of interests in real-life negotiations volitions always have to (and will) be justified. Claims and demands have to be legitimized with reference to facts and values" (Holzinger, 2001a, p. 256, my translation). The justification of demands takes the form of arguing: actors may explain why their demands constitute factual needs, or they may refer to normative standards of reasonable desires and distributive justice. Arguments are used to support bargaining positions; thus, Holzinger (2001b, p. 427) speaks of "bargaining through arguing" (my translation).

Actors may go one step further and completely substitute self-interested claims with principled arguments (Elster, 1999–2000, p. 406). Elster (1999–2000, pp. 408–10) discusses four reasons why actors choose such a strategy. First, principled arguments work like precommitments. They convince others that one is not to back away from the position taken (see also Goddard, 2006, pp. 42–3). Second, principled arguments gloss over the special interests behind political positions. Third, one might actually be able to persuade others using principled arguments. Fourth, there is a social norm that commits actors to using principled arguments in discussions. In order to conceal their self-interest, actors are willing to modify their proposals so that they fit with principled arguments. Elster (1999–2000, p. 406) even argues that actors do well to design their argumentation so that it deviates somewhat from their self-interest. For this makes the substitution of principled arguments for self-interested claims more convincing.

The Geneva diplomats I interviewed had no illusions about the interaction orientations of their counterparts: "People are very serious about these negotiations and nobody is willing to cede the iota of their territory. So, everybody is trying to maximize and well, that's very natural. Everybody tries to maximize their interests."[7] Nevertheless, the submissions and statements countries make during WTO negotiations usually contain explanations – often elaborate ones – about how the proposed measures are legitimate in terms of the common good, shared norms, reciprocal concessions, or special needs.

Before the launch of the Doha Round, for instance, the US submitted a "proposal for a comprehensive long-term agricultural trade reform" (WTO, 2000a). One and a half pages of preliminary remarks explained the rationale behind the proposal before any specific suggestions were presented. A more market-oriented agricultural trading system, the US argued, would not only provide farmers everywhere with expanded economic opportunities but also "alleviate food security concerns by providing greater access to food and enhanced purchasing power" and offer consumers "wider choice, access to new products with new benefits, and more competitive prices" (WTO, 2000a, p. 2). The EU, which unlike the US had little interest in liberalizing agricultural trade, submitted its own proposal, in which it claimed that the reform process needed to balance trade concerns and "non-trade concerns, which reflect important societal goals." The EU referred to the "multifunctional role of agriculture, which covers the protection of the environment and the sustained vitality of rural communities, food safety and other consumer concerns including animal welfare" (WTO, 2000b, p. 1; regarding the argument of multifunctionality see also Potter & Burney, 2002). As these examples show, WTO members feel obliged to justify their offensive as well as defensive demands with arguments beyond their national interests.

While the acceptance of their claims as legitimate is an important first step for actors in order to get others to agree to their proposals, it is not sufficient. Other actors may accept the claims as legitimate but still not agree to a proposal, which they feel hurts their own interests. So in addition to legitimating their claims, it is important for actors to convince other members that the proposal is in their interests, too. They need not convince all other actors, but they do have to bring together a coalition that is able to assert its will within the institutional decision-making procedures. In a voting scenario, this would mean the number of votes necessary for passing the decision. In the WTO, which operates according to the consensus principle, this means a coalition that carries enough political weight to spur the momentum necessary to build a consensus and bring opponents in line. Goddard (2006, pp. 42–3) has coined the term "coalitional outbidding" for this practice of strategic arguing.

In coalitional outbidding, actors use arguments to win new members for their coalition. Strategic arguing here complements the bargaining tactic of coalition building, which serves to enhance an actor's bargaining power. Coalitions play a very important role in WTO negotiations. Many interviewees named coalition building as their number one strategy.

> I think, the way WTO works is, obviously, you have a point of view and that may be very important for any nation, I mean, that might be for [country of the interviewee]. So, obviously, you take a position on that issue, but the way the dynamics in WTO work is you find other people who support you or you become part of groups and then use those groups or pick up an issue from there and then push those.[8]

All WTO members, including the big trading powers, resort to coalition building in some way. That said, the smaller the power of an individual member the greater the reliance on coalitions. As one developing country diplomat put it: "Coalition building is more popular among developing countries. You know, we are not sure whether we are – you know – confident enough, big enough et cetera. So [to] build coalitions with others who have the same interests would be the best thing to do and it normally happens."[9]

In order to be successful at coalition building, first, actors have to invoke feelings of shared concern; then, it is likely that a coalition will come together. A good example in this regard is the Group of 20 (G20) developing countries, which, despite their previously differing stances on the issue, came together after the US and the EU presented an unambitious joint proposal for the Doha Round negotiations on the liberalization of agricultural trade. As Hopewell (2016) spells out, the driving force behind the G20 was Brazil and its agricultural industry. The highly competitive Brazilian agribusiness sector would greatly profit from the liberalization of agricultural trade. In particular, a reduction of other countries' agricultural subsidies and the price increases on the world market that would follow would boost their exports. Even though the same is not true for all developing countries, Brazil managed to establish the demand that the countries of the Global North cut their subsidies as the key development issue of the Doha Round. By forgoing any demands on other developing countries (some of which subsidize their agriculture quite heavily, too) and portraying the issue as a matter of North/South justice, Brazil managed to win a multitude of other important developing countries for the G20. India became a co-leader of the group, even though its interests in agriculture are mainly defensive.

If actors are unable to win over others for their coalition or convince them of the legitimacy of their claims, their arguments can still be effective in other ways. One involves rhetorical entrapment, as conceptualized by Schimmelfennig (2001, 2003). Rhetorical entrapment is the practice of shaming actors into compliance by portraying any contrary behaviour as inconsistent with previous commitments of the actor (Schimmelfennig, 2003, pp. 217–22). It works because states care about their reputation. As Schimmelfennig (1997, pp. 233–5; 2003, pp. 206–8) argues, states need to legitimize themselves vertically vis-à-vis their citizens as well as horizontally vis-à-vis other states. These multiple audiences make a variety of demands, which often contradict one another as well as the bureaucratic culture of the foreign policy apparatus. In their external relations, states, just like international organizations, are thus prone to organized hypocrisy (Weaver, 2011, esp. p. 182). In their efforts to appease other actors and deal with contradictory demands, they often make rhetorical concessions that do not match their actual foreign policy behaviour. In order to maintain a good reputation, however, they also need to uphold an image of sincerity and consistency. This makes them vulnerable to other actors' strategies of rhetorical entrapment.

Similar mechanisms have been described as "argumentative self-entrapment" by Risse, Sikkink and colleagues (Risse, 1999; Risse, Jetschke, & Schmitz, 2002; Risse, Ropp, & Sikkink, 1999; Sikkink, 1993) and as "rhetorical coercion" by Krebs and Jackson (2007). Krebs and Jackson's concept of rhetorical coercion is somewhat broader than Schimmelfennig's concept of rhetorical entrapment as it is not limited to situations in which actors try to bring others into compliance with norms they have already accepted rhetorically:

> Rhetorical coercion is successful when C's [the claimant's] rhetorical moves deprive O [the opponent] of materials out of which to craft a reply that falls within the bounds of what P [the relevant public] would accept. In the end, O finds itself, against its better judgment, endorsing (or at least acquiescing in) C's stance regardless of whether O has been persuaded or believes the words it utters. (Krebs and Jackson 2007, 45)

In this understanding, rhetorical coercion is possible in all situations in which actors can portray other actors' positions or behaviour as incompatible with community norms, whether the actors in question have formally accepted them or not. While this is plausible, rhetorical coercion can be expected to be especially powerful if actors can rhetorically entrap others by reminding them of previous commitments.

One successful instance of rhetorical entrapment within WTO negotiations is the way India and other developing countries forced the US and the EU to drop most of the Singapore issues from the agenda of the Doha Round. These negotiation topics – investment, competition policy, transparency in government procurement, and trade facilitation – were introduced at the first ministerial conference of the WTO in 1996 in Singapore. Many developing countries were reluctant to take up these new issues. They were included in the Doha agenda, but, at the insistence of India (Panagariya, 2002a, 2002b), only with the proviso that "negotiations will take place ... on the basis of a decision to be taken, by explicit consensus ... on modalities of negotiations" (WTO, 2001b, § 20, 23, 26, 27). Developing countries that opposed negotiations on the Singapore issues insisted that this gave them a veto (WTO, 2003m), and after the ministerial conference of 2003 in Cancún broke down over the Singapore issues (ICTSD, 2003d), three of the four issues were removed from the agenda. Negotiations were started only on the least controversial one, trade facilitation.

Moreover, the development master frame of the Doha Round (Eagleton-Pierce, 2012, p. 316), to which members agreed in the Doha ministerial declaration of 2001 (WTO, 2001b), has been a recurrent point of reference in the Doha Round negotiations. Developing countries took this to mean they should be the ones who profited most from the negotiation round and incessantly held developed countries to this promise. Interviewees from developed countries remarked:

> Many portray this many times as a north–south issue and they always come back to this issue of the development round and saying that in the Doha mandate there is this about less than full reciprocity.[10]

> They're going to go: that round, we're developing countries, you've accepted that the objective here is to help us become more economically powerful. So, you are going to give more, we're going to get more and that it's going to be an uneven agreement, if you want an agreement.[11]

Another practice of strategic arguing, one that like rhetorical entrapment does not depend on actually convincing opponents of a proposed solution, is the veiled threat. Actors substitute threats (a central instrument in bargaining) with warnings about negative consequences (a factual argument) (Elster, 1999–2000, p. 406). That is, instead of announcing that they will sanction another's behaviour if it does not conform to their wishes, they claim that such behaviour will have negative consequences beyond their control. In this way, actors can avoid the need to prove the credibility of their threats as well as the negative connotation of using naked power (Elster, 1999–2000, 414–18). Veiled threats can be effective because the actors at which they are aimed believe the warnings. In this case, it is the argument that causes the effect. Veiled threats can also achieve their objective if the addressees see through the tactic and recognize the threat behind the warning. In this case, however, the effect is caused not by the argument *per se*, but rather by the bargaining power that backs the threat. In reality, the persuasive power and bargaining power at work in veiled threats are often hard to disentangle. The recipients of veiled threats will often be unsure whether negative consequences are actually within the power of the actor warning about them. What is more, those who make veiled threats can "invest in the truth of warnings" (Elster, 1999–2000, p. 415) by setting in motion mechanisms that will lead to the negative consequences they threaten, for example, by stirring up unrest among relevant publics.

In WTO negotiations, the most popular threat is that of blocking consensus and letting a meeting or even entire negotiation fail. This threat can be heightened by indicating that the other actors will be publicly blamed for the failure, a strategy that Wilkinson (2006) has described in detail. Interviewees confirmed that "no countries would want to be seen as an obstacle towards having an agreement."[12] Another important threat, one that can be used by the more powerful members in particular, is the exit threat. While it is not realistic for members to actually leave the organization, they can resort to "forum shopping" (Forman and Seegar, 2006; Rüland, 2012): the announcement by powerful members that they will concentrate on bilateral and regional free trade agreements (FTAs) if WTO negotiations do not lead to satisfactory results constitutes a credible threat.

Threats to block consensus or seek other forums are often made in an at least partly veiled manner. Trade negotiators use domestic constituencies as a pretext, claiming that they will not be able to sell a deal at home if it does not meet the expectations of certain domestic groups or institutions. US representatives, for example, warned that the US Congress would not accept a Doha Round outcome without substantial liberalization in NAMA (WTO, 2002h, § 1.12). For negotiating partners, it can be difficult to discern whether the negotiators actually have to bow to domestic interests or whether they are only using them as an excuse and possibly are manipulating them themselves.

Another example of a veiled threat is described by Crystal (2003): In the Uruguay Round negotiations about trade in services, many developing countries were reluctant to liberalize their telecommunications and financial services sectors. They caved, however, after the US portrayed open markets in these fundamental sectors as a precondition for foreign direct investment. This strategic move fit the concept of the veiled threat, because the effect of service liberalization on investment decisions was not really pregiven. It was the US International Trade Administration that alerted investors to the issue by publicly declaring developing countries' regulations to be inadequate.

The practices of legitimizing claims, coalitional outbidding, rhetorical entrapment, and making veiled threats are four central ways in which actors can use arguments to get others to agree. Whichever of these strategies actors pursue, they have to follow another set of practices in constructing their argument. In performing these, however, they have to keep in mind their strategic objectives in terms of legitimizing claims, coalitional outbidding, rhetorical entrapment, and veiled threats. An effective argument requires the skilful linkage of both sets of practices.

How to Construct an Argument

An utterance has to include a number of basic elements for it to be acknowledged as an argument. Rooted in culturally influenced expectations about reasoning, these basic elements recur in arguments beyond

Figure 2.2 Practices of constructing an argument

Practices of constructing an argument

- Framing
  - Discourses
  - Issue linkage
  - Negotiation history
- Presentation of facts
- Effectiveness
- Fairness
- Practicability
- Identification of a solution
- Motivation for action
  - Self interest
  - Moral commitment

Practices of getting others to agree

Sources of persuasive power → Making an effective argument → **Outcome** Persuasion

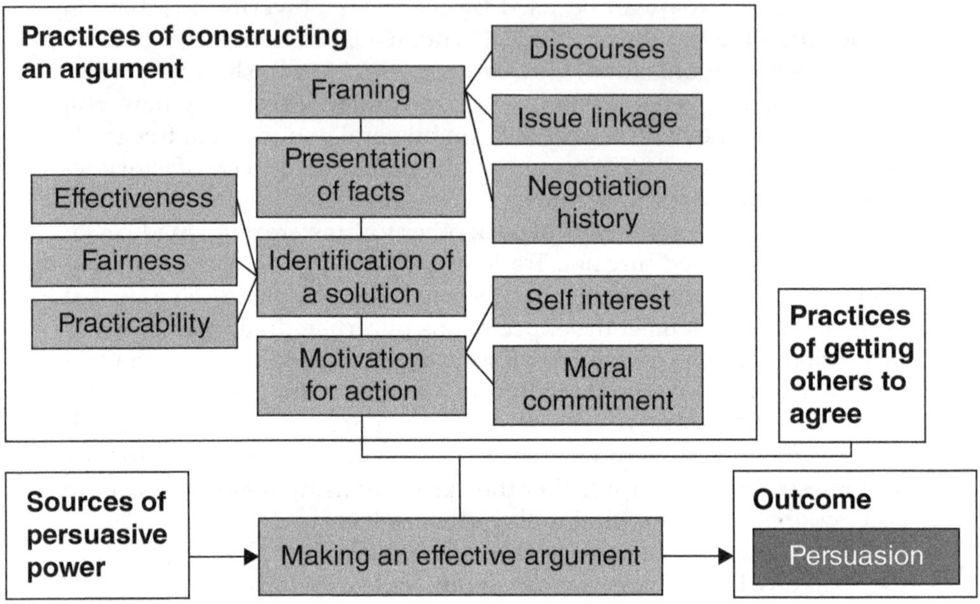

the context of the WTO. Schimmelfennig (1997, p. 230, 2003, pp. 208–9) proposes a formal model according to which an argument consists of a claim (c), which is backed by the grounds (g(w)) and the warrant (w) that stipulates that g(w) is sufficient backing for c. Put differently, every argument takes the form of: "C because g according to w!" Taking into consideration other contributions to strategic arguing, I slightly modify and expand on this model, distinguishing four practices involved in constructing an argument: the framing of the issue, the presentation of facts, the identification of a solution, and the provision of a motivation for action (see figure 2.2). Each of these is elaborated below with regard to the forms it takes in WTO negotiations and the way it is connected to the practices of legitimizing claims, coalitional outbidding, rhetorical entrapment, and veiled threats.

Fundamental to every argument is the framing of the issue. The idea of cultural "frames," defined as "basic frameworks of understanding available in our society for making sense out of events," goes back to Goffman (1974, p. 10). "I assume," he explains, "that definitions of a situation are built up in accordance with principles of organization which govern events – at least social ones – and our subjective involvement in them; frame is the word I use to refer to such of these basic elements as I am able to identify" (Goffman, 1974, pp. 10–11). The concept of frames has gained much prominence in social movement studies (Benford & Snow, 2000) as well as media studies (D'Angelo, 2002; Scheufele, 1999). Goffman uses the term frames to refer to scripts for everyday situations of human life (e.g., a business meeting or a party), whereas social movement and media studies utilize that term to describe frameworks of meaning in which social problems are embedded (e.g., sovereignty or human rights). Another difference is that while Goffman views the choice of frames as largely a routinized, unconscious activity, social movement and media studies analyse "framing" as a conscious tactic.

Some scholars of strategic arguing have incorporated framing into their conceptions. For instance, Krebs and Jackson (2007, p. 43) hold that "any argument that C puts forward contains two analytically separable parts: a frame (or set of terms) that characterizes the issue at hand and a set of implications that C suggests follows from that frame." In Schimmelfennig's model, the warrant corresponds to the concept of a frame. It establishes the principles according to which the situation is to be judged (Schimmelfennig, 2003, p. 209) and thus the context in which it is to be located.

In the WTO context, negotiators normally frame their proposals with reference to institutional norms and related discourses like liberal economics or development. Speakers very often invoke frames by referring to specific principles or recounting selected facts in order to set the stage before making their claims. The US proposal for agricultural liberalization, for instance, begins as follows: "In accordance with the long term objective of establishing a fairer, more market-oriented agricultural trading system ... the United States hereby submits a comprehensive agricultural reform proposal for correcting and preventing restrictions and distortions in world agricultural markets" (WTO, 2000a, p. 1).

This introductory paragraph clearly invokes normative ideas about trade liberalization and market orientation, which are connected to the discourse of liberal economics and enshrined in the norms of the multilateral trade regime. Another proposal for agricultural liberalization, submitted about a year later by the African Group (WTO, 2001a), starts by explaining the importance of agriculture for the economies of African countries. Here the introductory paragraphs talk about rural livelihoods, employment opportunities, economic performance, growth, and poverty reduction. References to the discourse of development and the social purpose of the world trade regime are obvious.

An important framing strategy, one related to but going beyond the attribution of an issue to a specific discursive context, is argumentative issue linkage. At least ostensibly, such linkage is not an interest-based package deal, but rather is grounded in substantive connections between the issues. A prominent example is how the US and business interests linked the protection of intellectual property rights to trade liberalization and promoted the inclusion of TRIPS into the WTO (Eagleton-Pierce, 2019, pp. 25–6; Sell & Prakash, 2004).

Another framing strategy involves referring to the negotiation history. Here, connections between earlier decisions and present questions are not necessarily self-evident but are actively constructed by state representatives in ways that serve their positions. While the countries that opposed negotiations on the Singapore issues referred to the language of the Doha Round mandate in order to establish their veto rights on the issue, for instance, the EU highlighted the fact that the Singapore issues constituted an element of the agenda and that the mandate stated negotiations were to commence after the clarification of modalities (WTO, 2003e). Both opponents and proponents thus referred to the same previous decision to substantiate their contrary claims.

Framing is important for any arguing strategy, but in every strategy it fulfils a slightly different purpose. For the legitimization of claims, it is important that the argument resonate with other actors' beliefs. Actors, therefore, need to choose a framing that is grounded in shared norms and ideas. Coalitional outbidding depends on the ability of actors to invoke a sense of common identity and interests. The framing has to hinge on attributes or goals that unite the proponents with those they wish to convince. To rhetorically entrap others with their argumentation, actors need to frame the issue in terms of shared norms or the negotiation history. For veiled threats, the appropriate framing depends on the nature of the threat.

The second element of an argument is the presentation of facts. In Schimmelfennig's (2003, pp. 208–9) model, facts constitute the grounds. How facts are substantiated is a function of culturally specific expectations. In Western society today the production of truth is centred in the discourse of science and its institutions (Foucault, 1978b, pp. 51–3). Statistical data and research findings are the established means to present factual statements because these are considered to constitute objective proof. The diplomats interviewed for this book attached great importance to the presentation of facts in the form of supposedly objective and independent data. "You have to have factual information," one interviewee observed.[13] Discussions at the technical level, another interviewee explained, are all about "trying to convince them with facts and figures."[14] One interviewee described how external research findings greatly increase the cogency of arguments:

> When, for instance, any of us bring this forward, this result of the study, in the negotiations saying that look here are the conclusion from them and they will have to take this into consideration. So, it really, well, contributes and makes the difference … It is a study based on facts, technical, so, it's not just come up, just we describe it by the way, so it merits consideration.[15]

The strategy of underpinning one's position with independent research findings is also nicely illustrated by a Brazilian statement in support of the West African initiative for the elimination of cotton subsidies: "The recognition of the trade distorting aspects of the subsidies in question does not stem from the African or developing countries themselves. Many studies that have been developed confirm assessments in the same sense" (WTO, 2005k, Annexe 2).

The presentation of facts generally is a standard feature of submissions within WTO negotiations. Member countries present figures for economic indicators such as production amounts and trade shares, employment levels and growth rates, consumption trends and price developments, tariff and subsidy levels, as well as the projected effects of proposed liberalization steps, as means to underpin their strategies of legitimizing claims and coalitional outbidding. The African Group's proposal on the agricultural negotiations mentioned earlier, for instance, contains numbers regarding the percentage of the labour force employed in the agricultural sector as well as agriculture's share of the gross national product (GDP) and the exports of African countries.

Strategies that aim less at convincing opponents than at forcing them into acquiescence depend on different kinds of facts. As can be seen in the example of the Singapore issues, previous WTO decisions are recalled as a basis for rhetorical entrapment strategies. To substantiate veiled threats, actors can provide factual information about the likelihood of negative consequences. They can, for instance, cite declarations by domestic stakeholders that they would block specific decisions.

Besides framing and the presentation of facts, every argument includes a conclusion or solution, a statement about what is the rational and/or normatively right thing to believe or do. Schimmelfennig (2003, pp. 208–9) calls this the claim, Krebs and Jackson (2007, p. 43) the implication. The social movement literature on framing (Snow & Benford, 1988, pp. 199–204) distinguishes prognostic framing (the definition of a solution) as a separate framing task besides diagnostic framing (the contextualization of the problem, which I refer to as framing in this book). While conceiving of them as two separate tasks, Snow and Benford (1988, p. 203) point out that an argument will be the more effective the better the diagnostic and prognostic framing match.

In the context of WTO negotiations, the claims or implications actors put forward in their arguments usually involve demands for liberalization commitments or new trade rules. They constitute a solution to some kind of problem with the status quo, which the proponents have formulated through their framing of the issue and presentation of the facts. In this context, I therefore speak of the identification of a solution as the third element in constructing an argument. Formally, in the WTO, the identification of a solution corresponds to a proposal for the content or wording of a part of the agreement under negotiation. Such a proposal might refer to general formulations or to concessions from specific members.

Solutions are justified in three ways. First, actors usually emphasize that the solution they are proposing is the only one that effectively addresses the problem they have identified. The G20, for example, held that the draft text on modalities for the agricultural negotiations presented by the chairperson of the ministerial conference in 2003 in Cancún "does not reflect the level of ambition of the Doha mandate, for it fails to deliver substantial cuts on trade distorting domestic support, substantial increase in market access and elimination of export subsidies" (G20, 2003). Their own proposal, in contrast, would ensure a fundamental reform of agricultural trade, eliminate prevailing distortions, and make agricultural trade fairer and more equitable. Second, actors often highlight the fairness of their proposed solution. The G20 emphasized that it was mainly developed countries that were responsible for existing distortions in agricultural trade and thus it was fair for the G20 proposal to require a substantial contribution from them, while providing ample special and differential treatment for developing countries (G20, 2003). Besides such a principle of responsibility, other principles of distributional justice such as equity, need, or ability can be referred to. Third, actors sometimes address the practicability of different solutions. In this, they may point to practical problems of implementation but also to the need to satisfy domestic stakeholders. In their agricultural proposal, for instance, the EU explained the need to take into account non-trade concerns partly as a requirement for "muster[ing] public support to the process of further liberalisation of trade in agricultural products" (WTO, 2000b, p. 4).

Arguments about the effectiveness, fairness, and practicability of a solution are connected primarily to the legitimization of claims and coalitional outbidding, but they can also be used in strategies of rhetorical entrapment and veiled threats. Negotiators can rhetorically trap others if they show that their proposed solution is the only one that achieves a goal to which their negotiating partners have committed themselves.

Veiled threats can be made about the negative consequences of ineffective, unfair, or unpractical solutions.

The final element in the construction of an argument is the provision of a motivation for action. In the context of social movement studies, Snow and Benford (1988, pp. 199–204) identified supplying a rationale for individuals to engage as a third framing task (in addition to diagnostic and prognostic framing), which they called motivational framing. With regard to arguing, the provision of a motivation for action is not necessarily a component of every argument, but if actors propose a solution that depends on the cooperation of others, they will have to explain why those others should engage. In their explanation, they can point to self-interested reasons as well as social norms.

In WTO negotiations, actors depend on the cooperation of others to introduce new rules or new rounds of reciprocal liberalization. They need to give other members reasons why they should agree to a proposed solution. This mostly takes the form of pointing out why the solution is in the others' own interests. As one interviewee described it: "Everybody tries to maximize their interests, yeah. But then the challenge is not to make it a zero-sum game, you know. The challenge is that everybody must see that there is some benefit for them in getting into the agreements."[16] Besides references to interests, however, arguments of moral commitment can also play an important role. Ethical arguments in the context of the HIV/AIDS crisis, for instance, were the basis on which developing countries led by Brazil, India, and South Africa were able to secure the flexibilities in the application of TRIPS to pharmaceuticals (Odell & Sell, 2006) laid down in the 2001 Declaration on the TRIPS Agreement and Public Health (WTO, 2001c) and the subsequent specification of rules that allowed for exports under compulsory licence to countries that lacked their own production capacity (WTO, 2003w; 2005t). Similarly, the Ministerial Decision on the TRIPS Agreement, adopted at the ministerial conference in 2022 in Geneva (WTO, 2022m), which further elaborated on TRIPS flexibilities in the context of public health crises, was the result of a waiver request by India and South Africa (WTO, 2020c), which brought forward strong moral arguments about access to affordable vaccines in the context of the COVID-19 pandemic (for an analysis of the negotiation process and outcome see Yu, 2024).

A motivation for actions that hinges on moral commitment can help legitimate claims or serve strategies of rhetorical entrapment. When actors point out how their proposed solution is also in the interest of others, they are usually aiming at coalitional outbidding. Veiled threats are also connected to an argument about interest. When they make veiled threats, actors argue that it is in the interest of all to agree to their proposed solution as this is the only way to avoid negative consequences.

How to Rebut Arguments Made by Others

Actors engaged in strategic arguing are not oriented towards finding the truth or reaching understanding with other actors, but towards asserting their own position. Even when they find the arguments of their opponents convincing, they may not admit it. As long as the others' arguments do not lead them to redefine their own interests, they will seek ways to rebut them (Schimmelfennig, 1997, pp. 228–9; 2003, pp. 201–6). For this, they have two fundamental options: make a counterargument, or try to prevent the others' argument from being discussed.

When making a counterargument, actors utilize the same practices as for making an original argument. Usually, they contradict some parts of the others' argument while adopting others. Depending on which parts of the others' argument they challenge, various constellations ensue. Krebs and Jackson distinguish between "framing contests," where actors disagree about the frame of reference, and "implication contests," where actors disagree about the implications to be drawn from a frame (Krebs & Jackson, 2007, p. 43). Schimmelfennig (1997, pp. 230–2; 2003, pp. 208–13) proposes three ways in which actors can challenge an argument on the factual level. If they object to the warrant, Schimmelfennig speaks of a "controversial argumentation." This corresponds to Krebs and Jackson's concept of a framing contest. In what Krebs and Jackson call implication contests, according to Schimmelfennig's terminology, actors agree on a warrant but disagree about which claims can be drawn from it for the given situation. Schimmelfennig sees two possible reasons for such a situation: a "competitive argumentation," where actors disagree about the grounds, and a "pseudo-competitive argumentation," where actors interpret the same warrant differently. Actors can also combine these strategies, for instance by objecting to parts of the proponents' framing while accepting other parts, but reinterpreting those and/or challenging the factual picture painted by the proponents.

Besides making a counterargument, actors sometimes resort to practices of preventing others from making an effective argument. Different from making a counterargument, these practices aim at defeating opponents not by making a more effective argument but rather by preventing their argument from being heard, taken seriously, and discussed. With respect to the process of translating sources of persuasive power into the outcome of persuasion via the act of making an effective

Figure 2.3 Practices of preventing others from making an effective argument

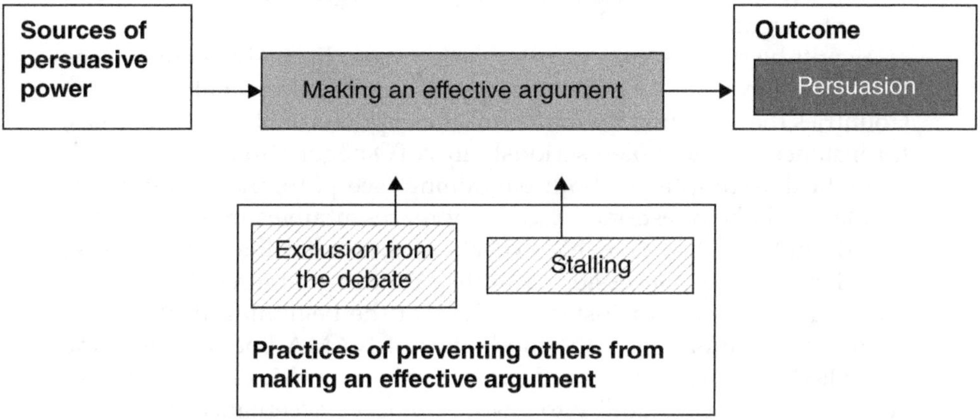

argument, the practices of preventing others from making an effective argument are intervening variables (see figure 2.3). There are two main strategies for preventing others from making an effective argument: stalling, and excluding the others from the debate.

The practice of stalling aims at preventing a specific debate from taking place by claiming that other issues or aspects of the topic have to be discussed first, that other decisions have to be awaited, or that additional information has to be solicited before the topic can be addressed. If these other issues or informational requirements are complex enough, a debate can be stalled indefinitely. In any case, stalling strategies buy actors time to plan their further strategy, gather their forces, and manipulate relevant contextual factors.

An example of a stalling strategy is the US reaction to the Cotton Initiative (described in detail in chapter 3). The US initiated a comprehensive analysis of the conditions and challenges of West African cotton production; among other purposes, this bought them time. In addition, they managed to link the central issue of subsidy elimination to the overall negotiations on agricultural domestic support, which are very difficult and have yet to arrive at a conclusion.

The other major practice for preventing others from making an effective argument involves excluding them from the debate. This can be done either by denying them participation in discussions or by disregarding their contributions. Usually this is accompanied by a line of argumentation that denies others' legitimacy or credibility as speakers.

Schimmelfennig (2003, p. 209) describes such an attack on the speaker as an alternative option for responding to an argument besides making a counterargument.

As will be discussed in chapter 6, there are discursive conventions that actors have to follow in order to be accepted as legitimate speakers. Countries that question fundamental assumptions of liberal economics, for instance, are not taken seriously in WTO negotiations. In line with theoretical assumptions about bargaining (see p. 9), the credibility of speakers will be questioned if country representatives make demands that do not match reasonable expectations of what they can achieve, or if they promise concessions that they cannot guarantee they will be able to implement. For instance, when, at the beginning of the Doha Round negotiations over the modalities of NAMA liberalization, the US called for across-the-board tariff elimination, Mexico raised concerns about the US's ability to ensure domestic acceptance and hence implementation of this very ambitious proposal (WTO, 2003n, § 1.42). Later during the NAMA negotiations, the US aggressively demanded greater concessions from emerging economies like China, India, and Brazil. Again, some negotiators questioned the credibility of the US position. The US demands were viewed as unrealistically excessive: "Simply put, the Americans don't have either the economic and political strength nor the high moral ground to demand such things from other players without some degree of reciprocity."[17] It was suspected that the US was not constructively engaging in the negotiations but following other motivations:

> It is … too unrealistic, it is too over the top, meaning it does not really make sense and it gives rise to the assumption that possibly the US here are not trying with these demands to accelerate the negotiations or to come to a conclusion but rather to block them, to position themselves in a blame game, so that they will be able to say: but the others have not accepted our offer.[18]

Nevertheless, the exclusion of the US from the debate was never seen as an option, as one interviewee pointed out. While the power of the US had declined, "it is not in the past that we need the US. There still won't be a deal without the US."[19] Therefore, talks went on, even if enthusiasm was lacking. The countries targeted by the US attempted to call its bluff by demanding an increased US offer in return for any additional concessions (WTO, 2010a, §2.2).

A perceived mismatch between a country's demands and its power to achieve them, or a questionable ability to implement concessions, will make other countries reluctant to engage in serious negotiations with the country and may in extreme cases lead to the country's exclusion from the debate. Whether the exclusion of a country from the debate is an option, of course, does not depend solely on the severity of doubts about its legitimacy or credibility; it also depends on its power. The exclusion of central players is usually no option because it endangers the effectiveness of the agreement.

Smaller players can be excluded from the debate if their positions are perceived as lacking in credibility. But even if nobody doubts the credibility of their positions, they do not have the same access to negotiations. As discussed in detail in chapter 7, a formal rule requiring decisions to be made by consensus ensures that no WTO member can be excluded completely, but much of the actual decision-making takes place within the informal decision-making process of concentric circles. The parameters of the negotiations are often set by the most important members. Smaller players are included in the talks only at later stages, which sharply limits their influence on the outcome. This systematic exclusion of smaller powers from the debate is justified with reference to the major interest norm, which is based on the "belief that participation in certain aspects of decision making ought to be restricted to those most affected or most influential, or both, in respect of the issue being dealt with" (Finlayson & Zacher, 1981, p. 586). Smaller players are thus denied the legitimacy to participate in the inner circles of the decision-making process. As one interviewee explained: "Those that are going to sit around the table and, if possible, clinch a deal are those that can pay and that can contribute. Those that do not have anything to chip in, they ... It is a poker table and you have a flat fee to sit at the table. If you do not have that capacity, don't even get close. It's a professionals' thing, you know."[20]

An infamous example of a decision agreed to among the dominant powers and then presented to the rest of the membership as a *fait accompli* is the Blair House Accord, in which the US and the EU determined the details of the Uruguay Round Agreement on Agriculture (Jawara & Kwa, 2004, p. 26). When the EU and the US presented their joint proposal on modalities for the Doha Round negotiations on agriculture shortly before the Cancún ministerial, developing countries feared it would be Blair House all over again (Clapp, 2007, p. 43). As Jawara and Kwa expose in detail, developing country negotiators complained that they were excluded from decision-making in many instances before and during the ministerial conferences in 2001 in Doha and in 2003 in Cancún (Jawara & Kwa, 2004; Kwa, 2003).

Since then, the distribution of power between the Global South and the Global North has seen significant changes that have impacted on the composition of the inner circles of WTO decision-making, and there have also been some efforts to address developing countries' complaints about exclusionary procedures. Most of the diplomats interviewed for this book were of the opinion that the inclusiveness and transparency of the negotiations had improved during the Doha Round. However, most also held that smaller developing countries were still largely excluded from the inner circles of the decision-making process. Many diplomats, including some from smaller developing countries, weighed the inclusiveness of the negotiations against their effectiveness. Small group meetings were generally perceived as more effective. A central role for the major trade powers was further seen as an inevitable reality of power politics. Thus, the perceived legitimacy of members to participate in all stages of the WTO negotiation process does depend on their economic power. The inclusion of smaller players is weighed against the effectiveness of the negotiations, and many are still largely excluded from important parts of the debate.

Internalization versus Contestation of Arguing practices

Most of the practices of strategic arguing prevalent in the WTO are not questioned by actors. In particular, the practices of constructing an argument have been habitualized to the point that actors no longer think of them as choices. Negotiators ponder which of the trade regime's norms, other negotiation issues, and previous decisions they can use for framing their demands, but they do not question the general need to find some kind of contextual framing. When they describe the situation, they seek to present facts, backed by data and research findings, without reflecting on the way truth is established or possible alternatives. Before proposing solutions, diplomats might consider whether the WTO is the right forum for solving their problem, but not whether humankind should try to solve problems through rational measures. They think about ways to present their proposed solution as the most effective, fair, and practicable one, but they hardly deliberate as to whether effectiveness, fairness, and practicability are useful criteria. When trying to motivate others for action, they point to the others' self-interest or to moral obligations without pondering the ethical assumptions behind these terms.

The practices of getting others to agree are slightly less internalized and more open to reflection and articulation. They constitute part of the established way "things are done" at the WTO, but actors perceive them as strategies and tactics they choose to employ. Still, there is little debate about these practices. The usefulness of the conventional way claims are legitimized is not questioned; the same goes for coalitional outbidding and rhetorical entrapment. The only practice that is occasionally criticized is the veiled threat. Several interviewees indicated that they disapproved of the way the US instrumentalized its Congress in order to extract additional concessions from emerging economies in NAMA: "Then the Americans would say: Well, ok, I see all this, but the point is that I cannot convince my Congress or my public opinion. So, but whose fault is this? I mean, how have you sold this round to your Congress and to your domestic public opinion? Now, it is your mistake, that is not mine."[21] This criticism is directed at the fact that the US negotiators portray congressional approval as beyond their control. Other diplomats think that it should be the US representatives' responsibility to develop a productive negotiating position together with their Congress. WTO members suspect the US of investing in the truth of their warning of congressional disapproval or at least doing nothing to prevent it, because it serves them well as a veiled threat.

Also subject to criticism are the practices of preventing others from making an effective argument, excluding others from the debate, and stalling. While most interviewees held that small group meetings among the most important players were necessary for reasons of effectiveness and political realism, not all diplomats concurred:

> I do not think that there is fairness in the process, since I think that transparency is still very mediocre and there are some members that are left completely aside and this is not good. To be honest with you, there have been many complaints along the process and in different negotiating groups. At the end of the day, if you are negotiating something, you do not want to be informed on what went on in the next room. You want to participate. So, no matter how complete and detailed your reports are, the truth is that some of the members are left behind.[22]

> We still have what we call Green Rooms. Green Rooms will take on board a few members, which are being seen as influential in the process. And for us it is only the coordinator of our group, like the ACP [African, Caribbean and Pacific] Group, the LDC Group, the African Group and the rest. They will be the only ones invited, but that is not enough. For if you have one coordinator for LDCs, which have around fifty members, it is not fair.[23]

While the practice of excluding smaller players from the debate is, to some extent, well established in the WTO, with many actors seeing it as legitimate, it is not without controversy.

The practice of stalling, as used by the US with respect to negotiations over the elimination of cotton subsidies, has been criticized by the proponents of the Cotton Initiative:

> Although we were aware of it at the time, it is now becoming even clearer that pushing us, up to the very last minute, to accept that the cotton issue be addressed within agriculture was a move planned in advance: while saying and knowing full well there would be no progress in agriculture, we have locked cotton into the entanglement of agriculture. We do not wish to be the subject of such a plot. We want the cotton issue to move forward and be resolved. There is no question of linking cotton with agriculture and then saying that since agriculture is not going to progress, nor will the cotton issue. (WTO, 2005o, Annexe 2)

Generally, it can be observed that the practices that are contested are those that obstruct arguing processes. These are the practices of preventing others from making effective arguments and the practice of veiled threats; the latter brings threats, an aggressive bargaining element, into the arguing process under the guise of factual warnings about negative consequences. This is another indicator that arguing as a preferred practice among diplomats has been firmly established. While there may be other forums (e.g., the political process between ministers) where bargaining is seen as correct conduct, the technical level of negotiations between diplomats in Geneva is clearly dominated by practices of – albeit strategic – arguing.

3 The Cotton Initiative and the Reaction of the US

Cotton has received attention during the Doha Round in a way no other single commodity has. This is due to the "Sectoral Initiative in Favour of Cotton" (WTO, 2003i) that Benin, Burkina Faso, Chad, and Mali – subsequently called the Cotton Four (C4) – launched in 2003. The initiative called for the complete and express elimination of cotton-related domestic support and export subsidies, which the C4 claimed severely curtailed the market chances of their otherwise competitive producers and condemned them to poverty. It was presented shortly before the ministerial conference in Cancún, which was supposed to constitute a mid-term stock taking of the Doha Round and played no small part in the failure of the ministerial to produce any consensus outcome and in the ensuing troubles of the Doha Round.

The C4 established the cotton issue as a test case for the development focus of the Doha Round, which had been promised at its launch in 2001. The C4 received a lot of support from other developing countries, and cotton has become an important item on the Doha Round agenda, with a lot of time and effort invested in talks. The US, the largest provider of cotton subsidies in 2003 and the main target of the C4 initiative, however, has been unwilling to scrap its domestic support programs. Over the course of the negotiations, the US was able to sideline the issue of subsidy reduction and draw the attention of the WTO membership to the domestic problems of the C4 countries instead. The discussions have achieved very little so far in terms of actual subsidy reductions.

The case of cotton is striking in two regards. On the one hand, the importance that cotton assumed in the Doha Round negotiations is astonishing. The C4 are four small LDCs and have little clout in the WTO, so it is remarkable that they managed to turn a single commodity into a central topic of the negotiation round. On the other hand, given the broad support their position has received among the WTO membership and the amount of work invested in the issue, it is startling how little the C4 has been able to gain from the negotiations. In this chapter, I demonstrate that an analysis of central actors' arguing strategies goes a long way towards explaining both the attention the cotton issue has received and the lack of tangible negotiation outcomes.

The chapter proceeds as follows: First, I describe the background against which the Cotton Initiative arose and the route the debate about it took. Then I explain this process by examining the negotiating strategies of the C4 and the US. Based on the conceptual outline provided in chapter 2, I analyse how the C4 skilfully employed the practices of strategic arguing described there in making their claim (practices of constructing an argument) and trying to convince the rest of the members (practices of getting others to agree). I go on to examine how the US has set about rebutting the C4's argument by constructing an equally skilful counterargumentation (using practices of constructing an argument and getting others to agree) and by stalling (which is a practice of preventing others from making an effective argument). Along the way, I discuss how the counterargumentation of the US can be categorized in terms of Schimmelfennig's distinction between controversial, pseudo-competitive, and competitive forms of argumentation.

Background

Cotton was a hot topic in 2003. World cotton prices had been declining since a peak in 1995, when the annual average was US$0.97 per pound, and hit their lowest mark since 1973 at an annual average of US$0.46 per pound in 2002 (World Bank, 2022b) (see figure 3.1).

Many observers identified subsidies as the central reason for the price decline. There were at the time three actors that paid substantial subsidies to their cotton farmers: the US, the EU, and China. While Greece and Spain, the major EU countries producing cotton, received high levels of government support per unit,[1] the quantities they produced and exported were so small (FAO, 2022) that their effect on world market prices was minimal. China, in 2002, already produced more cotton than the US (FAO, 2022), and it was paying substantial overall amounts of subsidies, in some years surpassing the support provided to US farmers.[2] However, China was a net importer of cotton and was not a central player in the export market (FAO, 2022). Attention thus focused on the US, which was by far the largest exporter of cotton (see figure 3.2).

In May 2002, the US Congress passed a new farm bill that was estimated to raise US agricultural subsidies by 80 per cent. Members of the Cairns Group of agricultural exporters voiced disapproval and called

Figure 3.1 Development of cotton prices (annual averages) before 2003 (based on data from the World Bank (2022b))

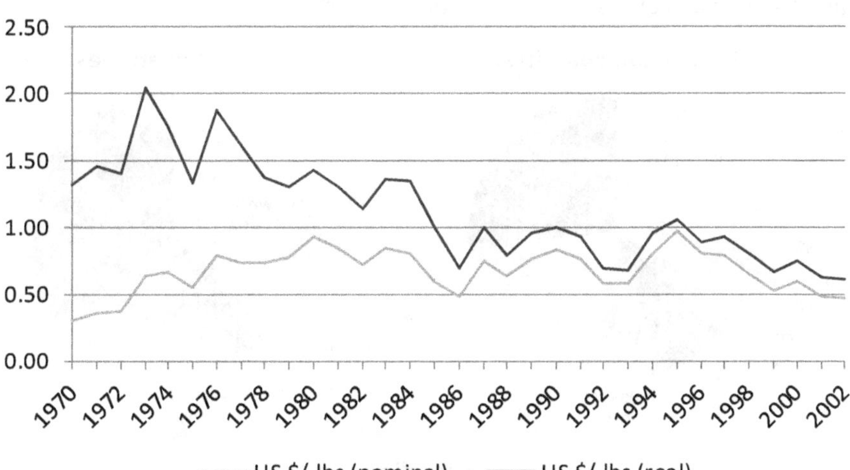

into doubt whether the new legislation was in keeping with US's WTO commitments (ICTSD, 2002a). In September 2002, Brazil filed a WTO dispute settlement case (WTO, 2002e) against the US on the issue of cotton subsidies, claiming that US subsidies were violating WTO rules, depressing world market prices, and injuring Brazilian cotton farmers (ICTSD, 2002b).

At the same time, both World Bank and International Monetary Fund (IMF) researchers (Badiane et al., 2002) and Oxfam International (Oxfam, 2002) released papers that highlighted the impact of US subsidies on cotton growers in West Africa. The World Bank and the IMF had been involved in cotton sector reforms in several West African countries and saw the sector as the "key to rural poverty reduction" in the region (Badiane et al., 2002, p. 4). In July 2002, four World Bank and IMF researchers published a paper (Badiane et al., 2002) that discussed further reform steps that West African states needed to take in the cotton sector, while also emphasizing that the cotton subsidies of the US as well as, to a lesser degree, China and the EU constituted a major external obstacle for the success of West African cotton producers.

Oxfam International released a briefing paper in September 2002 with the title "Cultivating Poverty" (Oxfam, 2002). It focused on the impact of US cotton subsidies on Africa and described the relationship in drastic terms. The paper played an important role in putting cotton on the global agenda (Lee, 2012, pp. 97–8). While criticizing the

Figure 3.2 The biggest cotton producers, exporters, and subsidy providers 2002 (based on data from FAO (2022) and ICAC (2003, 2004), subsidy levels are the averages of seasons 2001–2 and 2002–3)

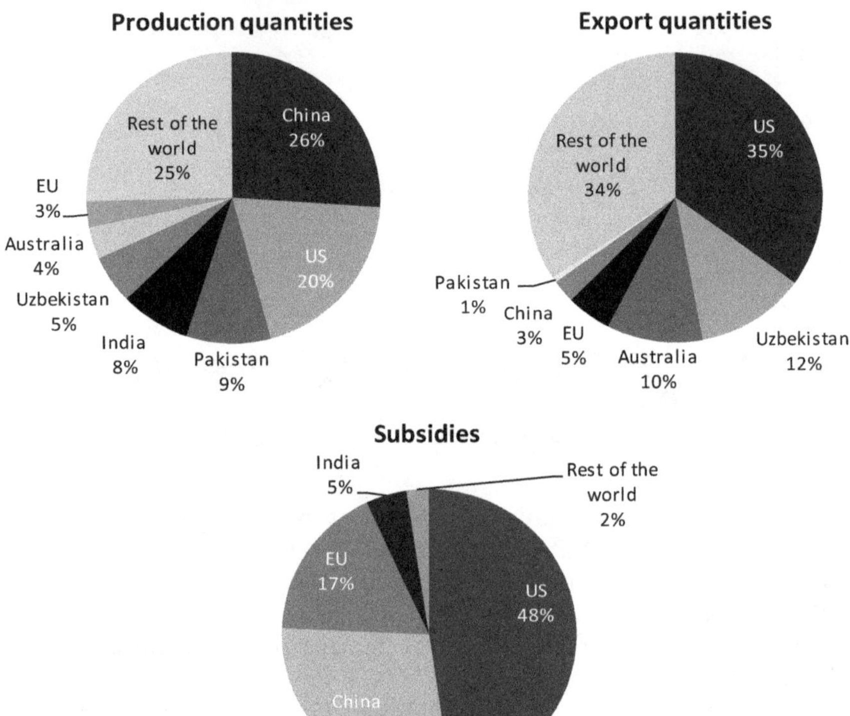

reform process driven by the World Bank and the IMF, Oxfam agreed with the Bretton Woods Institutions that cotton played a central role in economic development and poverty reduction in West Africa (Oxfam, 2002, pp. 9–10). Oxfam claimed that, as the largest exporter, the US in practice set the world market prices for cotton (Oxfam, 2002, p. 13); it also pointed out that the US was the only cotton producer that had increased production in the face of declining world market prices. This was only possible, it argued, because of extensive subsidies that led to the displacement of competitors (Oxfam, 2002, p. 11). Using data from the International Cotton Advisory Committee (ICAC), Oxfam estimated that the losses incurred by African cotton-producing countries as a result of US subsidies amounted to US$302 million in 2001.

Relating losses to international aid, Oxfam pointed out that the eight major cotton-exporting countries of West Africa had suffered losses due to US cotton subsidies greater than the overall amount of development aid they received from the US Agency for International Development (USAID) (Oxfam, 2002, p. 17). With regard to World Bank projects, Oxfam (2002, p. 10) remarked: "There is something inherently unbalanced in the World Bank using loan conditionality to drive cotton market liberalization in Africa when its major shareholder – the United States – is using subsidies to destroy local markets."

The Ministers of Agriculture of the West African Economic and Monetary Union (UEMOA) and the Conference of Ministers of Agriculture of West and Central Africa (CMA/WCA) met in Abidjan, Côte d'Ivoire, in June 2002 to discuss a common strategy to address the cotton price decline. Some observers anticipated that after Brazil filed its WTO dispute settlement case on US cotton subsidies, West African states would bring their own case (ICTSD, 2002b). According to Gross (2006, p. 374), Brazil invited Benin and Chad to join its dispute settlement case as co-complainants. In its briefing paper, Oxfam practically encouraged West African cotton-producing countries to join the Brazilian dispute settlement case or to file their own request for consultations: "African governments would be equally justified in claiming serious injury ... Relative to the size of national economies, Africa has suffered far more" (Oxfam, 2002, 3, 6).

The West African countries seriously considered raising their claims within the framework of dispute settlement procedures. Indeed, the idea of addressing the cotton issue in the Doha Round negotiations only evolved somewhat later (Sneyd, 2011, p. 113). Given their limited experience with the WTO system, it was not easy for the West African countries to decide on a course of action. In the end, Benin and Chad declined Brazil's invitation to join it as co-complainants, and no West African country filed its own dispute settlement case on US cotton subsidies. While Benin and Chad later joined the Brazilian dispute settlement case as third parties (WTO, 2014b), it was the Cotton Initiative launched by Benin, Burkina Faso, Chad, and Mali in 2003 that became the central strategy of cotton-producing West African countries.

According to Gross (2006, pp. 374–9), who reviews possible factors in great detail, the C4 decided to pursue its interests within the multilateral trade negotiations of the Doha Round rather than through the Dispute Settlement Body (DSB) because this offered them greater leverage as well as prospects for a more convenient solution. The enforcement of DSB decisions within the WTO hinges on authorized retaliation by the claimant. For countries with small trade volumes, like those of the C4, this is not a viable course to take against a defendant with the market size of the US. If they raise tariffs, they will hurt their own economies much more than that of the defendant, by cutting themselves off from necessary inputs. The threat to block multilateral trade agreements offers more leverage to small countries. What is more, a dispute settlement case against the US would only have treated US cotton subsidies, whereas an agreement within the framework of multilateral negotiations would regulate the cotton subsidies of *all* WTO member countries (see also Imboden & Nivet-Claeys, 2008). Fears about US reprisals also contributed to the C4 preferring the less confrontational route (Eagleton-Pierce, 2012, p. 320). Finally, the Cotton Initiative enabled the C4 countries to emphasize their specific situation as LDCs (Imboden & Nivet-Claeys, 2008, p. 125). This point notwithstanding, both the C4 and Brazil always perceived their strategies as complementing each other (Eagleton-Pierce, 2012, p. 320).

In preparing its strategy, the C4 was aided by several civil society organizations. The most important roles were played by Oxfam International and the Geneva-based IDEAS Centre (Eagleton-Pierce, 2012, p. 320; 2013, p. 93; Heinisch, 2006, p. 268; Sneyd, 2011, pp. 104–24). Oxfam is credited with raising global awareness of the cotton issue through publications like *Cultivating Poverty* and public relations work within the framework of its Make Trade Fair campaign. As well, Oxfam in collaboration with the African-based networks Réseau des Organisations Paysannes et des Producteurs de l'Afrique de l'Ouest (ROPPA) and Environnement, Développement et Action dans le Tiers Monde (ENDA-TM) alerted the UEMOA and the CMA/WCA to the issue and encouraged them to take action (Sneyd, 2011, p. 110). The IDEAS Centre worked closely with the C4 from 2003 until 2012 (IDEAS Centre, 2020). In this, Imboden, a former Swiss ambassador with excellent connections in Geneva, played a decisive role. Oxfam had suggested that West African countries join the Brazilian dispute settlement case or initiate a separate case, but it was Imboden who argued in favour of addressing the cotton issue within the framework of the Doha Round negotiations (Eagleton-Pierce, 2012, p. 320; Sneyd, 2011, 113, 116). As the IDEAS centre itself recounts the story on its project website, C4 representatives were initially dubious about the prospects of this strategy, but IDEAS centre staff convinced them to give it a try. In a project funded by the Swiss and other European governments, the IDEAS centre supported the C4's work through strategic advice and capacity-building measures. According to some insiders, Imboden was heavily involved in writing the C4 submissions and orchestrating their presentation to the WTO membership (Eagleton-Pierce, 2012, p. 320; 2013, pp. 93–4; Sneyd, 2011, pp. 116–17). Over the course of several years, the IDEAS centre hosted and trained several C4 officials. At the time the C4 launched the Cotton Initiative, only Benin and Mali had permanent representatives in Geneva (IDEAS Centre, 2020; Sneyd, 2011, pp. 117–18). Besides Oxfam and the IDEAS centre, the International Centre for Trade and Sustainable Development (ICTSD) played a role in advising the C4, connecting it with other actors in Geneva (Eagleton-Pierce, 2012, p. 320; 2013, p. 93). A consultant engaged by the C4, Goreux, who prepared central background studies, was a former IMF and World Bank employee. His work for the C4 was financed partly by a World Bank project in Burkina Faso (Goreux, 2004, p. 4).

Course of Negotiations

Between May and August 2003, the C4 submitted a number of formal proposals on the Cotton Initiative to the WTO demanding the progressive elimination of all domestic and export subsidies in the cotton sector over a three-year period and, until the complete elimination of subsidies, financial compensation for cotton-producing LDCs equivalent to their export revenue losses. They proposed to adopt the sectoral initiative on cotton as an "early harvest" prior to the single undertaking of the Doha Round at the upcoming ministerial in Cancún (WTO, 2003i; WTO, 2003q; WTO, 2003u).

In Cancún, the Cotton Initiative was generally well received. WTO Director-General (DG) Supachai underscored the importance of the issue (ICTSD, 2003a; WTO, 2003x), and a separate working group on cotton was established. A number of other African countries, the LDC Group, and members of the G20 and the Cairns Group expressed their support for the Cotton Initiative (WTO, 2003x). The EU signalled its willingness to consider the C4 proposal (ICTSD, 2003a). The US, however, made it clear that it was not willing to discuss cotton, at least not as a separate issue (ICTSD, 2003b). The ministerial working group on cotton was chaired by DG Supachai. Reportedly all ministers approached for the job had declined because they did not want to risk opposing the US (Jawara & Kwa, 2004, p. xxx).

Cotton was not the only issue that proved difficult in Cancún. The conference eventually broke down over irreconcilable differences on the Singapore issues,[3] and no consensus on a ministerial declaration was reached. After Cancún, the chairperson of the WTO General Council undertook to pursue consultations on the issue (WTO, 2003ab). In March 2004, the WTO secretariat organized an "African Regional Workshop on Cotton" in Cotonou, Benin, (WTO, 2004b), which focused on the "development assistance aspects" of the Cotton Initiative. An array of problems faced by African cotton producers were debated, other countries' subsidies being only one of them (WTO, 2004b, § 7).

The first decision on the cotton issue was taken in the "July 2004 Package" in which WTO members agreed on initial modalities for liberalization in agriculture and NAMA. The cotton issue was divided into "trade-related aspects" and "development aspects of the issue" (WTO, 2004d, § 1b). Regarding the development aspect of cotton, the July 2004 package instructed the WTO secretariat to work with the development community and the DG to consult with other IGOs on how development aid ought to be directed towards affected cotton-producing countries. It also encouraged developed country members to provide aid (WTO, 2004d, § 1b). A Consultative Framework for the coordination of bilateral and multilateral aid was established (WTO, 2004h). Within this framework, donors met regularly over the following years and reported on their aid programs for affected countries. Regarding the trade-related aspects of the Cotton Initiative, the July package promised that these would "be addressed ambitiously, expeditiously, and specifically, within the agriculture negotiations" (WTO, 2004d, Annexe A, § 4). A Subcommittee on Cotton (SCC) to the Special Session of the Committee on Agriculture was established to deal with the trade aspects (WTO, 2005a, 2005j).

In September 2004, the DSB panel in the case of Brazil against the US ruled that several forms of domestic and export support the US provided to its cotton farmers were incompatible with its WTO commitments (WTO, 2004f). The US appealed this decision; but the Appellate Body in essence upheld the panel's findings in March 2005 (WTO, 2005c). Subsequently, the US announced it would bring its programs into compliance with the DSB ruling (USDA, 2005a, 2005b). The actual impact of the changes made by the US on the situation of West African cotton farmers has been limited (Eagleton-Pierce, 2013, p. 116); even so, the ruling strengthened the C4's case in the negotiations over the Cotton Initiative. The dispute settlement case had brought publicity to the cotton issue; it had also confirmed that many aspects of the US cotton support programs violated existing WTO norms and substantiated the C4's argument that the situation was untenable. The C4 referred to the ruling in its public statements (Eagleton-Pierce, 2013, p. 116; Imboden & Nivet-Claeys, 2008, p. 126). Lee (2007, p. 148) holds that "the Uplands Cotton ruling was a judicial shot in the arm of the DDA cotton negotiations. Had Brazil not won this case it is unlikely that there would have been any progress towards African goals in the cotton negotiations."

In the run-up to the 2005 ministerial conference in Hong Kong, the C4 presented an updated proposal. It called for the immediate elimination of export subsidies, an elimination of trade-distorting domestic supports by the end of 2008, substantial improvement in market access, and the establishment of an emergency fund (WTO, 2005r, 2006d, Annexe 2, Statement by Benin). The EU submitted its own proposal on cotton in which it declared that it was willing to give duty-free-quota-free (DFQF) market access to LDC cotton and eliminate all export subsidies and trade-distorting domestic support for cotton from the first day of an agreement (WTO, 2006d, Annexe 2). This was an easy proposal for the EU to make, for it was already giving DFQF market access to LDC products, had no export subsidies on cotton, and was about to shift its amber box cotton subsidies (considered trade-distorting) to the green box (considered non-trade-distorting) in a reform of the Common Agricultural Policy (CAP) (ICTSD, 2003c). At the ministerial conference in Hong Kong, US Trade Representative Portman offered West African countries DFQF access for their cotton and the elimination of export subsidies on cotton until 2006. This was seen as an insignificant offer, for no West African country exported cotton to the US and the US was already required to eliminate its export subsidies on cotton in the wake of the DSB ruling (Ledermann & Moseley, 2007, p. 44).

The Hong Kong ministerial conference produced a general decision to eliminate all export subsidies in agriculture by the end of 2013 (WTO, 2005u, § 6) and to provide DFQF access to the markets of developed countries and developing countries declaring themselves in a position to do so for at least 97 percent of LDC products (WTO, 2005u, Annexe F). Regarding cotton, the elimination of export subsidies by developed countries was accelerated to 2006; also, DFQF market access for LDC cotton producers to developed country markets was to take effect immediately from the beginning of the implementation period of a Doha agreement. Domestic support in cotton was to be cut more and faster than in other agricultural products (WTO, 2005u, § 11). All this, however, was part of the Doha Round single undertaking and would only come into effect once the round was concluded.

The C4 attempted to build on the Hong Kong decision to cut domestic support in cotton more and faster than in other agricultural products. In February 2006 it presented a proposal for a concrete reduction formula for the trade-distorting domestic support for cotton. It suggested that the reduction of domestic support for cotton should be three times higher than the reduction rate stipulated in the general formula for cutting domestic support for agricultural products. The reduction should take place in one third of the general time frame (WTO, 2006b). After some discussion with other members, the C4 presented a modified proposal in March 2006 with a more sophisticated formula according to which the difference between the reductions in cotton and the general reductions would be smaller the higher the reductions under the general formula were (WTO, 2006c). The proposal was supported not only by the African Group and members of the G20, but also by the EU. The US, however, declared that it would not discuss a formula for cotton before a general reduction formula for agriculture had been agreed upon (WTO, 2006m, 2006n).

The chairperson of the agriculture negotiations, Falconer, issued new draft modalities in July 2007 (WTO, 2007b), which, after a number of revisions, became known as the December 2008 draft modalities (WTO, 2008f). On cotton, these modalities contained the reduction formula and implementation period for the trade-distorting domestic support proposed by the C4 with special and differential treatment for developing countries. It stipulated that developed countries would eliminate their export subsidies from the start of the implementation period and developing countries would do so within one year after this date. Developed countries and developing countries declaring themselves in a position to do so were to allow DFQF market access for cotton from LDCs from the start of the implementation period.

The C4 proposal on domestic support had already been included, in brackets, in a July 2006 draft (WTO, 2006k, §§ 86–93). Now it was unbracketed, a change that usually indicates an agreement among the membership on the element in question. However, Walker, who succeeded Falconer as chairperson of the agriculture negotiations in April 2009, explained that the text – even though not bracketed – was "annotated, with the annotation stating that further work was needed in order to reach a multilateral consensus solution" (WTO, 2010b, §14).

At the July 2008 mini-ministerial meeting, cotton was not discussed even though it was identified as one of twenty critical issues. Progress had been made on eighteen issues when talks broke down over the next to last, the special safeguard mechanism (SSM) for developing countries in agriculture. Cotton was the sole remaining issue the talks never turned to (Scott & Wilkinson, 2010, p. 11). The C4 and its supporters were disappointed (WTO, 2008h, § 8–43). The following year, consultations on cotton were held (WTO, 2009a, § 30; 2010b, § 4). However, in October 2009, Brazil observed that the cotton negotiations seemed to be "deadlocked and even back-tracking" (WTO, 2010b, § 23). This was also true for the Doha Round in general. In 2009, the WTO held a ministerial meeting in Geneva, but this only addressed "housekeeping issues." The Doha Round was officially off the agenda (ICTSD, 2009a, 2009b). At the next ministerial, also in Geneva, in 2011, members officially acknowledged that the Doha Round was "at an impasse" (WTO, 2012).

Meanwhile, Brazil judged the steps taken by the US to bring its cotton subsidy programs into compliance with the DSB ruling insufficient and requested that a compliance panel be established. In December 2007, the compliance panel found that the US had taken some appropriate measures but had failed to fully bring its export as well as domestic subsidy programs on cotton into compliance with WTO rules (WTO, 2007g). Both the US and Brazil appealed the decision. In June 2008, however, the Appellate Body confirmed the central findings of the panel (WTO, 2008a). Despite the panel ruling of December 2007 and the pending Appellate Body report, the US congress passed a new farm bill in May 2008 that largely continued the existing subsidy system in cotton as in other agricultural products (ICTSD, 2008c). In November 2009, the DSB authorized Brazil to take far-reaching retaliation measures. Under the threat of retaliation, the US offered to negotiate a mutually satisfactory solution. The two parties notified the DSB in August 2010 that they had concluded a Framework for a Mutually Agreed Solution to the Cotton Dispute (WTO, 2014b).

That framework did not in itself constitute a solution to the cotton dispute, but it laid out parameters for discussions. The aim was to include a mutually satisfactory solution in the next US farm bill, which was supposed to be passed in 2012 (WTO, 2010c). The US also agreed to provide US$147.3 million annually to a fund for technical assistance and capacity-building activities related to the cotton sector in Brazil. The memorandum on the fund stipulated that the money could also be used for international cooperation related to the cotton sector in countries in Sub-Saharan Africa and other developing countries (Office of the USTR, 2010).

In 2013, the ministers of the WTO member countries met in Bali. They now took a more pragmatic approach at the Doha Agenda. This meant starting to unravel the Doha single undertaking and focusing on specific issues that were deemed deliverable. Cotton was among the agenda items for the ministerial, and the C4 presented a proposal in which it demanded the immediate realization of the Hong Kong decisions on the elimination of developed countries' export subsidies as well as DFQF market access for LDC cotton. In addition, it demanded that the Special Session of the Committee on Agriculture and the Sub-Committee on Cotton be instructed to submit a draft decision on domestic support for cotton by the end of 2014 (WTO, 2013a).

The "early harvest" realized by the Bali package was celebrated as a breakthrough for the Doha Round negotiations. The package also included a decision on cotton (WTO, 2013c), but its content was meagre. It merely reaffirmed the commitment to address cotton "ambitiously, expeditiously and specifically." The text on cotton in the December 2008 draft modalities for agriculture was mentioned as a "reference point" for further work. In order to "examine relevant trade-related developments" in cotton, the decision introduced dedicated biannual discussions in the context of the Committee on Agriculture in Special Session. Since 2014, twice a year, the WTO has held such sessions together with those of the Consultative Framework Mechanism on the development aspects of cotton (WTO, 2022g).

After long debates in Congress, the US finally passed a new farm bill in February 2014 (Branco, 2014; Soto, 2014). That bill abolished direct payments and counter-cyclical domestic support to cotton farmers. Instead, it introduced a cotton crop insurance program, called the Stacked Income Protection Plan for Upland Cotton (STAX). Even though 80 per cent of the insurance premiums would be covered by the government, overall subsidy levels to US cotton farmers were expected to decline substantially under the 2014 farm bill (UNCTAD, 2014, p. 7). In October 2014, Brazil and the US notified the DSB that they had agreed that their dispute on cotton had ended (WTO, 2014b). In a Memorandum of Understanding, the US agreed to a series of rules regarding the administration of its export guarantee program, and a final payment of US$300 million was made to the Brazilian fund for technical assistance and capacity building in the cotton sector (WTO, 2014a).

The 2015 Nairobi ministerial meeting of the WTO finally saw some decisions on cotton; these would take effect irrespective of an overall Doha Round agreement. A general decision on export subsidies required developed countries to eliminate them for all products by 2020. Developing countries were given until 2023 (WTO, 2015a). A separate decision on cotton stipulated that export subsidies on cotton were to be eliminated immediately by developed countries and by developing countries by 1 January 2017 (WTO, 2015b, § 9). The decision on cotton also called for developed country members and developing country members that declared themselves in a position to do so to immediately provide DFQF market access for cotton from LDCs "to the extent provided for in their respective referential trade arrangements in favor of LDCs" (WTO, 2015b, § 2). The most important and difficult issue, domestic support, remained unsolved.

In 2017, the C4 presented a new proposal on domestic support. This one called for an immediate 70 to 90 per cent cut in amber and blue box subsidies by developed countries (the more, the higher the bound aggregate measurement of support [AMS]). Developing countries were to be given a five-year implementation period and a reduction rate two thirds of that of developed countries. Amber and blue box support in total was not to exceed *de minimis* provisions. The same proposal

Figure 3.3 WTO decisions on cotton

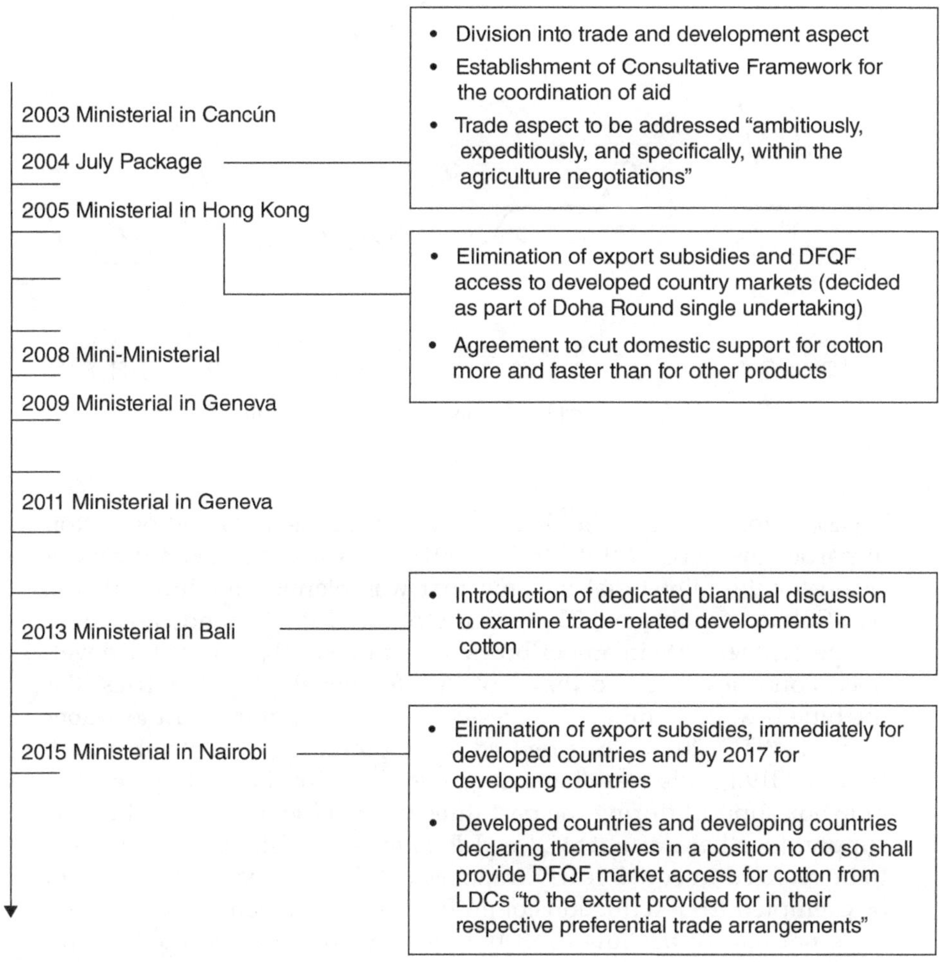

demanded the introduction of far-reaching discipline on green box support, including direct payments (WTO, 2017a). In the run-up to the ministerial conference in Buenos Aires in 2017, domestic support in agriculture, including cotton, was discussed with new impetus (ICTSD, 2016, 2017a). However, this ministerial produced no decision on domestic support. The only new development in cotton was the launch of an online cotton portal by the WTO and the International Trade Centre (ITC), which provides cotton producers and policy-makers with information (WTO, 2017b).

Figure 3.4 Development of cotton prices (annual averages) before and after 2003 (based on data from the World Bank (2022b))

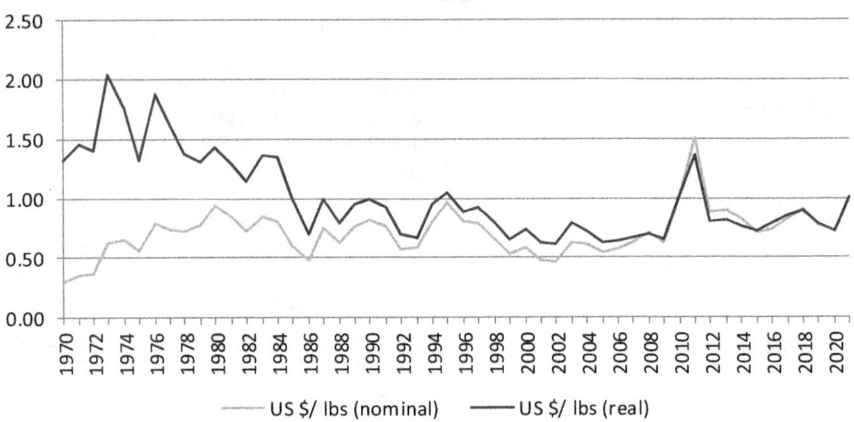

Discussions continue on domestic support in general and on cotton in particular (WTO, 2019f). In July 2019, the C4 submitted a draft decision for the ministerial meeting that was planned for June 2020 in Nur-Sultan, Kazakhstan. The C4 now reduced its demands regarding the percentage cuts in amber box support to 30–40 per cent for developed countries and two thirds of that for developing countries. For the blue box, they initially suggested a cut of two thirds of the amber box cut (WTO, 2019c). In a revised draft, presented in September 2019 (WTO, 2019d), this was changed to two thirds of the average level of blue box support during the past three years. Blue box and amber box support together was not to exceed *de minimis* provisions. The cuts were to be realized in equal yearly tranches within five years. LDCs would be exempted from reduction commitments. New green box disciplines were not part of the July draft but were reintroduced in the September revision (WTO, 2019c; 2019d). Due to the COVID-19 pandemic, the ministerial conference was postponed several times; it finally took place in June 2022 in Geneva. There was a draft ministerial decision on agriculture (WTO, 2022k) that contained little on cotton and did not achieve consensus at the ministerial.

Over the twenty years that WTO members have now been discussing cotton subsidies, cotton prices have fluctuated (see figure 3.4). After the drop below the US50¢ mark in the yearly average for 2002, prices recovered somewhat, ranging around US60¢ per pound for a few years (World Bank, 2022b). The global recession of 2009 caused a decline in

Figure 3.5 The biggest cotton producers, exporters, and subsidy providers in 2019 (based on data from FAO (2022) and ICAC (2020–21), subsidy levels are the averages of seasons 2018–19 and 2019–20)

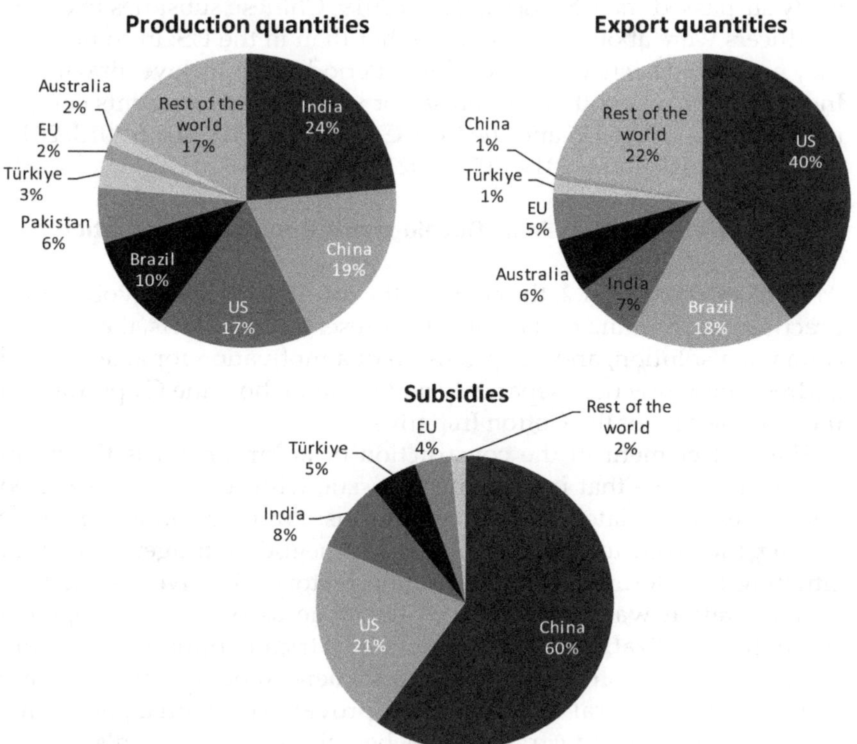

production, and when the economy started to recover, demand for cotton surpassed supply (MacDonald & Meyer, 2018, p. 8). In 2010, cotton prices averaged US$1.04 per pound, and in 2011 they spiked to US$1.51 per pound (yearly average). This caused production to increase again, and cotton prices have been ranging around US80¢ per pound since 2012 (World Bank, 2022b). The decline in prices might have been much sharper if not for China. To be prepared for future shortages in supply, the Chinese government had begun building up large stocks of cotton, which significantly raised global demand (ICTSD, 2013a, p. 5). Since 2021, cotton prices have been on the rise again, for several reasons, including the general commodity price hike caused by the Russian invasion of Ukraine (World Bank, 2022a).

Brazil and India have become important producers and exporters of cotton, while Uzbekistan has fallen in importance. China plays an even lesser role as exporter, its share in world cotton exports now being only 1 per cent. The US has been able to increase its world share of cotton exports further. With regard to subsidies, however, China has continuously surpassed the US since 2010. In 2019, Chinese subsidies to cotton producers were about three times higher than in the US; in some years they have even been ten times as high. Periodically, Türkiye, Brazil, and India have provided their cotton sector with subsidy amounts comparable to those of the US and the EU (ICAC, 2010, 2011, 2012, 2013, 2014, 2015, 2016, 2017, 2018, 2019, 2020, 2021) (see figure 3.5).

The Case of the Cotton Four: Development through Liberalization

As detailed in chapter 2, the construction of an argument involves four practices: the framing of the issue, the presentation of facts, the identification of a solution, and the provision of a motivation for action. I will address these practices separately and examine how the C4 performed them in the case of the Cotton Initiative.

The first element in the construction of an argument is the framing of the issue – that is, defining the issue with reference to selected discourses and related institutional norms. Framing can also involve linking the issue to other issues on the negotiation agenda and/or situating it in terms of the negotiation history. Decisive for the C4's argumentation was its framing of the issue as one of development through liberalization. "The example of African cotton offers a conspicuous illustration for the rare cases where trade liberalization and respect of multilateral trade rules can provide substantial and immediate trade benefits to African States belonging to the world's poorest countries" (WTO, 2003l), Burkina Faso's President Compaoré declared when presenting the Cotton Initiative to the Trade Negotiation Committee (TNC) in June 2003. While development through liberalization is a common theme of export-oriented development policies, the twist here was that liberalization was required of developing countries' trading partners. With this framing, the C4 drew on two distinct discursive contexts. One is liberal economic thought, which occupies a central place in the norms of the world trade regime. The other is the development discourse (which is also represented in the norms of the word trade regime but not as central to the regime). A central theme of the development discourse, poverty, is invoked in the title of the proposal: "Poverty Reduction: Sectoral Initiative in Favor of Cotton" (WTO, 2003i). References to the importance of the cotton sector for development and poverty reduction occupy a prominent place (WTO, 2003i, § 1, 2003q, § 4) in the C4's written submissions. At the same time, the C4 used liberal economic rhetoric as they emphasized that their cotton farmers were "among the most competitive producers" (WTO, 2003i, § 2), pointed out the liberalization efforts of their governments, condemned the subsidies paid by the US and other countries as market-distorting, and asked for a free market (WTO, 2003i, §§ 2–5; 2003q, §§ 8–9). In his speech to the TNC, Compaoré emphasized that the C4 sought no more than the implementation of the WTO's liberalization norm: "Our countries are not asking for charity, neither are we requesting preferential treatment or additional aid. We solely demand that, in conformity with WTO basic principles, the free market rule be applied. Our producers are ready to face competition on the world cotton market – under the condition that it is not distorted by subsidies" (WTO, 2003l).

At a meeting of the SCC in 2005, Benin explicitly referred to liberal economics in pointing out that "economic theory stated that countries which were not competitive in one area had to stop producing in that area and African countries, despite underdevelopment, produced cotton three times cheaper than cotton produced in the United States. Hence, according to economic theory, Benin noted that the United States should stop producing cotton and leave it to countries which were more competitive" (WTO, 2005n, § 25).

With its framing, the C4 identified the nature of the problem: its competitive cotton farmers being victimized by the distortion in world market prices caused by other countries' subsidies. Eagleton-Pierce (2012, pp. 319–23) has fittingly described the C4's framing as a "competitive victim" frame.

Framing the issue in terms of liberalization and development was a conscious decision. The merits of this decision were debated between the C4 and its advisers. Diouf, a trade lawyer connected to ICTSD, advised against incorporating references to development into the framing and argued for a stringent argumentation that focused on the WTO's liberalization norm. Imboden from the IDEAS centre, however, held that a linkage of the issue to questions of development and poverty reduction would guarantee that the issue could not be ignored (Eagleton-Pierce, 2012, p. 321; 2013, 96, 98; Heinisch, 2006, p. 268).

Another ingenious aspect of the C4's framing was its linkage of the cotton issue to the development master frame (Eagleton-Pierce, 2012, p. 316) of the Doha Round. While developing countries in all contexts frequently reminded their negotiation partners of the development promise of that round, the C4 managed to establish a special tie between the cotton issue and the overall issue of the Doha Round by presenting cotton as a "test" for the round's development dimension.

Thus, at the first meeting of the SCC in February 2005, Benin, speaking on behalf of the C4, argued:

> For the least developed countries, cotton will test the international community's readiness to create an international trading system that addresses the legitimate interests of all of its Members, including the weakest. It is crucial for us to find a solution to the cotton issue; this will demonstrate our actual capacity to turn this negotiating round into a genuine development round, for cotton is a perfect example of what should be the focus of our quest and our action, namely to combat poverty by furthering trade, while ensuring the participation of poor countries in international trade. (WTO, 2005a, Annexe 2)

This framing not only constituted a form of issue linkage but also entailed a reference to the negotiation history. All WTO members had agreed in the Doha Declaration to "place their [developing countries'] needs and interests at the heart of the Work Program adopted in this Declaration" (WTO, 2001b, § 2).

The second element in the construction of an argument as understood here is the presentation of facts. The C4 made a number of factual claims and presented a wealth of statistics and research findings to substantiate them. In its initial submission, the description of the situation takes up as much space as the explication of its demands. The C4 asserted that cotton was of central importance for its members' economies and provided figures on the percentage of cotton in their respective GDPs and export earnings as well as the number of people employed in cotton and downstream industries. It cited studies that had found that the cultivation of cotton had positive effects on farmers' nutrition and on rural poverty reduction. It further declared that its cotton farmers were competitive on the global market, describing the growth in the cotton production of West African countries, their share of world cotton production and trade, and the low production costs and high quality of their cotton. Finally, the C4 claimed that other countries' subsidies were responsible for the recent suffering of their cotton farmers. It presented figures on the amount of subsidies the US and other countries paid to their cotton farmers, the decline in global cotton prices, and the resulting decline in West African export earnings from cotton. It pointed out that a number of studies had found that eliminating cotton subsidies would result in much higher cotton prices. Researchers had consequently calculated that West African cotton producers suffered considerable losses due to the continuation of subsidies (WTO, 2003i, §§ 9–26).

The third element in the construction of an argument is the identification of a solution. This involves justifying that solution in terms of effectiveness in addressing the problem identified in the framing, its fairness, and its practicability. The solution the C4 identified was simple: the prohibition of cotton subsidies. For the period until the elimination of subsidies, it proposed a transitory measure of financial compensation to ensure the survival of the West African cotton farmers until a free market was established (WTO, 2003u, §§ 1–2). This solution corresponded to the factual description of the situation by the C4 and its liberal economic argumentation: its cotton farmers were competitive, and all they needed to prosper was a free market in which other states did not subsidize their producers. The transitory measure was, at first, simply described as "financial compensation to offset the income they are losing" (WTO, 2003i, § 7), not as any kind of development aid.[4]

The C4 argued that its proposal was the only effective solution because it targeted the central problem it had identified when framing the issue: the subsidies, which violated liberal economic principles and thwarted the development prospects of its cotton sector. When the EU and the US at the first meeting of the SCC announced that they wanted to undertake further analysis of the problems of the West African cotton sector, Benin, speaking on behalf of the C4, replied: "In the case of cotton, the core problem is relatively simple. The international cotton market is distorted by billions of dollars of subsidies which unquestionably affect world market prices. This is the issue that we need to resolve. All the other matters are ancillary" (WTO, 2005a, Annexe 2).

Regarding the fairness of the solution, the C4 argued that its countries had undertaken painful reforms in order to conform to the WTO's rules but were being kept from enjoying the fruits of that liberalization effort because other members were interfering in the global market in a way that was incompatible with the norms, if not the concrete rules, of the WTO:

> The WCA [West and Central Africa] countries emphasize that they have made the necessary, sometimes painful, adjustments in order to adapt their rural economies to global market requirements. In undertaking these reforms, they have shown their determination to become integrated in the global market and observe the WTO's rules. The results of these reforms have been virtually nullified by the refusal of other cotton–producing countries to accept market forces and competition, as defined in the WTO's objectives, by maintaining high levels of support for production and export … A solution to the problems affecting cotton would enable the multilateral system to show that the objectives fixed apply to all Member countries. (WTO, 2003i, § 15)

African countries thus argued that the elimination of cotton subsidies (and agricultural subsidies in general) would be fair because it would mean an application of the same liberal rules to all trade in goods. In addition, the C4 claimed that the elimination of cotton subsidies, without causing "too much 'suffering'" (WTO, 2003q, § 6) in the subsidy-providing countries, would save the West African cotton sector and raise many West African farmers from poverty. It would thus be the solution that brought the greatest good to the greatest number: "One half of cotton subsidies to American producers (around US$1 billion) goes to a few thousand farmers who cultivate around 1,000 acres of cotton and are thus well above the poverty threshold. In the WCA countries, on the other hand, these subsidies penalize one million farmers who only have five acres of cotton and live on less than US$1 per person per day" (WTO, 2003i, § 20).

Finally, the C4 pointed out that any practicable solution had to ensure a rapid and effective remedy to its cotton farmers' plight. This would need to entail the elimination of subsidies as well as a transitory measure. At an SCC meeting in 2005, the representative of Burkina Faso reported that, at a seminar on cotton held in his country, "people on the ground complained that negotiators and diplomats were showing too slow a progress in Geneva, while at home poverty was taking an increasing toll on families. Burkina Faso stressed that Members needed to speed up their efforts on the cotton issue" (WTO, 2005k, § 7).

The final element in the construction of an argument is the provision of a motivation for action. This can take the form of arguments about self-interest or morality. The C4 used both types of arguments. On the one hand, it pointed out that according to liberal economic theory, the elimination of subsidies, which supported an otherwise uncompetitive sector, was in the interest of the subsidy-paying countries, too: "In the long-term, in a market economy, these adjustments will be beneficial not only to the cotton-producing countries of West and Central Africa, which will be able to profit fully from their comparative advantages in the cotton trade, but also to the countries which have reduced or abandoned their 'uneconomical' production of cotton for other products and sectors where they have comparative advantages and where they are competitive without having to resort to subsidies" (WTO, 2003q, § 9).

Moreover, President Compaoré of Burkina Faso, in his speech to the TNC (WTO, 2003l), as well as Minister Akplogan of Benin in his opening address to the African Regional Workshop on Cotton (WTO, 2004g, Annexe 2), stressed that the subsidy-paying countries were destroying the efforts of their own development programs in West African countries.

At the same time, the C4 stressed the moral commitment of richer countries to rectify the situation. They emphasized that the very survival of the cotton sector in the C4 countries, and with it the livelihood of millions of poor cotton farmers, depended on a rapid solution (WTO, 2003i, § 35). "I am launching an appeal, in the name of several millions of women and men, who live in least developed countries and for whom cotton is the main means of subsistence," (WTO, 2003l) Compaoré said. This constituted a strong request for action. While the C4's proposed solution did not need any backing beyond liberal economic logic, in providing a motivation for action, the development aspect of the framing was decisive.

Having analysed the construction of the C4's argument through the practices of framing, presentation of facts, identification of a solution, and motivation for action, I now turn to the second set of practices involved in making an effective argument. These are the practices of getting others to agree, which build upon the practices of constructing an argument. The practices of getting others to agree include the legitimation of claims, coalitional outbidding, rhetorical entrapment, and veiled threats. Of these, the C4 mainly employed the first three. Again, I will examine the C4's use of these practices one after the other. The first practice to consider is the legitimation of claims, at which the C4 succeeded. Its framing, which combined liberal economic thinking with the moral appeal of the development discourse, provided it with a convincing legitimation of its claims. While liberalization is generally considered a legitimate objective in the WTO context, proponents of specific liberalization steps are nevertheless expected to explain how these will serve not only their national interest but also the common good. As development is considered a higher objective, for which the international community should provide support, it supplies the necessary legitimation for liberalization demands. At the same time, this combination also prevented arguments about the WTO not being the right forum, which developing countries that frame their demands solely in terms of development have often been confronted with. The C4's arguments about the fairness of the solution and its appeal to the moral commitment of the international community lent additional support to the legitimacy of its claims.

The second practice of getting others to agree, coalitional outbidding, also played an important role for the proponents of the Cotton Initiative. Their framing of the cotton issue as a case in which liberalization would foster development induced an understanding of shared interest in other countries with offensive interests in the agricultural negotiations. The G20, most prominently Brazil and Cuba (WTO, 2006d, § 4), as well as the Cairns Group (WTO, 2005q, §17), officially supported the Cotton Initiative. Even more importantly, the strong linkage of the cotton issue to the development master frame of the Doha Round through its presentation as a "test" for the development promise of that round invoked a strong feeling of shared identity and interest in all developing countries. The African Group submitted its own proposal on cotton in April 2005 (WTO, 2005i). The African, Caribbean, and Pacific (ACP) Group and the LDC Group also stood firmly behind the C4 (WTO, 2003ab). The strong attention the cotton issue received was certainly due, in part, to the great support it could muster among the WTO members.

The C4 further engaged in the third practice of getting others to agree, rhetorical entrapment. This strategy was employed with regard to the US and other subsidy-paying cotton producers. Fertile ground for their rhetorical entrapment was provided by the C4's framing in terms of development through liberalization as well as the stylization of the cotton issue as a test for the development promise of the Doha Round. The US and the other subsidy-paying developed countries were all advocates of economic liberalism and had upheld the trade regime's normative orientation towards liberalization in the past. In his speech to the TNC, President Compaoré accused the subsidy-paying countries of deviating from the liberalization norm: "The multiform subsidies still provided by some WTO member States to their agriculture … [were] in total contradiction with WTO basic principles" (WTO, 2003l). Speaking in support of the Cotton Initiative at an SCC meeting in 2005, Uganda emphasized that "it was the same countries which had pushed for developing countries to liberalize their economies which were still hanging on to such supports" (WTO, 2005k, § 6), thus pointing out inconsistencies in the position of the subsidy-paying countries.

The most powerful tool for rhetorically entrapping opponents of the Cotton Initiative, however, was the C4's successful resort to cotton as a test for the development promise of the round. This allowed the C4 to portray the failure to find a satisfactory solution to the cotton issue as the breaking of a promise and the consequent loss of credibility for the members involved, the Doha Round, and even the WTO as a whole (Lee, 2012, p. 95). Thus President Compaoré highlighted that the cotton issue was a "test that will allow member States to prove their sincerity behind the commitments taken at Doha" (WTO, 2003l). Rwanda, speaking on behalf of the African Group at the second meeting of the SCC, called cotton "a test for our Organization" and warned that "the credibility of this Organization would unquestionably suffer an enormous blow if, by next July, no tangible result had been achieved, if no progress had been made towards finding a genuine solution" (WTO, 2005h, Annexe 4).

WTO members had agreed to address cotton "ambitiously, expeditiously, and specifically" (WTO, 2004d, Annexe A, § 4) in the July 2004 package. The C4 now used this decision to rhetorically entrap members that were reluctant to reform their subsidy programs. Benin thus declared at a SCC meeting in 2005 that "the July mandate clearly stated that the issue of cotton had to be dealt with 'ambitiously' and Benin hoped that there would be more ambition for cotton than in the agriculture negotiations as a whole" (WTO, 2005n, § 8). Demanding an acceleration of discussions, Benin at the next SCC meeting warned: "We should not go back on the decision we all adopted within the framework of the July Package" (WTO, 2005o, Annexe 2). Mali seconded: "In July last year we all agreed that the cotton issue was to be addressed expeditiously, specifically and ambitiously. Until now, work on cotton has been postponed pending resolution of the problems in the agriculture negotiations. To my mind this is a departure from the letter and spirit of the commitments we made in July 2004" (WTO, 2005o, Annexe 2).

Veiled threats, the fourth strategy of getting others to agree, did not play an important role in the C4's strategy. Rather than make veiled threats, the C4 openly threatened to let the 2005 ministerial meeting in Hong Kong fail if no progress was made on cotton. "In view of the seriousness of the situation on the ground, the Ministers of the four countries reaffirmed that they would only be able to join a consensus in Hong Kong if the concerns of their countries and populations were effectively taken into account" (WTO, 2006d, Annexe 2). During the later course of the negotiations, the G20 (WTO, 2008h, § 19) and the African Group (WTO, 2009a, § 56) joined the C4; that is, they could not agree to a Doha outcome without a proper solution on cotton. In 2011, the C4 reaffirmed: "In the absence of an ambitious result for cotton, the C4 will use every means at its recourse to change the situation because those were defensive interests for millions of producers of cotton in Africa and at the heart of their very survival" (WTO, 2011c, § 8). Open threats like these belong in the realm of bargaining. However, representatives of the C4 backed up their threats with factual claims about the position of domestic stakeholders, which can be categorized as veiled threats. At an SCC meeting in 2005, Mali pointed out that West African cotton farmers believed that "the cotton sector was 'programmed' to disappear. As political representatives of their States, Mali and the other countries had played down such statements and did not share such an understanding of the situation because they believed that their partners had not 'programmed' the disappearance of cotton in West and Central Africa" (WTO, 2005n, § 7).

The message was: Political representatives of the C4 countries had tried to reassure their cotton farmers but had failed to dispel their perception that other countries' cotton subsidies were a conscious attack on their businesses. Domestic opinion, therefore, was beyond the control of political representatives and could pose a serious problem if the political representatives did not secure a solution to cotton.

The US Strategy: Elaborate Smoke and Mirrors

The US, which was the main target of the C4's Cotton Initiative, was unwilling to discuss a reduction of its cotton subsidies – at least, not as a stand-alone issue (ICTSD, 2003b). So instead, it constructed a counter-argumentation, which is analysed below. Again, the first practice to examine is the framing of the issue. The US reframed the issue in a subtle but important way. In its first response to the presentation of the Cotton Initiative at the Cancún ministerial, the US argued that factors beyond subsidies such as the general economic downturn, competition from artificial fibres, and a worldwide increase in supply were responsible for the suffering of the West African cotton farmers. Thus a "comprehensive" approach to the problem was needed. The US suggested that the West African countries diversify their economies away from cotton towards textile production (ICTSD, 2003a). After Cancún, the US was influential in the division of the topic into a trade aspect and a development aspect (Eagleton-Pierce, 2012, pp. 326–9). At the third meeting of the SCC, the US declared:

> We understand the critical role cotton plays in the economic and social development of the African region. We are committed to addressing development obstacles facing these countries through assistance programs …
>
> If we are committed to solving the difficulties faced by West African farmers, we must admit that trade in cotton is affected by many factors. While subsidies may play a role, other factors include high or unpredictable tariffs and discretionary TRQ administration, as well as market trends in fabrics, including competition with synthetics. And, specifically, domestic marketing arrangements in many West African countries negatively impact the price actually paid to farmers. (WTO, 2005k, Annexe 2)

The US thus reaffirmed the C4's framing of cotton as a development issue but reinterpreted that issue. Ignoring the fact that the C4 had presented the cotton sector as a vehicle for development that needed a free market and no other assistance, the US immediately spoke of "development obstacles" and "assistance programs." Sidelining the issue of subsidies that the C4 had raised, the US drew attention to a number of problems usually associated with development, such as outdated technology, poor infrastructure, and bad governance. In doing so, the US countered the C4's competitive victim framing with an uncompetitive victim framing.[5] By introducing other development issues, the US managed to separate the development dimension of the C4's framing from the liberalization aspect. Within the development aspect, the US talked about domestic reform and international aid rather than unfair global economic structures, thus drawing on different strands of the development discourse. The liberalization aspect of the C4's framing was silently marginalized. The US counterargumentation thus included aspects of what Krebs and Jackson (2007, p. 43) call a framing contest and what Schimmelfennig (1997, pp. 230–2; 2003, pp. 208–13) calls a controversial argumentation. At the same time, it included aspects of what Schimmelfennig calls a pseudo-competitive argumentation. The US did not openly reject the liberalization aspect of the C4's framing but did actively sideline that framing. The development aspect of the C4's framing was taken over and given a different meaning.

Another important aspect of the US counter-framing was that it sought to link the cotton issue, or at least what it called its trade aspect, to other issues in the negotiation. Initially, the US argued that cotton was part of the textile sector (ICTSD, 2003b) and needed to be addressed in the context of "agriculture, NAMA, development, and possibly rules (subsidies and trade-remedies)" (WTO, 2005a, Annexe 2). At the African Regional Workshop on Cotton, held by the WTO in March 2004, the position emerged that the trade aspect of the cotton issue should be treated as part of the agriculture negotiations (WTO, 2004b, § 9). During the further course of the negotiations the US vehemently insisted that no solution to cotton was possible without a general agreement on agriculture. They argued that an early harvest on cotton would threaten the cross-cutting approach of the overall negotiations (WTO, 2005k, Annexe 2) and that only comprehensive improvements in agricultural market access would ameliorate the situation facing African countries (WTO, 2005n, Annexe 2).

The presentation of facts played an important role in the counter-argumentation of the US. Its construction of the uncompetitive victim counter-frame was closely connected to the presentation of additional facts, which were meant to substantiate the claim that, contrary to the C4's analysis, subsidies were not the central problem. The African Regional Workshop on Cotton, which brought together the C4 and twenty-six other African countries as well as the US, the EU, Canada, Japan, China, and eighteen multilateral organizations including the IMF and the World Bank (WTO, 2004b), perfectly served this objective. Its opening session on "factors in African cotton production and trade" (WTO, 2004g, II, B) was supposed to "establish the facts on the basis of which the solution-oriented dialogue between representatives of the trade and development communities, at the subsequent sessions, would be based" (WTO, 2004g, § 4), explained chairperson Dadusch from the World Bank. In a number of presentations, given by representatives from multilateral organizations, a "complex range of factors influencing cotton production, consumption, trade and price trends" (WTO, 2004b, § 8) were identified, including "internal taxation policies, decline of cotton as a share of total fibre consumption relative to chemical fibres in textiles and clothing, new technologies, increased transgenic varieties, internal structural difficulties (trade and finance) within individual countries, the impact of HIV/AIDS, and external trade barriers, particularly trade distorting government intervention" (WTO, 2004b, § 8).

Despite all the expertise provided at the workshop, at the first meeting of the SCC in February 2005, the EU (WTO, 2005a, § 10) as well as the US (WTO, 2005a, § 18, Annexe 2) argued that further analysis of the global cotton market and the situation in West Africa was necessary before solutions could be discussed. At a SCC meeting in July 2005, the US presented a comprehensive "analytical input" (WTO, 2005a, § 18) on the cotton issue. It reiterated that the problems of West African cotton farmers had multiple sources, including increased global competition, flagging demand, and domestic problems such as outdated production techniques, sub-standard infrastructure, and missing domestic competition. Its argument was that West African farmers were lagging behind in productivity while globally, production and yields had increased and prices had fallen. "Increasing global supply means West Africa must increase its competitiveness" and "development assistance is needed to assist West Africa and its cotton sector to be more economically viable," the US concluded. In addition, the US cited studies by the Food and Agriculture Organization (FAO), the IMF, and the World Bank which found that the elimination of subsidies would not result in a significant price increase. According to these studies, the elimination of subsidies without liberalization of market access could even hurt African countries and LDCs. The largest benefits would be reaped by comprehensive tariff reductions (WTO, 2005n, Annexe 2), as favoured by the US. The US counterargumentation thus also included aspects of Schimmelfennig's (Schimmelfennig, 1997, pp. 230–2; 2003, pp. 208–13) concept of competitive argumentation, where the opponent questions the proponent's description of the factual situation.

The next practice of constructing an argument that needs to be examined is the identification of a solution. Based on its analysis of the situation, the US argued that the solution identified by the C4 would be ineffective (WTO, 2005n, Annexe 2). Instead, the US proposed a two-tiered solution that would address not only the trade aspect but also the development aspect of the cotton issue. While it insisted that the trade aspect – that is, the issue of subsidies elimination – could only be discussed within the overall agricultural negotiations, it readily engaged in the organization of development aid aimed at increasing the productivity of cotton farmers in West African countries (WTO, 2005k, Annexe 2, 2005n, Annexe 2). The US welcomed the domestic reform efforts of the West African countries and over the course of the negotiations made increasing demands to see results in this regard (WTO, 2007f, §§ 31–2; 2008h, §§ 87–9). This focus on development aid and domestic reform matched the US framing of the issue as essentially a domestic development problem.

A central element of the solution identified by the US regarding the development aspect of cotton was the Director-General's Consultative Framework for the coordination of development aid to the cotton sector, which was established as part of the July 2004 package. This constituted an institutional process in which the practice of presentation of facts again played an important role. Donors presented figures and information on their relevant aid programs and activities. Recipient countries were, in turn, expected to provide information on actions taken and envisaged to include cotton in their World Bank/IMF Poverty Reduction Strategy Papers and Diagnostic Trade Integration Studies, and to prepare national strategies for their cotton sectors and cotton-sector specific projects to be funded. They were also expected to report on their domestic reform efforts (WTO, 2004h, § 18). The donor countries provided a steady stream of information about their activities during the consecutive meetings of the Consultative Framework; meanwhile, the recipient countries struggled to review this information (WTO, 2006g, § 13) and to provide the information expected from them (WTO, 2004h, §§ 19–26). The US repeatedly reminded recipient countries that "the funding process required 'give and take'" (WTO, 2004h, § 51) and that it would like to see more "frequent and comprehensive reports" (WTO, 2008h, § 88) about domestic reform projects and the implementation of aid projects, all the while using its superior capacity to present facts in order to put the C4 countries on the defensive.

With regard to the final practice for constructing an argument, the provision of a motivation for action, the US did not challenge the C4's argumentation, nor did it present any new arguments. The construction of their counterargument thus hinged on the three practices of framing, presentation of facts, and identification of a solution.

Among the practices of getting others to agree, the US argumentation was centred on one in particular, the practice of rhetorical entrapment. To be precise, the US engaged in a somewhat atypical strategy of rhetorical entrapment. It did not hold the C4 to any norm or to earlier commitments, but instead turned the C4's framing of cotton as a development issue back on it. The competitive victim frame of the C4 claimed that West African cotton producers were competitive and the sector could be a vehicle for development, if it weren't for the unfair subsidization of cotton farmers in the US. The uncompetitive victim framing of the US instead claimed that West African cotton farmers suffered from domestic problems and needed development aid. Cotton went from a development opportunity to a development problem. This way, the US was able to sideline the issue of subsidies and hold the C4 responsible for its own misery.

While the C4 understood this to be a strategy and repeatedly reminded other members that the trade aspect of the cotton negotiations should not be sidelined by the development aspect (WTO, 2005a, § 36; 2005d, § 3; 2005o, Annexe 2, Statement by Benin; 2006d, § 20), it accepted the development aid offered and hurried to prioritize cotton in the donors' various programs. In some of its statements, aid was more central than trade rules (WTO, 2006e, §§ 5, 15; 2006n, § 18). When the C4's demand for a transitory measure in its original framing as compensation encountered the firm resistance of the US and other developed countries, the C4 was quick to reframe it as an "(emergency) support" (WTO, 2003aa; 2005i, § 27) or "rescue fund" (WTO, 2005d, § 9) – a concept that fitted the categories of the development discourse rather than the discourse of economic liberalism and that defined the C4 as uncompetitive rather than competitive victims. In the course of the negotiations, the LDC Group, in an attempt to support the C4, even presented data proving the low competitiveness of West African cotton farmers and their need for aid (WTO, 2009a, § 39), completely forgetting that the C4 had made a point of demonstrating their competitiveness. The C4 itself "acknowledged the necessity of measures and contributions to improve productivity in the cotton sector" (WTO, 2009a, § 24). The proponents of the Cotton Initiative and their allies had so internalized the development discourse and its concepts of deficiency, reform, and aid that they were unable to avoid constructing themselves as helpless victims and offering polite thanks for the aid that was being used to deflect attention from their original demands. They were easy picking for rhetorical entrapment by the US.

Eagleton-Pierce (2012, p. 322; 2013, pp. 99–100) speculates that the compensation part of the C4 proposal constituted an "implicit 'plan B'" from the beginning. The C4 knew that subsidy elimination was not feasible in the short-run, and it may also have been aware that the US would hardly agree to pay compensation, especially as such a mechanism is not rooted in WTO procedures; but it might have hoped that its demand for a transitional measure would result in additional development assistance, and anything that would ameliorate the plight of its cotton farmers was a win. However, Eagleton-Pierce also emphasizes that the way the US drew upon the development aspect in the C4's own framing and reinterpreted it was "perhaps the subtlest distortion of the C4's position"; he observes that development assistance measures felt like a "natural" part of the solution even for C4 diplomats in a "pre-reflexive, doxic sense" (Eagleton-Pierce, 2013, p. 110). Imboden from the IDEAS centre, who had advocated for the inclusion of the development aspect in the C4's framing, in an interview with Eagleton-Pierce, expressed his astonishment that aid was being presented as central to development within the Doha Round negotiations, even though, in this context, "trade is supposed to be development, not aid!" (Eagleton-Pierce, 2013, p. 111).

Of course, the problems of West African cotton farmers are not limited to the price-depressing impacts of other countries' subsidies. As Sneyd (2011, pp. 107–108), who criticizes the influence of northern NGOs in this regard, points out, the Cotton Initiative focused on trade liberalization as the solution and disregarded other problems such as price volatility, the impact of fluctuating exchange rates, secular price declines for raw materials, and the challenge of moving up the value chain by developing domestic processing industries. This take on the issue was controversial even within Oxfam (Sneyd, 2011, pp. 111–14). Sneyd (2011, p. 119) attributes the insistence of IDEAS centre staff on the centrality of the subsidy issue and their characterization of cotton-specific development aid as counterproductive to negotiations to their liberal convictions, which he perceives as objectionable.

Without ignoring the complexity of the problem, however, it is obvious that the US strategically seized on the domestic development deficits in the West African cotton sector as a means to detract attention from the issue of subsidy reduction. A combined effort at reducing global market distortions and ameliorating domestic conditions was called for, but this is not what happened. Instead, the trade aspect of the issue was sidelined while the WTO organized development assistance, which is not their field of expertise and would better have been left to other international organizations. The injection of the development aspect into the WTO negotiations on cotton was thus much more of a win for the US than for the C4.

In another, less central and more classical move of rhetorical entrapment, the US instrumentalized the wording of the July 2004 package in order to preclude any discrete negotiations on the cotton issue. As mentioned previously, the proponents of the Cotton Initiative emphasized the commitment to an ambitious, expeditious, and specific treatment of the cotton issue contained in the July 2004 package; the US instead highlighted another aspect of the July 2004 package, that is, that the trade aspect of cotton was to be discussed "within the agriculture negotiations" (WTO, 2004d, Annexe A, § 4). Thus, it declared at an SCC meeting in 2006:

> The July 2004 Framework provides, and the Hong Kong Declaration affirms that cotton will be addressed "ambitiously, expeditiously and specifically *within the agriculture negotiations.*" It is important to remind ourselves that before any result can be reached on cotton, we must first reach agreement on the core modalities of the agricultural negotiations, where much work remains to be done. (WTO, 2006m, Annexe 2, emphasis in original)

The other practices of getting others to agree, namely the legitimation of claims, coalitional outbidding, and veiled threats, did not play a role in the counterargumentation of the US. The rhetorical entrapment of the C4 within the strings of the development discourse was, instead, complemented by the strategy of stalling – which constitutes a practice of preventing others from making an effective argument.

The US engaged in stalling in two ways. First, it initiated an excessive presentation and analysis of facts that was not necessitated by the problem as defined by the C4. This process served the presentation of a different factual situation and the construction of the uncompetitive victim frame, both of which were instrumental in the US strategy of rhetorically entrapping the C4; it also bought the US time. Second, the US effectively stalled discussion on subsidy elimination by linking the trade aspect of the cotton issue to the overall agricultural negotiations as part of its counter-framing of the issue. Since the agricultural negotiations have progressed only very slowly and the US has kept insisting that it will not discuss the issue of cotton subsidies separate from the overall issue of agricultural subsidies, there has been very little progress on the elimination of cotton subsidies. In the meantime, the buzz created around the development aspect of the cotton issue through the Consultative Framework process for coordinating development aid has created the impression that something is being done about the situation of the West African cotton farmers.

On the issue of eliminating cotton subsidies, the US never presented any proposal. The proposals of the C4 and the African Group were the only ones on the table for a long time. At a number of consecutive SCC meetings in 2005, African countries called for written responses or alternative proposals from other members (WTO, 2005n, §§ 9–10; 2005o, Annexe 2; 2005p, §6, Annexe 2; 2005q, § 16). The EU submitted a written proposal by the end of the year (WTO, 2005r), whereas the US responded that the outcome on cotton would depend on the outcome of the overall agricultural negotiations (WTO, 2005l). The same discussion repeated itself after the C4 submitted its proposal for a formula for reducing domestic support for cotton in March 2006. In April 2006, Chad, speaking on behalf of the C4, called for responses to their paper (WTO, 2006n, Annexe 2), and the representative of the Côte d'Ivoire questioned the entire point of the SCC if nothing could be discussed before the completion of the agricultural modalities:

> The first reactions we received left us perplexed: we were told, as indeed we already knew, that the negotiations on cotton were inexorably linked to the negotiations on agriculture. Yes, we knew this very well, but we had proposed a calculation formula which did not require, for the time being, any results in agriculture. All we are asking at this stage is whether the proposed method could be discussed, because we also wanted to enrich the discussions. The fact that this question received no response bewilders us somewhat. One thing I was going to say today, is that although it may be true that we must know the results for agriculture before determining the results for cotton, why do we have a Sub-Committee on Cotton? What is the point, if not to take preliminary steps such as those which you have taken in giving us reference papers on which we are tirelessly working in order to have one or more texts when the time comes. (WTO, 2006n, Annexe 2bis)

In December 2007, the C4 asked the US and the EU to submit counterproposals in writing. The EU promised to respond shortly to the C4 proposal, but the US declared that it would only respond "after general commitments for agriculture as a whole were clear" (WTO, 2007f,

§§ 15–16). In 2009, the C4 was still left to reiterate its expectation for counterproposals by the US and EU (WTO, 2009b, § 8 h).

The decision on export subsidies for cotton taken in 2015 in Nairobi was possible only because WTO members concurrently agreed to eliminate export subsidies on all agricultural products. When negotiations on domestic support, including for cotton, picked up after Nairobi, the US reverted to demanding more information and analysis before negotiations could start. In 2018, the US submitted a communication on "the situation in cotton" (WTO, 2018), in which it declared:

> In order for Members to have productive discussions to address the challenges facing cotton farmers, an understanding of the current state of Members' trade policies is needed. Transparency by Members with regards to their notifications on market access, domestic support, and export subsidies is the best way to begin engagement … In addition to greater transparency, Members need to improve their understandings of the factors affecting cotton trade over the last decade and going forward in order to most effectively define a negotiating context. (WTO, 2018, §§ 19–20)

By conducting an analysis of all members' trade policies regarding cotton, the US can draw attention to the fact that China is now providing much higher subsidies to its cotton farmers and that a number of other countries spend sums comparable to those paid by the US. But demanding more information from other members and yet another extensive analysis is also a way to stall the negotiations again.

4 The Debate about Sectoral Tariff Elimination in Industrial Goods

Since WTO members resumed negotiations on Doha Round issues in the form of packages of deliverables at the 2013 ministerial conference in Bali, non-agricultural market access (NAMA) has not been on the table. When the mini-ministerial in 2008, which turned out to be the last attempt at negotiating modalities for a Doha Round single undertaking, broke down, conflicts within the NAMA negotiations played an important role. In 2007, the US started demanding that emerging economies, in particular Brazil, India, and China, make larger concessions in NAMA. They argued that these countries, whose economies had boomed and gained much greater weight since the start of the Doha Round, could no longer expect the same treatment as other developing countries and had to make concessions that matched their new economic power (ICTSD, 2009c; Office of the USTR, 2009a, 2009b). In particular, the US suggested that in order to increase their concessions, the emerging countries should participate in sectoral tariff elimination initiatives in NAMA (ICTSD, 2008e).

A number of developed and advanced developing countries had been seeking to include initiatives for tariff elimination in selected sectors in the modalities for NAMA since the start of the Doha Round. Most developing countries opposed the idea, and they had been able to secure an agreement that participation in such sectorals was to be voluntary. When the US demanded greater commitments from emerging economies, these were not willing to increase their offers. Regarding sectorals, they insisted on their voluntary nature. The proponents of sectoral tariff elimination, however, kept insisting that a critical mass of WTO members, including large emerging economies, had to participate. The conflict was never resolved and contributed decisively to the deadlock in the Doha Round negotiations.

In comparison to the Cotton Initiative, which I analysed in chapter 3, the outcome of the debate about sectoral tariff elimination in NAMA is less surprising. Nevertheless, it is an interesting case, for it is one of the central issues in which the conflict between the established trading powers and the emerging economies that is at the core of the WTO's current difficulties has been fought out. In contrast to the cotton case, developing countries were on the defensive and articulated a very different notion of the relationship between trade and development than the C4. The argumentation strategies of the two parties were more openly antagonistic.

In this chapter, I analyse the negotiation strategies of both the proponents and the opponents of sectoral tariff elimination in NAMA. The chapter begins with some background information about tariff structures in NAMA and the negotiation mandate. Then I describe how the debate over sectoral tariff elimination as an element of the NAMA modalities progressed between 2002 and 2011. To explain this process, I turn to the negotiation strategies of the two parties. As in chapter 3, I will start with the argumentation of the opponents, examining their use of the practices of strategic arguing outlined in chapter 2 (practices of constructing an argument and practices of getting other to agree). I will then analyse the counterargumentation of the opponents. For this, again, I will draw on the conceptual scheme of the practices of strategic arguing. In addition, I will discuss how the counterargumentation of the opponents can be categorized in terms of Krebs and Jackson's as well as Schimmelfennig's typologies of argumentative conflicts.

Background

Developed countries have long had a competitive advantage in most industrial goods sectors, with notable exceptions, like textiles. In the trade negotiating rounds of the GATT, developed countries have by and by reduced most of their NAMA tariffs to very low levels. Because negotiations were organized according to the major-interest norm (Finlayson & Zacher, 1981), and because developing countries were exempted from reciprocity in commitments, developed countries mainly struck deals among themselves. Developing countries were given a free ride, as tariff reductions were extended to all WTO members on a most-favoured-nation (MFN) basis. As a result, at the start of the first WTO negotiation round, the Doha Round, the NAMA tariffs of developed country members were on average much lower than those of developing country members. While developed countries had bound their tariffs at an average of 12.5 per cent of the product price, the bound tariffs

Figure 4.1 WTO members' tariffs for non-agricultural products at the start of the Doha Round (data on bound tariffs is taken from the World Trade Report (WTO, 2003a), data on applied tariffs from UNCTAD (2020), countries are classified according to UNCTAD (2020))

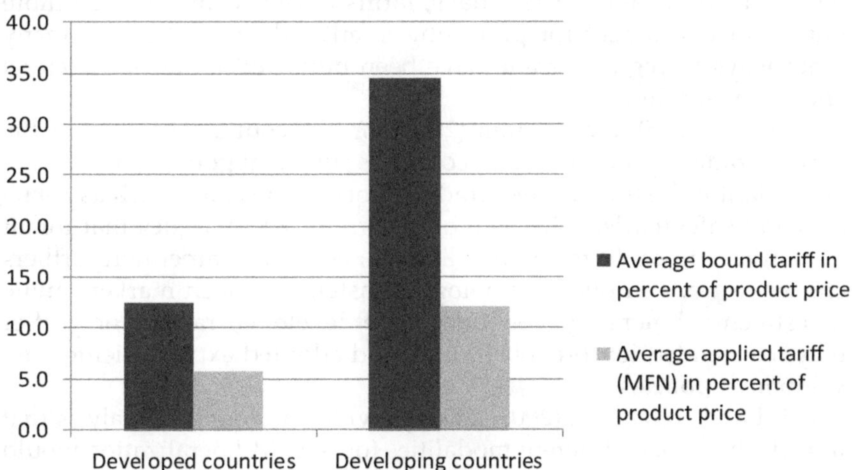

of developing countries averaged 34.6 per cent of the product price. The difference was smaller, but still substantial, in applied tariffs – here developed country members' tariffs averaged 5.8, those of developing country members 12.2 per cent of the product price (see figure 4.1).

In the Doha Round, many developed countries were aiming at further tariff reductions in NAMA and a harmonization of tariff levels. They were eager to ensure the participation of developing countries, not least because they were afraid that a further reduction of their own tariffs would leave them without bargaining chips to trade against market opening in developing countries.

Most developing countries, however, were reluctant to liberalize access to their markets because they wanted to retain flexibility in their industrial policies. Among observers, the benefits of NAMA liberalization for developing countries are debated. Economic theory holds that free trade is generally beneficial because it enables the optimal exploitation of comparative advantages. As Akyüz (2005) argues, however, this assumption neglects important requirements of the development process. In order to industrialize, developing countries need to move beyond the resource- and labour-intensive industries, where they currently hold comparative advantages. During this process, they require policy space to protect infant industries in a flexible manner. The particular industries that need protection will change as an economy moves up the value chain. Binding specific tariff lines at an early stage in the development process is therefore not advisable. Akyüz further holds that today's leading economies themselves relied on protectionism during their industrialization. These days, tariffs have become an even more important instrument for protecting infant industries, because many other ways to regulate trade have been outlawed under multilateral and regional rules.

Amsden (2005) and Legrain (2006), on the contrary, claim that the current trade regime still leaves countries sufficient policy space to support infant industries via less trade-distorting measures such as subsidies and safeguards. What is more, Legrain (2006) argues that infant industries will profit from liberalization, because competition furthers efficiency, trade implies technology transfer, and open markets invite investments. Emerging economies have developed rapidly only after they have ended import substitution and adopted export-oriented development policies.

Laird and colleagues (2003; 2006) provide an economic analysis that models the impact different modalities for NAMA liberalization would have on imports and exports, domestic production and sectoral output, government revenues, economic welfare, real wages, and employment in developing countries. They conclude that trade effects are likely to be positive in the aggregate but that important differences exist between countries. In particular, LDCs that currently profit from trade preferences could lose export markets if access is liberalized. Besides, adjustment costs and reduced government revenues would frequently pose serious problems. Hammouda and colleagues (2007), who assess the NAMA negotiations from an African perspective, also raise the issue of preference erosion. In addition, they emphasize that supply side constraints limit African prospects of profiting from liberalization. Consequently, they contend that aid for trade and capacity-building measures are an important element of special and differential treatment.

The Doha negotiation agenda regarding NAMA stipulated that "the negotiations shall take fully into account the special needs and interests of developing and least-developed country participants, including through less than full reciprocity in reduction commitments" (WTO, 2001b, § 16). The modalities were to include "appropriate studies and capacity-building measures to assist least-developed countries to participate effectively in the negotiations" (WTO, 2001b, § 16). Thus, developing countries were promised less than full reciprocity but no free ride. Every effort was made to ensure that even LDCs would participate in the negotiations.

The mandate did not prescribe any specific modalities for the further liberalization of NAMA. It did, however, state that negotiations should aim to "reduce or as appropriate eliminate tariffs … as well as non-tariff barriers, in particular on products of export interest to developing countries" (WTO, 2001b, § 16). As the Uruguay Round had seen "zero for zero" plurilateral agreements, in which participants agreed to eliminate tariffs on a number of NAMA sectors, the wording of elimination of tariffs as appropriate was read by some as a reference to such sectoral zero-for-zero agreements. Besides products of export interest to developing countries, "environmental goods and services" were mentioned in the Doha agenda as candidates for specific liberalization efforts (WTO, 2001b, § 31).

Course of Negotiations

The NAMA negotiations started in 2002 with a debate on whether the negotiations would best be organized according to a formula, sectoral, or request-and-offer approach, or a combination of these. Among those who wanted to include sectoral initiatives for tariff elimination or harmonization into the modalities were almost all developed countries, including Australia (WTO, 2003c, § 1.40), Canada (WTO, 2002f, §§ 8, 11–12), the EU (WTO, 2002a, § 11; 2002i, §§ 9–10), Japan (WTO, 2002b, § 4; 2002l, §§ 2–3; 2003f), Norway (WTO, 2002c, § 8), Switzerland (WTO, 2002m, §§ 5, 12), and the US (WTO, 2002o, §§ 8–9), as well as some developing countries like Chinese Taipei (WTO, 2002p, § 5), Colombia (WTO, 2003n, § 1.29), Ecuador (WTO, 2003c, § 1.43), Pakistan (WTO, 2003n, § 1.47), Singapore (WTO, 2002d, § 11), and Thailand (WTO, 2003d, § 6). The most ambitious proposals came from Hong Kong (WTO, 2002j), New Zealand (WTO, 2003c, §§ 1.12–1.14), and the US (WTO, 2002o), which wanted to eliminate NAMA tariffs altogether. While only the US proposal included sectorals as a first step, these proposals shared with most proposals for sectoral initiatives the idea of complete tariff elimination.

Many developing countries were not willing to participate in tariff elimination and were wary of the modalities of sectoral initiatives. An influential Indian submission in October 2002 provided a critical analysis of sectorals from the perspective of developing countries (WTO, 2002g, § 7.a). Kenya declared that African countries were against the inclusion of sectorals in the NAMA modalities (WTO, 2003c, § 1.38). In December 2002, China proposed to consider sectorals but only as supplement to a formula approach and with participation on a voluntary basis (WTO, 2002q, §§ 4–6). This position soon became common ground among the majority of developing countries (WTO, 2002h, §§ 1.17, 1.29, 1.34; 2002k, § 3.9; 2002n, § 13; 2003c, § 1.52; 2003d, § 6; 2003g, § 7; 2003h, § 4; 2003n, §§ 1.86, 1.101; 2003p, § 1.62; 2003ac, §§ 1.27, 1.42, 1.83, 1.87).

When the chairperson of the Negotiating Group on Market Access (NGMA), Girard, presented the first draft modalities for the NAMA negotiations in May 2003, they included a formula cut but also a mandatory sectoral component. Sectoral agreements with mandatory participation for all but LDCs were envisaged in a number of sectors the WTO secretariat had identified as being of particular interest to developing countries, namely electronics and electrical goods, fish and fish products, footwear, leather goods, motor vehicle parts and components, stones, gems, and precious metals, as well as textiles and clothing. The modalities also foresaw the possibility of adding further sectoral initiatives on a voluntary basis (WTO, 2003j, 2003ad, § 1.4). The developed countries that had previously proposed sectoral negotiations welcomed the way Girard had included them in the draft (WTO, 2003v, § 7;, 2003ad, §§ 1.56, 1.61, 1.84, 1.91) and demanded that additional sectors – including ones of interest to developed countries – be added on a mandatory or at least voluntary basis (WTO, 2003ad, §§ 1.12, 1.23, 1.61, 1.70, 1.108). A large number of developing countries, however, including many of those that had previously supported sectorals, objected to the mandatory nature of the sectorals listed in the draft (WTO, 2003t, §§ 3.6, 5.3; 2003ad, §§ 1.29, 1.32, 1.33, 1.35, 1.37, 1.41, 1.44, 1.48, 1.51, 1.55, 1.65, 1.66, 1.67, 1.74, 1.76, 1.80, 1.87, 1.89, 1.104, 1.105) or sectorals *per se* (WTO, 2003s, § 36; 2003ad, § 1.54). In particular, LDCs and other developing countries profiting from trade preferences saw sectoral tariff elimination as a problem, even if they were not required to participate, because it would lead to an erosion of their preferences (WTO, 2003o, § 6; 2003r, §§ 11–12; 2003ad, § 1.116; 2003ae, § 1.22; 2005b, § 7). The ACP countries therefore rejected any form of sectorals (WTO, 2004a, § 7).

While sectorals were retained in the further discussion, mandatory participation was progressively abandoned. The framework for NAMA modalities, drafted during the 2003 ministerial conference in Cancún (WTO, 2003z, Annexe B) and subsequently adopted as part of the July 2004 package (WTO, 2004d, Annexe B), said on sectorals:

> We recognize that a sectorial tariff component, aiming at elimination or harmonization is another key element to achieving the objectives of paragraph 16 of the Doha Ministerial Declaration with regard to the reduction or elimination of tariffs, in particular on products of export interest to developing countries. We recognize that participation by all participants will be important to that effect. We therefore instruct the Negotiating Group

to pursue its discussions on such a component, with a view to defining product coverage, participation, and adequate provisions of flexibility for developing-country participants. (WTO, 2004d, § 7)

Participation by all countries was thus highlighted as important, but not proscribed. Over time, the proponents of a sectoral component changed their approach to one of critical mass. At an NGMA meeting in June 2004, Hong Kong reported that it had, together with Canada and the US, organized a plurilateral session on sectoral initiatives based on a critical mass approach. Twenty invited delegations had discussed questions concerning the choice of sectors, participation thresholds for critical mass, product coverage, and special and differential treatment (WTO, 2004e, § 3.1). At the same meeting, the United Arab Emirates tabled a proposal for a critical mass–based zero-for-zero sectoral on raw materials (WTO, 2004c, 2004e, § 2). In 2005, Canada and the US circulated a paper on "How to Create a Critical Mass Sectoral Initiative" (WTO, 2005g).

In the ministerial declaration adopted at the 2005 ministerial meeting in Hong Kong, members unambiguously determined that participation in sectorals was to be voluntary:

In furtherance of paragraph 7 of the NAMA Framework, we recognize that Members are pursuing sectoral initiatives. To this end, we instruct the Negotiating Group to review proposals with a view to identifying those which could garner sufficient participation to be realized. Participation should be on a non-mandatory basis. (WTO, 2005u, § 16)

Negotiations on specific sectorals picked up speed. In January 2006, Singapore submitted an "Update on the Negotiations on the Sectoral Tariff Component" (WTO, 2006a). Negotiations based on the critical mass approach (WTO, 2006a, § 6) were going on in the sectors of automobiles and auto parts, bicycles, chemicals, electronics and electrical equipment, fish, footwear, forest products, gems and jewellery, pharmaceuticals and medical equipment, raw materials, sporting goods and apparel, and textiles (WTO, 2006a, §§ 1–2). Several NGMA meetings in the first half of 2006 discussed sectoral proposals informally (WTO, 2006h, §§ 1.1–1.4; 2006i, §§ 1.1–1.2).

While developing countries' dissatisfaction with other elements of the evolving NAMA modalities led to the formation of the NAMA-11 Group (Vickers, 2009, pp. 165–9), most developing countries seemed to have made their peace with the non-mandatory sectorals. In a joint communication on the NAMA modalities in October 2007, the ACP

Figure 4.2 WTO decisions on NAMA sectorals

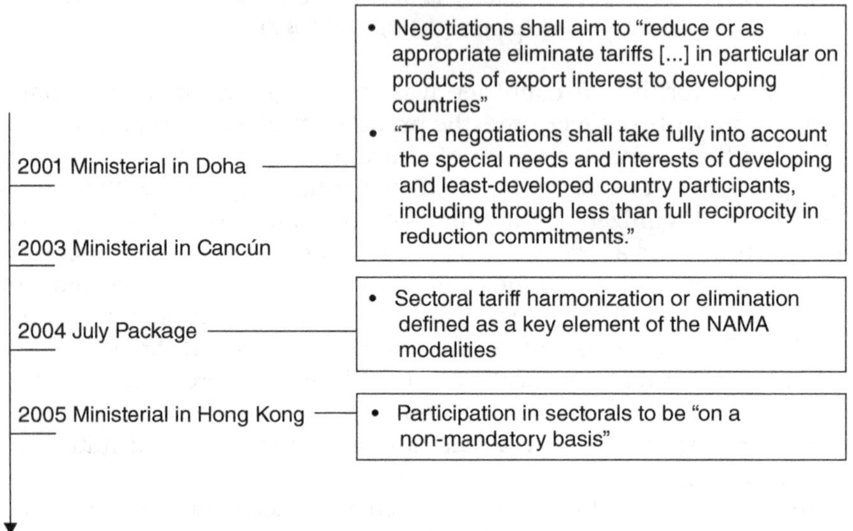

Group, the African Group, the NAMA-11 Group, and the Group of Small and Vulnerable Economies (SVE) acknowledged that "voluntary sectoral negotiations ... can be important to address the diverse needs and negotiating objectives of various Members." They emphasized the process needed to be sensitive to possible adverse effects on non-participating preference-dependent countries. But the definition of sectorals as voluntary seemed to have made them *per se* acceptable to the majority of developing countries (WTO, 2007c, § 7).

In the meantime, the global economy had changed. The economic power of developing countries in general, and a number of big emerging economies in particular, was increasing fast. Brazil, India, and China were the most important of these emerging powers (Pigman, 2009, p. 45). In the decade between 2000 and 2010, the GDP of developing countries gained 6.1 per cent annually on average, but that of developed countries only 1.6 per cent. Brazil's GDP on average grew by 3.7 per cent annually, India's by 7.8 per cent annually, and China's by 10.8 per cent annually (UNCTAD, 2013, pp. 424–6) (see figure 4.3).

At the same time, the merchandise exports of developing countries on average grew by 14.4 per cent and their imports by 14.1 per cent annually. The average annual increase in developed country merchandise exports was 8.5 per cent, and the average annual increase of their merchandise imports 8.6 per cent. Brazil's merchandise exports rose by

Figure 4.3 Annual average GDP growth rates of developed, developing, and big emerging economies, 2000 to 2010, in percentages (based on data from UNCTAD (2020))

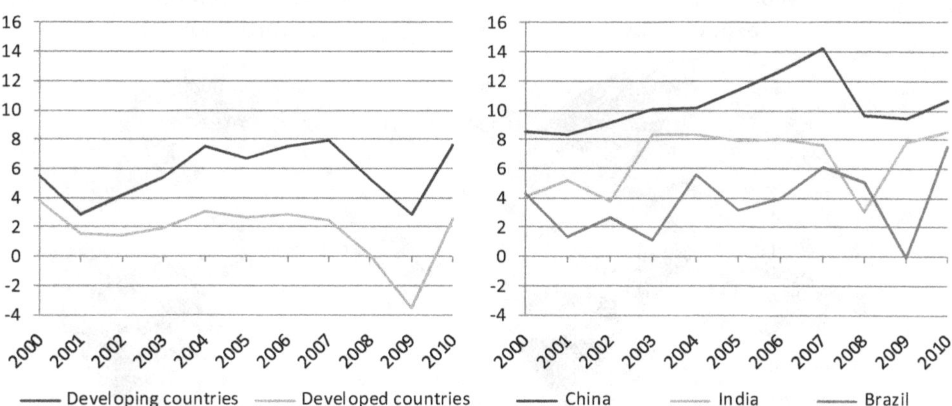

an annual average of 15.5 per cent, their imports by an annual average of 14.9 per cent. The respective figures for India's merchandise exports and imports were 20.1 and 24.6 per cent respectively. The Chinese merchandise exports on average rose by 22.4 per cent and their imports by 20.9 per cent annually (UNCTAD, 2013, pp. 28–31). While Brazil's main exports are agricultural products, and India's services, China's rapid growth is based on its exports of manufactures (Hopewell, 2010). At the start of the Doha Round in 2001, China was in fifth place in manufactures exporters, behind the US, Germany, Japan, and France. It surpassed France in 2002, Japan in 2004, the US in 2006, and Germany in 2008, becoming the top exporter of manufactured goods (WTO, 2022a) (see figure 4.4).

Competition from China has invoked fears in all developed countries, but most strongly in the US. The rise of China constitutes a threat to the US position as the world's largest economy and the hegemonic power in post–Cold War international relations (Pigman, 2009, p. 46). The direct economic relations between the two countries add to the perception of threat, as the US is importing large quantities of goods from China and in return exporting its debt to China, creating a worryingly high trade deficit. The US blamed Chinese currency policy for its unbalanced trade relations with the rising power and was eager to use the Doha Round to gain additional market access to China and other emerging markets, such as Brazil and India, to redress the situation (Scott, 2007). Meanwhile, other emerging and developing countries

Figure 4.4 Share of top exporters in world merchandise trade 2001 and 2008 (based on data from the WTO (2022a))

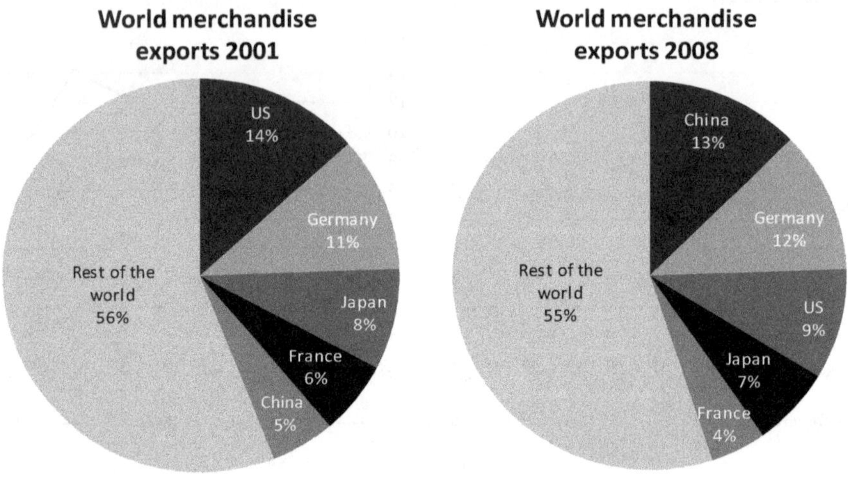

feel threatened themselves by China's ever-increasing output of cheap manufactured goods, which are displacing their products in many markets (Blustein, 2009, pp. 244–5; Hopewell, 2010, pp. 19–20).

In January 2006, in a speech at Georgetown University (Rice, 2006) US Secretary of State Condoleezza Rice declared that the rise of emerging economies necessitated new diplomatic strategies by the US. The US and the EU both increased pressure on China and other emerging economies to play a more active role in the WTO negotiations and take on more commitments, reflecting their changed role in the global economy (Blustein, 2009, p. 238; Chin, 2009, pp. 128–9; Gao, 2011, p. 159). At a meeting between the trade ministers of Brazil, the EU, India, and the US in Potsdam in June 2007, the established powers clashed with the emerging economies over the level of ambition in NAMA liberalization (Office of the USTR, 2008, part II, p. 2).

Tariff elimination sectorals came to play a central role in this quarrel. In December 2007, Canada, the EU, Iceland, Japan, New Zealand, Norway, Switzerland, and the US submitted a joint communication on the NAMA modalities in which they highlighted that they expected the round to deliver ambitious market openings for all members and that they would judge the results on, among other factors, the participation in sectorals (WTO, 2007d, §§ 1–3). In particular, the US wanted Brazil, India, and China to participate in sectoral tariff elimination (Blustein,

2009, p. 253). When members started to discuss new draft modalities for NAMA in the spring of 2008, Canada, Iceland, Japan, Norway, Switzerland, and the US proposed to reward developing countries that agreed to participate in sectorals with access to a less demanding formula (ICTSD, 2008a). Shortly before the mini-ministerial in Geneva in July 2008, where it was hoped that full modalities would be produced, NGMA chairperson Stephenson issued another revision of the draft modalities in which the wording on sectorals was modified in a small but important aspect: After "Participation in sectoral initiatives is on a non-mandatory basis," a qualification was added: "However, for some Members, sectoral initiatives that reach a critical mass of participation will help to balance the overall results of the negotiation on non-agricultural market access, which includes the coefficients in paragraph 5 and the levels of flexibilities and related provisions of paragraph 7," that is, the level of special and differential treatment provided for regarding the formula (WTO, 2008b, § 9).

In their Ministerial Communiqué, the NAMA-11 countries objected that "sectoral negotiations should remain voluntary and that there could be no linkage between sectoral negotiations and the coefficients and flexibilities" (WTO, 2008c). The mini-ministerial consisted mainly of discussions among the inner circle of the US, the EU, Japan, Australia, Brazil, India, and China. On NAMA, the US and the EU considered it a priority to ensure participation of a "critical mass" of WTO members in NAMA sectorals (ICTSD, 2008b). But India and China succeeded in fighting off the inclusion of a linkage between developing country participation in sectorals and formula flexibilities in the draft modalities (Ismail, 2009, p. 208), as well as efforts to commit the big emerging economies to participation in sectorals.

In December 2008, NGMA chairperson Wasescha presented another revision of the 2008 draft NAMA modalities. He generally saw a wide convergence of positions but identified sectorals as the one area in which further work was required. As Wasescha reported, some members had indicated that their ability to finalize NAMA modalities depended on a commitment by "those Members who took part in the negotiations on formula and flexibilities in July" to participate in sectorals. Besides the US, the EU, Japan, and Australia, these were Brazil, India, and China, which continued to resist the demand (WTO, 2008g, § 1). In the final revision of the 2008 modalities draft, the entire paragraph on the non-mandatory nature and the purpose of the sectorals was placed in brackets (WTO, 2008g, § 9). A paragraph with proposals for special and differential treatment and dealing with preference erosion was added (WTO, 2008g, § 11). In an annexe, a list of members who had agreed to participate in sectoral negotiations was provided (WTO, 2008g, Annexe 7).

After no modalities were agreed upon in 2008, the Doha Round saw a long period of deadlock. Negotiations on specific sectorals continued on a bilateral and plurilateral basis outside the framework of the NGMA until the spring of 2011 (WTO, 2011b, § 2). In April 2011, DG Lamy held consultations on "the size of the gaps in market access in the NAMA sectoral negotiations" with Australia, Brazil, China, the EU, India, Japan, and the US (WTO, 2011a, §§ 1–2). "All of them indicated to me that they were ready to participate in one or more sectorals, depending on the specifics of the treatment and how sensitivities on specific tariff lines would be accommodated," Lamy reported (WTO, 2011a, § 6), but members disagreed about the role of the sectoral negotiations in achieving the overall level of ambition in the NAMA negotiations (WTO, 2011a, § 12). Lamy concluded that a fundamental gap in positions existed, which was not easily bridgeable (WTO, 2011a, §§ 13–14). At the 2011 ministerial conference in Geneva, the balance in contributions between developed and emerging economies was widely held to be the key question for unlocking the impasse of the round, as the conference chairperson, Minister Aganga of Nigeria, noted in his concluding remarks (WTO, 2011d, part II). Since then, NAMA has not returned to the negotiating agenda.

The Case for Sectoral Tariff Elimination: Liberalization as Win–Win

In order to analyse the negotiation strategy of the proponents of sectoral tariff elimination, I will proceed as in chapter 3 and start by examining how the proponents constructed their argument (framing, presentation of facts, identification of a solution, and motivation for action).

To recall, the first element in the construction of an argument is the framing of the issue. In framing an issue, actors situate it within specific discourses and refer to related institutional norms. All proposals for sectoral tariff elimination or harmonization in NAMA were presented in the language of liberal economics: sectorals were to serve the goal of liberalization, which was assumed to be beneficial for all participants. For example, Canada, Chinese Taipei, Japan, Norway, Singapore, Switzerland, and the US in their proposal for tariff liberalization in the chemicals sector argued that chemicals are inputs to various manufacturing and agricultural industries. Liberalization of the chemicals market, resulting in lower prices, would thus benefit large parts of participants' economies (WTO, 2005m, §§ 1, 3, 12). Moreover, the proponents of sectoral tariff elimination in NAMA pointed out that most WTO members had already committed to duty-free trade in many sectors within the framework of FTAs. Norway thus held that duty elimination on an MFN-basis was the "logical next step" (WTO, 2002c, § 7). The US declared that it "believed it was time for the WTO to return to its core role as a central global liberalizing force, bringing benefits to all and had now to set the standard for duty free trade, rather than lag behind regional initiatives" (WTO, 2002b, § 1.3). This framing spoke to two core norms of the world trade regime: liberalization and non-discrimination.

In addition, the proponents sought to frame sectoral tariff liberalization as a development opportunity. As the Doha mandate called for negotiations to aim to "reduce or, as appropriate, eliminate tariffs ... as well as non-tariff barriers, in particular on products of export interest to developing countries" (WTO, 2001b, § 16), several members suggested that the choice of sectorals should include sectors of interest to developing countries. In this context, the EU proposed a sectoral initiative to bring tariffs on textiles, clothing, and footwear "within a narrow common range as close to zero as possible" (WTO, 2002i, § 10). Japan believed that its proposal for sectorals in textiles, toys, and rubber would be especially beneficial to developing countries (WTO, 2002h, § 1.2). Switzerland expressed that special consideration should be given to pharmaceutical products referred to in the Doha Declaration on TRIPS and Public Health (WTO, 2003n, § 1.1). The sponsors of the chemicals sectoral tariff elimination proposal argued that, given the increasing role of developing countries in the global chemicals trade, liberalization of the sector would promote development (WTO, 2006j, § 1–2).

However, developed countries also wanted to reap liberalization gains for themselves, including through better access to developing country markets. While at the beginning of the round this was seldom explicitly mentioned, the US became outspoken about it later. The norms of the world trade regime include the expectation of reciprocity in reduction commitments. Developing countries are not required to engage in full reciprocity. Given the increasing participation of the emerging economies and many other developing countries in global trade, however, the US as well as other developed countries argued that they should bring their tariff levels into a similar range as the other trading nations. In 2011, NGMA chairperson Wasecha reported that some developed members regarded the formula as insufficient because it would not achieve harmonization between the NAMA tariff levels of developed and emerging economies. Given their already low levels of NAMA tariffs, these countries feared that if they further reduced their own tariffs but no harmonization was achieved during the Doha Round, they would lose all leverage towards emerging economies in reducing NAMA tariffs (WTO, 2011a, § 13). They had in this way identified the sectorals as a means to achieve harmonization: "The objective of sectorals would be to rebalance the disparity in the contribution between developed and emerging countries and to achieve, if not equalization, a harmonization of their tariffs. In other words, the goal of sectoral negotiations would be for emerging countries to 'catch up' with developed members regarding the level of market opening" (WTO, 2011a, § 12).

This was a recurring topic in my interviews with diplomats at various countries' permanent missions to the WTO in Geneva. "The US is totally convinced that this is a graduation round,"[1] one interviewee observed. Representatives of other developed countries showed sympathy with this position. Interestingly, though, even at this stage, other framings dominated in official negotiation proposals.

The presentation of sectoral initiatives as a development opportunity on the one hand and a means for restoring reciprocity between emerging and developed economies on the other is somewhat contradictory. If one follows the classical liberal economic idea that reciprocal liberalization is beneficial for all market participants, the contradiction can be resolved. Based on such thinking, which is inscribed in the norms of the world trade regime, the proponents sought to portray sectoral tariff elimination as a win–win opportunity for developed as well as emerging and developing countries. The overall framing of sectorals by the proponents can thus be boiled down to sectoral tariff liberalization as a win–win situation.

Besides references to discourses and norms, framing can involve issue linkages. This was also the case in the framing advanced by the proponents of sectoral tariff elimination. In their liberalization-centred framing, the issue of NAMA sectorals was closely linked to the issue of the overall level of ambition of the NAMA negotiations. For example, as the US was not satisfied by the level of ambition in the formula, it viewed the sectoral component as "an effort to set up a sufficient level of market access liberalization to offset the highly modest formula" (WTO, 2003ad, § 1.61).

Another aspect of the proponents' framing was a reference to the negotiation history of the GATT and the WTO. Japan (WTO, 2002b, § 4; 2002l, § 3), Norway (WTO, 2002c, § 8), and Switzerland (WTO, 2002h, § 1.19) pointed out that the sectoral tariff harmonization and elimination initiatives of the Uruguay Round had achieved good results. The formulation in the Doha Round NAMA mandate that the aim of the negotiations was to "reduce or as appropriate eliminate" tariffs (WTO, 2001b, § 16) was interpreted as a suggestion for a like approach.

As Norway explained: "The mandate from Doha calls for elimination of tariffs where appropriate ... In previous rounds, in particular in the Uruguay Round, tariff elimination has generally been achieved through sector agreements based on a zero-for-zero approach at a multilateral or plurilateral level. This might be a supplementary method also in this round" (WTO, 2002c, §§ 7–8).

The second element in the construction of an argument is the presentation of facts. The proponents of NAMA sectorals performed this practice as they presented figures and research findings substantiating the factual claims involved in their description of the situation. To substantiate the claim that sectoral liberalization would have economic benefits, Japan for instance, in its proposal for a far-reaching sectoral component in the NAMA modalities, declared: "Our empirical study indicates that if 'zero-for-zero' and 'harmonization' in these proposed sectors will be achieved, the gross domestic product (GDP) of the world would grow 0.24 per cent" (WTO, 2003f, § 5). The proponents of the chemicals sectoral provided figures on production and employment in the global chemicals industry (WTO, 2005m, § 1), the percentage of value added by chemical inputs in various finished products (WTO, 2005m, § 3; 2006j, § 1), and the scope for tariff reductions (WTO, 2005m, §§ 4–5) to illustrate the size of gains to be realized from the liberalization of the sector. Regarding the need for a multilateral tariff elimination, the US presented a comparison between the percentage of duty-free trade in FTAs and the percentage of tariffs bound at zero in the WTO (WTO, 2003n, § 1.3).

Because many developing countries were sceptical about the benefits of a sectoral approach to NAMA liberalization, the proponents of sectorals spent considerable time and effort to make plausible the benefits of sectoral tariff harmonization or elimination for developing countries. The US (WTO, 2002o, § 12) and Japan (WTO, 2002l) cited a World Bank study according to which the largest share of the benefits from across-the-board tariff reductions or elimination would accrue to developing countries. The US further pointed out that NAMA products accounted for 89 per cent of developing countries' exports (WTO, 2002o, § 12). Japan calculated in its own study that the GDP of developing countries would grow by 0.7 per cent (compared to a global average of 0.24 per cent) as a result of the sectorals proposed by Japan (WTO, 2003f, § 5). The proponents of a sectoral in chemicals cited figures by the UN Conference on Trade and Development (UNCTAD) on the growing share of developing countries in global chemicals trade in order to demonstrate the gains developing countries could reap from liberalization of the chemicals sector (WTO, 2005m, § 2).

The proponents of sectorals further presented facts to dispel developing countries' concerns about protection of their industries and revenue earnings. The US pointed to research by the World Bank according to which developing countries that liberalized during the 1990s enjoyed a greater increase in their per capita incomes than those that did not (WTO, 2002o, § 6). Regarding the problem of revenue losses, Australia (WTO, 2003p, § 1.63), New Zealand (WTO, 2003ac, § 1.35), and the US (WTO, 2003p, § 1.59; 2003ac, §§ 1.12–1.15) argued that revenue systems could be reformed to accommodate tariff reductions and become more effective at the same time. "A number of studies had found that reducing high tariffs might actually increase government revenues in the early stages by stimulating substantial growth in trade and GDP" (WTO, 2003ac, § 1.14), the US claimed. Data and research findings by the IMF and the World Bank about the percentage of tariffs in different countries' revenue incomes, and about reforms undertaken, were provided.

Last but not least, an important argument for the participation of developing countries in tariff elimination sectorals was construed around the fact of growing South–South trade. The EU (WTO, 2002h, § 1.90), New Zealand (WTO, 2003c, § 1.13), and Singapore (WTO, 2003ac, § 1.65) cited statistics indicating a rapid increase in trade among developing countries. The US cited studies by the World Bank and others which found that over 70 per cent of the remaining tariff barriers were between developing countries. They thus argued that liberalization of South–South trade was where the greatest gains were to be reaped for developing countries themselves (WTO, 2002h, § 1.12; 2002o, § 12). In their proposal for a chemicals sectoral, Japan pointed out that South–South trade in the sector was increasing (WTO, 2003f, Annexe 5, § 1).

The third element in the construction of an argument is the identification of a solution. The solution the proponents of a sectoral element in the NAMA modalities identified on the basis of these facts and the underlying framing of liberalization as a win–win opportunity can be described as the harmonization or elimination of tariffs by a critical mass of countries, including the big emerging economies, in a number of specific sectors. The solution was not formulated in this way at the beginning of the NAMA negotiations. As described earlier, at the start of the Doha Round, a number of countries independently presented proposals for a sectoral component or specific sectorals. Most of them did not specify whether participation in the proposed sectorals was meant to be mandatory or voluntary. At this stage, only Norway referred to the critical mass approach (WTO, 2002c, §§ 8–9). Only after it had become clear that most developing countries opposed mandatory sectorals did a core group of countries interested in a sectoral component agree to base further discussions on the critical mass approach (WTO, 2004e, § 3.1).

They were not content, however, to pursue sectoral initiatives in those sectors where a critical mass of interested members existed. Rather, they insisted that a critical mass of members had to participate in at least some of the sectorals on their wish list (WTO, 2008b, § 9). Furthermore, when the rapid growth of big emerging economies became an issue, their participation in particular was requested (WTO, 2008g). The way critical mass was discussed in a progress report on the negotiations about a chemicals sectoral, circulated by the US in 2006, is telling: "Participants have discussed that to obtain a meaningful outcome, a balance needs to be struck between the need for significant market opening by a critical mass of participants and the need to address concerns of developing countries" (WTO, 2006f, § 8). In a proposal for tariff liberalization in the chemical sector, Canada, Norway, Singapore, Switzerland, Chinese Taipei, and the US stated: "Recognizing the importance of participation by key producers, and the limitations of cross–national production data, Members should work with their own industries to identify key producers, which will then be targeted for participation" (WTO, 2006j, § 4).

In identifying a solution, actors typically point out that their solution is effective, fair, and practicable. The proponents of sectoral tariff elimination argued that such a critical mass approach was the only effective way to bring about the multilateral liberalization they had identified as a need in their framing. The envisaged NAMA tariff reduction formula was perceived as too weak to reach the goal of ambitious liberalization. Sectorals were thus presented as a means to achieve tariff elimination in at least a number of important sectors. The participation of a critical mass of countries was necessary to prevent free riding by key traders as well as to provide participating members with the necessary incentives (WTO, 2005g). Since developing countries and – as had become apparent during the course of the Doha Round – large emerging economies played an increasingly important role in the globalized world economy, their participation was essential. Because of the growing importance of South–South trade, the participation of developing countries in sectoral tariff elimination was also necessary for the sake of development.

With regard to the fairness of their proposed solution, the proponents argued that the participation of developing and especially emerging economies in sectoral tariff harmonization or elimination initiatives was a fair demand. Even though developing countries' Uruguay Round tariff reductions were greater than those of the developed countries, their resulting tariffs were still much higher. Also, exports of developing countries had increased much more than those of their developed counterparts since the completion of the Uruguay Round (WTO, 2003c, § 1.29). Emerging economies had developed to a level where the developed countries regarded it as fair that they should take on liberalization commitments that matched their own.

The last element in the construction of an argument is the provision of a motivation for action. For this, the proponents of NAMA sectorals relied mainly on the argument that sectoral tariff elimination was in the interest of all. As described earlier, they proposed to include a number of specific sectors of interest to developing countries in the sectoral component and spent considerable time and effort explaining how developing countries would profit from participation in sectorals. Beyond these general arguments, the US presented figures on the export structures of Thailand, which had previously criticized the choice of sectorals in the US proposal, as well as Brazil, India, and South Korea, pointing out that the proposed sectors should be of great interest to them (WTO, 2003n, § 1.78).

The emphasis on South–South trade was another attempt to demonstrate the usefulness of sectoral tariff elimination for developing countries. More importantly, though, it was meant to construct a moral obligation for the emerging economies: given the growing importance of South–South trade, effective liberalization of products of export interest to developing countries depended on the participation of developing countries in liberalization efforts. If large emerging economies refused to take part in sectorals, they would be denying less advanced developing countries their development chances. The EU highlighted the moral obligation of the emerging economies in this regard:

> In a situation where protection in some developing countries is significantly higher than in other developing or developed countries at a comparable level of development and competitiveness, those countries need to justify the maintenance of such excessive barriers to the detriment of the more vulnerable developing and least developed countries whose exports and imports are in the main sheltered from liberalization altogether. (WTO, 2002i, § 8)

Criticizing the insistence of the emerging economies on their developing country status, the representative of the EU at an NGMA meeting in 2003 declared: "Some Members tried to hide behind weaker Members and this was not good. She wished to hear justification as to why a Member would not wish to participate in an initiative that could be of benefit to a Member who was worse off" (WTO, 2003c, § 1.59). In providing a motivation for action, the proponents of NAMA sectorals thus invoked arguments about self-interest as well as the moral commitment facing emerging economies.

In constructing their argument in this way, the proponents of sectoral tariff elimination were performing all four of the practices of getting others to agree: legitimization of claims, coalitional outbidding, rhetorical entrapment, and veiled threats.

Let us begin with the legitimization of claims. The framing of sectoral tariff elimination as a case of liberalization – which, according to liberal economic thinking, provides economic opportunities for all – provided the claims of the proponents with a basic legitimization in the WTO context. In order to provide additional justifications for the specific liberalization steps they proposed, the proponents of sectoral tariff elimination included other discursive references in their framing. Alluding to the idea of multilateralism and the WTO's non-discrimination norm, they argued that tariff elimination steps within the WTO were necessary to ensure the continued relevance of the organization given the proliferation of FTAs that had eliminated many tariffs among its members. Beyond their own profit they were thus seeking the best for the WTO as an organization. A further important attempt to legitimize their claims was the argument that developing countries in particular would profit from sectoral tariff elimination and it could thus be justified in the name of development. References to the WTO's reciprocity norm, arguments about the effectiveness and fairness of the proposed solution, and data about South–South trade legitimized the demand that developing countries, and especially the big emerging economies, be expected to participate in sectoral agreements.

The second strategy that can be employed for getting others to agree is coalitional outbidding. The proponents of sectoral initiatives in NAMA formed only a loose group; even so, coalitional outbidding constituted a significant element in their strategy. They sought not only to convince other members to include a sectoral component in the NAMA modalities, but also to win them over for participation in specific sectorals. Their success in this regard was limited, however. In 2011 the list of participants in sectorals included Canada, Chinese Taipei, the EU, Hong Kong, Iceland, Japan, New Zealand, Norway, Oman, Singapore, South Korea, Switzerland, Thailand, United Arab Emirates, Uruguay, and the US. Most of these had been proponents of a sectoral approach from the start. A few additional countries had come on board specific sectorals: Iceland, Oman, and Uruguay in fish and fish products, and South Korea in electronics. Seizing the development framing of the proponents (WTO, 2003k, § 17 b), the United Arab Emirates proposed a sectoral on raw materials (WTO, 2011b, Annexe 7). Overall, the number of WTO members that could be won over for participation in NAMA sectorals was small.

With regard to those countries that remained unconvinced, rhetorical entrapment (the third practice of getting others to agree) was an important means to ensure their acquiescence. For this purpose, the proponents of sectoral tariff elimination held WTO members to their commitment to the WTO's mission of liberalization as well as to the promise that the Doha Round would be a development round. Thus the US warned that "members would have failed the trading system, and failed to support the Doha development goals if significant South–South trade liberalization was not one key outcome of this negotiation" (WTO, 2002h, § 1.12). The proponents presented sectoral tariff elimination as the only effective way to liberalize NAMA and pointed to the Doha NAMA mandate, which called for ambitious liberalization and also mentioned tariff elimination. At an NGMA meeting in 2002, Canada stated "that at the last meeting there seemed to be an underlying level of debate as to whether all Members should participate in and contribute to this part of the Doha Development Agenda (DDA). This question was addressed, unequivocally, by Ministers in November 2001 when they agreed to undertake a broad and balanced work program" (WTO, 2002h, § 1.6).

In its first communication in the NAMA negotiations, Norway reminded members that "the mandate from Doha calls for elimination of tariffs where appropriate. These negotiations should therefore explore ways of achieving a significant increase in the number of duty-free non-agricultural products" (WTO, 2002c, § 7). In the further course of the negotiations, the proponents of NAMA sectorals also pointed to the July 2004 package (WTO, 2006a, § 1; 2007e, §§ 1–2), in which WTO members had recognized tariff harmonization or elimination sectorals as another key element in addition to the formula for the liberalization of NAMA and agreed "that participation by all participants will be important to that effect" (WTO, 2004d, § 7).

A rather effective vehicle for the rhetorical entrapment of developing countries reluctant to participate in sectorals was the concept of critical mass. This concept was readily accepted or even championed by the opponents of mandatory sectorals because it was taken to mean that sectorals would be pursued in sectors "where there was a critical mass to do so" (WTO, 2002h, § 1.29). But once the concept of critical mass was established as the basis for the sectoral component, the proponents started to argue that participation in a number of sectorals had to reach a critical mass and thus the big emerging economies at least had to take part (ICTSD, 2008b; WTO, 2008b, § 9).

Veiled threats, the fourth strategy of getting others to agree, played only a minor role in the arguing strategy of the proponents of NAMA sectorals. As was the case with the proponents of the Cotton Imitative, threats to block a Doha Round consensus should their demands not be met were made openly. Thus the US indicated that it would not accept a solution that did not meet its expectations in terms of ambition. What is more, it threatened to take its business to bilateral and regional FTAs if the WTO did not deliver. At a meeting in 2003, the US representative said:

> Her delegation strongly shared the view that in light of the growing number of RTAs [regional trade agreements], WTO Members could either embrace multilateral liberalization or be caught in a web of RTAs that would leave many, in particular many developing countries, outside the scope of liberalization. However, if significant liberalization did not come from this process, the US and others would proceed on the RTA route. (WTO, 2003n, § 1.77)

While such threats belong to the realm of bargaining – again, similar to the case of cotton we explored in chapter 3 – some elements of veiled threats were apparent. Note that the US did not just threaten to "proceed on the RTA route" itself; it was also warning that others would do the same. In effect, it was warning about negative consequences that were supposedly beyond the control of the US, although in reality, the actions of the US were likely to have a significant impact on the choices of others; this made it in essence a veiled threat. In addition, the US pointed to domestic stakeholders in order to portray the risk of a Doha Round failure resulting from lack of ambition in NAMA as something beyond the control of the negotiators. In this spirit, the US representative at a NGMA meeting in 2002 stated: "Her delegation was surprised to hear some developing country Members state that they saw no need for further liberalization. This was not a flexible position, nor was it one that the United States could accept. The outcome of any Round had to be judged on the basis of the liberalization achieved and that was how it would be judged by the US Congress and constituents" (WTO, 2002h, § 1.12).

The Case against Sectoral Tariff Elimination: Development First

The majority of developing countries were not in favour of the inclusion of sectoral tariff harmonization or elimination initiatives in the modalities – at least not in a mandatory form. Under the leadership of

India and Kenya, they devised a counterargument. I analyse the opponents' use of practices of constructing an argument and getting others to agree and discuss how their counterargumentation can be categorized in terms of the different types of argumentative contests categorized by Krebs and Jackson (2007) and Schimmelfennig (1997, 2003).

Again, the first element in the construction of an argument that needs to be examined is the practice of framing. The counterargument of opponents was based on a framing that differed decidedly from the framing of the proponents of NAMA sectorals. In what Krebs and Jackson (2007, p. 43) would call a framing contest and Schimmelfennig (1997, pp. 230–2; 2003, pp. 208–13) a controversial argumentation, the opponents rejected the primacy of liberalization in the proponents' framing. As Kenya declared at an NGMA meeting in 2003, "at the centre of the modalities should be the goal of enabling and facilitating the industrial development of developing countries. Liberalization should only be seen as a possible means towards this goal" (WTO, 2003p, § 1.26). Focusing on development, they also adopted part of the proponents' framing. The opponents, however, drew on different notions within the development discourse. Their counterargumentation, therefore, showed aspects of what Schimmelfennig (1997, pp. 230–2; 2003, pp. 208–13) calls a pseudo-competitive argumentation, where actors use the same framing but interpret it differently. The proponents, following liberal economic theories about development, portrayed sectoral liberalization as an opportunity for developing countries; the opponents, following more critical lines of development thinking, saw it as hazard.

In an influential contribution, India pointed out a number of reasons why sectoral tariff elimination initiatives were detrimental to developing countries' interests: developing countries needed the comparatively high tariffs to raise government revenue, protect their industries, and attract investment. Sectoral tariff elimination would thus deprive them of a key opportunity for development. In addition, sharp drops in tariffs in some sectors in combination with high tariffs in other sectors could cause problems in the supply chain (WTO, 2002g, § 7). Furthermore, a sectoral approach might divert the major concessions of developed countries to sectors of their interest and lead to a neglect of sectors of export interest to developing countries – a problem that might arise even if developing countries were not required to participate in sectorals (WTO, 2003c, § 1.5). A number of preference-receiving countries highlighted the problem of preference erosion. They argued that because their modest development successes and trade growth depended on their preferential market access, sectoral tariff elimination would endanger their prospects for development (WTO, 2003r, § 11; 2004a, §§ 9–11; 2005b, §§ 21–2).

Furthermore, India's argument placed great emphasis on adequate reciprocity between developing and developed countries. Here, they were adopting another part of the proponents' framing, which had also referred to the WTO's reciprocity norm. But again, the opponents' take on this norm was different: the Indian submission stated that developing country tariff reduction commitments in the Uruguay Round "when measured by how they will affect importers' expenditure were deeper than those of the developed countries … It would be important to ensure this time around that substantial gains accrue to the developing countries" (WTO, 2002g, §§ 2–3). It went on to explain that "from a developing country perspective," the approach to NAMA liberalization had to fully integrate the concept of less than full reciprocity, to ensure liberalization in products of export interest to developing countries, to fully take into account the "fiscal, developmental, strategic and other needs of developing countries," and to keep in view their "special needs of economic development" (WTO, 2002g, § 4). Sectoral tariff elimination would not fulfil these conditions. Because of their higher NAMA tariffs, sectoral tariff elimination would demand greater concessions from developing countries than from developed countries, which would turn the principle of less than full reciprocity upside down (WTO, 2002h, § 1.21).

The uniting principle of these arguments is that they put development first. Liberalization is seen not as a goal *per se* but as a means to development. Consequently, liberalization is only to be pursued if it serves development. In contrast to the proponents with their win–win framing, the opponents doubted that this would be the case with sectoral tariff elimination. Their development-first framing, therefore, involved a more antagonistic understanding of the relationship between liberalization and development.

In addition to references to discourses and regime norms, framing can also involve issue linkage and references to the negotiation history. The proponents of NAMA sectorals had linked them to the overall ambition of the NAMA negotiations. Opponents, for their part, linked the issue of the overall ambition in NAMA to the overall ambition of agriculture negotiations. With the Cotton Initiative, the US had tried to justify its linkage of cotton to the overall agricultural negotiations with reference to the substance of the two issues; with the NAMA sectorals, by contrast, the opponents did not bother to hide the tactic behind their issue linkage. In a joint communication, the ACP Group, the African Group, the NAMA-11 Group, and the SVE Group declared that agriculture was central to developing countries and that, in a development round, ambition in NAMA could not be greater than ambition in agriculture: "The Doha Round is about development of developing countries, especially Least Developed Countries, amongst them … Agriculture determines the ambition of the Round. NAMA modalities have to be built around and lead to a result comparable to what is achievable in agriculture" (WTO, 2007c, § 1). Because of the openly strategic manner of this issue linkage, it has to be categorized as a bargaining move rather than an arguing move.

At the same time, the NAMA-11 Group insisted that sectoral initiatives could not be linked to the overall ambition of the NAMA negotiations, because they were to be voluntary: "In this equation [the balance between outcomes in agriculture and NAMA] the sectoral results, which are additional in nature, cannot be taken into consideration and consequently sectoral negotiations have to be conducted separately" (WTO, 2008d, § 5).

Another element of the framing, which again constitutes an important arguing strategy, can be found in the references to the negotiation history that the opponents of mandatory sectorals constructed. In a joint communication, Ghana, Kenya, Madagascar, Mauritius, Nigeria, Rwanda, Tanzania, Tunisia, Uganda, Zambia, and Zimbabwe pointed out that it had been WTO practice in the past to conduct sectoral initiatives on a voluntary basis. "The current proposal is a radical departure from the previous practice of this organization that is fond of following precedents," they criticized (WTO, 2003r, § 12). India (WTO, 2003ad, § 1.65) argued similarly.

The most important reference point in the negotiation history for the opponents of sectorals, however, was the rule of less than full reciprocity. While this rule can be traced back to the developing countries' exemption from full reciprocity in Part IV of the GATT, added in 1965, and the enabling clause of 1979, the term "less than full reciprocity," which is cited over and over again by developing countries opposing mandatory sectorals, is taken from the Doha mandate on NAMA, which stipulates that "the negotiations shall take fully into account the special needs and interests of developing and least-developed country participants, including through less than full reciprocity in reduction commitments" (WTO, 2001b, § 16). Allusions to the supposed imbalances in commitments between developing and developed countries in the Uruguay Round, which the Doha Round was meant to correct, and to the development master frame of the round, constituted additional references to the negotiation history.

The next element in the construction of an argument is the presentation of facts. The opponents of sectorals presented facts and figures in order to substantiate their argument that participation in sectorals posed a threat to developing countries and constituted an unfair level of concessions. Kenya drew on academic publications and studies by UNCTAD to underpin the claim that the development of domestic industries required protection (WTO, 2002h, § 2.30). It cited an article by former WTO DG Supachai in which he argued that poor developing countries, which lacked the preconditions for trade integration, could come out of liberalization efforts as net losers (WTO, 2003c, § 1.38). According to studies, Kenya claimed, a number of African countries had experienced deindustrialization as a consequence of trade liberalization (WTO, 2003p, § 1.26). Bangladesh presented figures on the decline of LDCs' share in world trade, drawing attention to the fact that

> there were many studies that referred to the immense potential gains from trade liberalization. While these studies referred to the total gains possible, they did not break down the data, i.e. to indicate how much each country was likely to gain, or how the gains would be distributed. It was clear that those who traded more would gain more. There had been major growth in world trade during the last few decades, yet the LDC share was declining. (WTO, 2003p, § 1.19)

India (WTO, 2003n, § 1.10) and the ACP countries (WTO, 2004a, § 12) presented figures on the much greater reliance of developing countries on taxes for government revenue. They argued that the studies on revenue reform cited by the proponents of sectorals overlooked the particular difficulties of revenue reform in federal systems and the immense administrative complexity of introducing a value-added tax (WTO, 2003p, § 1.63).

The African Group (WTO, 2005b, § 17) as well as the ACP Group (WTO, 2005e, § 10) described the positive effects that trade preferences had had on exports in the past. Mauritius, speaking on behalf of the ACP countries, cited a study by the US Trade Representative (USTR) about the significant positive impact of US trade preferences on growth and economic development in African countries; that study included figures on jobs and investment created and exports generated (WTO, 2005e, § 11). The African Group presented the results of a simulation that projected considerable losses for preference-receiving African countries if MFN tariffs were significantly liberalized (WTO, 2005b, § 20).

In the context of adequate reciprocity between developed and developing countries, developing countries argued that their Uruguay Round concessions were much more extensive than those of the developed countries and that the Doha Round had to correct this imbalance.

India attempted to substantiate this claim about the Uruguay Round results by presenting the results of a number of studies that had calculated the "real terms" of concessions (WTO, 2002h, § 1.21; 2003c, § 1.4).

With these studies and figures, the opponents painted a different factual picture from the one the proponents had presented. The dispute between the two groups thus also displayed characteristics of what Schimmelfennig (1997, pp. 230–2; 2003, pp. 208–13) calls a competitive argumentation: proponents and opponents not only disagreed about parts of the framing and the interpretation of specific frames, but also about the factual situation.

Consequently, the opponents also contested the argumentation of the proponents with regard to the third element in the construction of an argument, the identification of a solution. In the view of the opponents, NAMA tariff liberalization was to be based on a formula approach. They proposed a so-called Swiss formula, which harmonizes tariffs, but with different coefficients for developed and developing countries in order to ensure less than full reciprocity. Sectorals, they held, could only be pursued as supplementary modalities by interested members on a strictly voluntary basis (WTO, 2007c). This solution corresponded to the opponents' development-first framing and their presentation of the factual situation: developing countries had made greater concessions in the Uruguay Round even though they required greater protection. Any approach to NAMA liberalization in the Doha Round would have to incorporate the principle of less than full reciprocity. Since tariff harmonization or elimination sectorals would require greater concessions from developing than from developed countries, those could not be a mandatory element of the modalities. Developing country participation in tariff elimination sectorals would have to be voluntary also because developing countries needed to retain tariffs for the purposes of domestic industry protection and revenue collection. Furthermore, sectoral modalities had to be sensitive to the interests of preference-receiving countries.

Opponents argued that their solution was fairer and more effective than that of the proponents. With regard to the solution's effectiveness, the opponents of NAMA sectorals had a different benchmark than the proponents. While the latter had argued that sectoral tariff elimination was necessary to achieve effective liberalization, the opponents argued that liberalization had to proceed cautiously in order to be effective for the development of developing countries. Kenya declared that while it agreed that "greater openness to trade should be the ultimate aim of all Members, it should not be the immediate aim of countries at early stages of industrialization" (WTO, 2003n, § 1.56). Developing countries with a weak industrial base were not ready for import competition. Premature liberalization had in the past led to a weakening of the industrial base in developing countries, as well as to market failures, rising poverty, and less equitable income distribution. If developed countries liberalized market access for products of export interest to developing countries, this could, in principle, contribute to development, but supply constraints often kept developing countries from taking advantage of improved market access. As import surges would not be offset by corresponding increases in exports, liberalization could easily worsen the trade balance of developing countries and stifle economic growth and development (WTO, 2002h, § 1.28; 2003n, § 1.56; 2003p, § 1.25). A joint communication by Ghana, Kenya, Madagascar, Mauritius, Nigeria, Rwanda, Tanzania, Tunisia, Uganda, Zambia, and Zimbabwe supported the view that "if the modalities are not designed correctly to assist countries with weak industrial base, any further liberalization will impact negatively on their economies, a situation that has to be avoided by all costs" (WTO, 2003r, § 1). The ACP countries declared: "Economists generally argue that trade liberalization leads to efficient allocation of scarce resources, lifts economic welfare and contributes to economic growth. Despite nearly 20 years' experience of reform, there is no clear-cut formula that guarantees that reform will bring about increased level of welfare. Thus, for many countries, especially ACP, a more cautious approach to liberalization is needed" (WTO, 2004a, § 1).

Indonesia (WTO, 2003p, § 1.50) agreed that supply side constraints made liberalization a problematic enterprise for many developing countries. Malaysia stated that liberalization in products of export interest to developing countries was well-meaning, but more important for developing countries, which harboured plans to become developed countries themselves, was the protection of their domestic industries (WTO, 2003n, § 1.43). Bangladesh pointed out that LDCs had had a dismal experience with liberalization and that it had been "preferential access, and not MFN reductions on tariffs, which had been responsible for the modest growth which had occurred in the trade of LDCs" (WTO, 2003p, § 1.20). For all these reasons, sectoral tariff elimination was not an effective solution to the problem of development.

In terms of fairness, the developing countries opposing NAMA sectorals held that the rule of less than full reciprocity emphasized in the Doha NAMA mandate prohibited any requirement for developing countries to participate in tariff harmonization or elimination sectorals as these would entail greater concessions from developing countries. In addition, they pointed out their own commitments during the Uruguay Round, which, they argued, had been greater than those of the developed countries. Based on this assessment, they expected developed countries to correct this imbalance and re-establish less than full reciprocity by making greater commitments in the Doha Round. Preference-receiving countries defended their adherence to preferences by pointing out the developed countries' adherence to their own agricultural subsidies. Thus, Uganda argued at a NGMA meeting in 2003:

> Looking at what was happening in other negotiations, agriculture for example, some Members were holding onto trade distorting domestic support measures and other Members were holding onto export subsidies for the similar reasons that they wanted to retain levels of development. Yet in the NGMA, when participants tried to do something similar, they were told that they were being an obstacle to liberalization. This did not show much coherence within the WTO. (WTO, 2003ae, § 1.23)

As their stance was a defensive one, the opponents of sectoral tariff elimination did not provide a motivation for action. This final element thus did not play a role in the construction of their counterargumentation. Their argumentative strategy consisted of a reframing of the issue, a presentation of a different factual picture, and the identification of a different solution.

Based on this construction of a counterargumentation, the opponents engaged in three practices of getting others to agree, namely legitimization of claims, coalitional outbidding, and rhetorical entrapment. The fourth practice of getting other to agree, veiled threats, did not play a role in their response to the proposal for sectoral tariff elimination.

In identifying their solution to the issue, the opponents raised their own, albeit defensive claim that participation in sectorals had to be voluntary. Consequently, they also sought to provide a legitimization for this claim. This was based on their development-first framing and their arguments about sectorals not being an effective solution to the problem of development as well as on their reference to the rule of less than full reciprocity, which proved that tariff harmonization between developed and developing countries was unfair.

Predictably, the proponents of sectorals responded with the assertion that liberalization, not development, was the organization's main purpose. The EU stated: "Ministers had indicated less than full reciprocity in the mandate, but it was going too far to make that aspect the hub of the mandate" (WTO, 2003ac, § 1.73). The EU was seconded by Hungary, which observed that "some Members had selective interpretations of the Doha Declaration ... Special and differential treatment provisions were not meant to set aside the common objectives and the negotiating mandate" (WTO, 2003ac, § 1.81). With regard to erosion of preferences, Canada (WTO, 2003ac, § 1.55), New Zealand (WTO, 2003ac, § 1.31), and the US (WTO, 2003n, § 1.82) reminded members that the Enabling clause stated explicitly that preferences should not constitute an impediment to MFN liberalization. In this context, New Zealand asserted that

> it was necessary to recall the overall purpose and objectives of the WTO and DDA. The preamble to the WTO agreement said "parties wish to contribute to those objectives by entering into reciprocal and mutually advantageous arrangements directed to the substantial reduction of tariffs and other barriers to trade and to the elimination of discriminatory treatment in international trade relations" and the parties go on to express that they are "determined to preserve the basic principles and further the objectives underlying this multilateral trading system (MTS)." This was the agreement which had been signed up to and which the current negotiation aimed to advance further. (WTO, 2003ad, § 1.107)

While the aspect of the framing that it put development before liberalization was thus contested, the aspect of fair reciprocity between developed and developing countries proved to be a powerful tool for legitimating the claim that participation in sectorals had to be voluntary. Developing countries opposing sectoral tariff elimination were able to make a convincing argument that participation in sectorals, which would demand greater concessions from them than from the developed countries, would undermine the principle of less than full reciprocity, which is grounded in the WTO's development norm and was specifically highlighted in the Doha NAMA mandate. This argument was further strengthened by references to the onerous commitments developing countries had undertaken in the Uruguay Round as well as by the linkage to the agricultural negotiations, where ambition did not prove very high.

The practice of coalitional outbidding also played an important role in the strategy of the opponents of NAMA sectorals. The opponents did not constitute a coherent group at the start of the negotiations, but India and Kenya soon emerged as leaders. In their influential contributions, these two countries did not speak for themselves only; rather, they argued that sectorals were not good for developing (WTO, 2002g, § 7) or African countries (WTO, 2003c, § 1.38; 2003r, § 11), respectively. In this way, they appealed to the shared identity of African and developing economies. Having framed the issue in terms of development first, they then pointed to a number of reasons why sectorals would not benefit these countries and why a formula-based approach would serve them better. Given that a large majority of developing countries, including some that had initially proposed sectorals themselves, aligned around the demand that sectorals be only a supplementary and voluntary element of the modalities, the opponents must be seen as quite successful at coalitional outbidding.

With respect to the developed countries and other remaining supporters of sectoral tariff elimination, the opponents relied on the practice of rhetorical entrapment. In this regard, they pointed to the WTO's development norm, the development master frame of the Doha Round, and, most importantly, the commitment to less than full reciprocity in the Doha NAMA mandate. In an exemplary statement at an NGMA meeting in 2002, Brazil reminded members of the centrality of less than full reciprocity in the Doha NAMA mandate:

> The representative of Brazil stated that on the question of less than full reciprocity, he recalled that paragraph 16 of the Doha Ministerial Declaration clearly stated that "the negotiations shall take fully into account the special needs and interests of developing and least–developed country participants, including through less than full reciprocity in reduction commitments ..." The current round of negotiations were dubbed "The Doha Development Agenda," and to give concrete expression to such a concept, to which his delegation attached importance, the aspect of less than full reciprocity had to be a central element of the work, in particular in the drafting of appropriate negotiating modalities. (WTO, 2002h, § 1.7)

The centrality of less than full reciprocity was highlighted by a number of developing countries, including Argentina (WTO, 2002h, § 1.15), Chile (WTO, 2002h, § 1.8), China (WTO, 2003p, § 1.15), Egypt (WTO, 2003n, § 1.58), India (WTO, 2003n, § 1.6) Thailand (WTO, 2002h, § 1.33), and the Philippines (WTO, 2002h, § 1.34). Brazil (WTO, 2003n, § 1.55), Egypt (WTO, 2003ad, §§ 1.35, 1.115), and India further emphasized that the harmonization of tariffs between developed and developing countries went against the rule of less than full reciprocity and that harmonization was not part of the Doha NAMA mandate (WTO, 2003b, § 3 b). The commitment to less than full reciprocity in the Doha NAMA mandate thus was an important instrument for the rhetorical entrapment of the proponents of sectorals.

In the context of the revenue argument, India further pointed out that Article XXVIII bis of the GATT acknowledged that developing countries needed to maintain tariffs to assist their economic development and for revenue purposes (WTO, 2003n, § 1.10). Preference-receiving countries argued that "non-reciprocal preferences under the GATT have been cemented by the principle of special and differential treatment, (S&D) for developing countries and LDCs, which has evolved over time, and remains an important part of the WTO legal framework" (WTO, 2005b, § 3; see also Kenya in WTO, 2005e, § 1; and Mauritius in WTO, 2005e, § 9).

After members agreed to consider the problem of preference erosion in the July 2004 package (WTO, 2004d, Annexe B, §§ 16), preference-receiving countries pointed to that document as a means to underpin their demands (WTO, 2005b, § 8; 2005e, §§ 2, 8). And after the decision of the Hong Kong ministerial 2005 that participation in sectorals should be voluntary (WTO, 2005u, § 16), the opponents of (mandatory) sectorals would not accept a derogation from this decision. When NGMA chairperson Stephenson added this sentence – "However, for some Members, sectoral initiatives that reach a critical mass of participation will help to balance the overall results of the negotiation on non-agricultural market access" – after "Participation in sectoral initiatives is on a non-mandatory basis" in his draft modalities of July 2008 (WTO, 2008b, § 9), the NAMA-11 promptly insisted that participation in sectorals had to remain voluntary (WTO, 2008c). The opponents further pointed to paragraph 24 of the Hong Kong decision in which members had pledged to "ensure that there is a comparably high level of ambition in market access for Agriculture and NAMA" (WTO, 2005u, § 24). They argued that any requirement for developing or emerging economies to participate in sectorals would disturb the balance between the levels of ambition in NAMA and agriculture (WTO, 2008e, §§ 2–3).

5 Assessing Persuasion

In strategic arguing, actors present factual or normative arguments in order to convince other actors of their positions and achieve their preferred negotiation outcomes (see chapter 1). All the practices of strategic arguing involved in making an effective argument as described in chapter 2 aim at one thing: persuasion (see figure 5.1). This chapter takes a closer look at the impact: Does persuasion actually take place, and does it have an effect on the overall outcome of WTO negotiations? First, I discuss how to define and empirically assess persuasion and its effect on negotiating outcomes as well as existing hypotheses about factors promoting persuasion. Then I look at the two case studies treated in the previous two chapters: the Cotton Initiative and the debate about sectoral tariff elimination in industrial goods. For each, I determine instances of persuasion that occurred over the course of the negotiations and their influence on outcomes. I also analyse which practices of strategic arguing have been decisive for these instances of persuasion and which factors have played a role in this.

Persuasion refers to a change in an actor's position that results from a process of arguing. The precise meaning of the term depends on the mode of arguing. In Habermas's concept of communicative action, which is characterized by an understanding-oriented interaction orientation (Habermas, 1984, 1987), a change in actors' positions can only be regarded as persuasion if it is rational and non-strategic (Deitelhoff, 2006, p. 115; Deitelhoff and Müller, 2005, p. 177). In strategic arguing, which is characterized by a goal-oriented interaction orientation (see p. 10), these limitations do not apply.

Schimmelfennig (2003, pp. 201–2) distinguishes three levels of persuasion: changes in the addressees' identities, values, and normative beliefs are the deepest form of persuasion; changes in their situational preferences occupy a middle ground; and mere cooperation without

Figure 5.1 Persuasion as the outcome of making an effective argument

<table>
<tr><td>Sources of persuasive power</td><td>→</td><td>Making an effective argument</td><td>→</td><td>Outcome
Persuasion</td></tr>
</table>

conviction is the most superficial form of persuasion. Holzinger (2004, p. 201) argues that normative beliefs are open to rational debate, whereas basic values, preferences, and identities are not. This is because basic values are determined by societal processes (Holzinger, 2001a, p. 271; 2004, p. 199) and "preferences are subjective volitions, which are difficult to change by cognitive processes alone" (Holzinger, 2004, p. 201). However, when processes of persuasion lead actors to change their behaviour, this can in the long run also alter their preferences. For preferences are strongly influenced by habit and socialization (Holzinger, 2004, p. 201).

Table 5.1 thus distinguishes four levels. Very deep persuasion (the first level) involves changes in basic normative values, preferences, and identities. It only occurs within long-term societal processes, through socialization and habit. Deep persuasion (the second level) effects changes in normative beliefs. Convincing arguments about the right frame of reference and its implications are decisive here. At the middle (that is, third) level lie changes in actors' normative and factual beliefs about the situation as well as in their situational preferences. As with the deeper normative beliefs, it is arguments about the right frame of reference and its implications that lead actors to reconsider their normative assessment of the situation. Their factual beliefs about the situation can be changed simply by the introduction of new information (Zangl & Zürn, 1996, pp. 352–8). If factual and/or normative beliefs about the situation change, so do situational preferences. Most of the practices of strategic arguing analysed in this book are situated at this middle level. This includes all the practices of constructing an argument (framing, the presentation of facts, the identification of a solution, and the provision of a motivation for action) as well as – among the practices of getting others to agree – the legitimization of claims and coalitional outbidding. Veiled threats work as convincing arguments if they are taken as objective warnings. If they are deciphered as concealed bargaining moves, however, then they, like bargaining, will change actors' behaviour but not their situational preferences. Rhetorical entrapment also

Table 5.1. Different levels of persuasion

Level of persuasion	Object of change	Mechanisms of change	Practices of strategic arguing
Very deep	Basic normative values, preferences and identities	Long-term societal processes, socialization and habit	
Deep	General normative beliefs	Convincing arguments about frames of reference (in terms of basic normative values) and their implications	
Middle	Factual and normative believes about the situation, situational preferences	Convincing arguments about frames of reference (in terms of normative beliefs) and their implications as well as new information	Framing, presentation of facts, identification of a solution, provision of a motivation for action, legitimization of claims and coalitional outbidding as well as veiled threats (if they are taken as objective warnings)
Superficial	Revealed preferences and behaviour	Coercive arguments, bargaining veiled as arguing	Rhetorical entrapment, veiled threats (if they are deciphered as bargaining)

operates at this fourth, superficial level. Actors who are rhetorically entrapped change their behaviour and often their revealed preferences as well, but only for strategic reasons. They are not really convinced, but only coerced into accepting their opponents' arguments.

Empirically, we cannot observe actors' beliefs and situational preferences because they are intra-personal phenomena. Only revealed preferences and behaviours are observable. Changes in actors' negotiation positions can be traced, but it is impossible to determine with certainty whether they have truly embraced their new positions. Müller, Risse, and colleagues have tried to solve this problem by applying a number of indicators. Convincing arguments, they hold, will probably be the explanation for changing positions if, first, actors change their frames and argumentation at the same time as they change their positions (Ulbert, Risse, & Müller, 2004, p. 20); if, second, actors explicitly state that they have been convinced (Ulbert, Risse, & Müller, 2004, p. 20; Deitelhoff & Müller, 2005, p. 171); and if, third, actors argue consistently (Deitelhoff & Müller, 2005, p. 171). Where these indicators are negative, Müller, Risse, and colleagues assume that changes in position are probably due to bargaining.

As Müller, Risse, and colleagues come from a Habermasian understanding of arguing, they do not specifically consider rhetorical entrapment and veiled threats, which according to my categorization can lead to a form of persuasion that does not involve a change in situational preferences. Actors who are rhetorically entrapped can be expected to change not only their behaviour but also their revealed preferences. If they do so in a consistent manner, Müller, Risse and colleagues would surmise that persuasion has occurred. Often in such cases, however, one can identify at least small lapses in the consistency of actors' arguments, which indicate that they have been rhetorically forced into accepting arguments they do not truly believe in. With regard to veiled threats, actors are likely to behave in a manner that Müller, Risse and colleagues would associate with persuasion, if they read such threats as objective and plausible warnings. If they read them as bargaining moves, however, their reaction will most likely resemble that which can be expected in a bargaining situation. They will change their behaviour, but not their revealed preferences, at least not in a consistent way.

In any case, in addition to applying the criteria developed by Müller, Risse and colleagues, it is important to cross-check alleged cases of persuasion through convincing as well as coercive arguments for possible alternative explanations, such as bargaining processes. We can expect the overall outcome of international trade negotiations to be influenced by bargaining as well as arguing. Even when instances of persuasion can be identified, it is necessary to examine their impact on the overall outcome.

Together with the fact that changes in actors' beliefs and situational preferences are intra-personal phenomena that cannot be observed directly, the ubiquity and interconnectedness of bargaining as well as arguing processes in international negotiations make it difficult to measure the precise impact of actors' arguing strategies on negotiating outcomes or to prove causation. Such an aspiration would also not fit the constructivist theoretical basis and qualitative methodological approach of this book. The aim of this chapter is thus much humbler: by describing changes in the actors' revealed preferences and behaviour and connecting these to other actors' arguing strategies, using Müller, Risse and colleagues' indicators and cross-checking for alternative explanations in terms of bargaining processes, I seek to identify instances where persuasion is likely to have taken place, thus making it plausible that arguing strategies have had a tangible impact on the course of the negotiations.

The extent to which processes of persuasion have influenced negotiation outcomes in the two case studies is difficult to ascertain for an additional reason: neither the negotiations on cotton nor the debate about sectoral tariff elimination in industrial goods have reached a final conclusion as of this writing. There have been a number of preliminary outcomes, however: the decisions WTO members took as part of the July 2004 package as well as the ministerial declarations of Hong Kong 2005, Bali 2013, and Nairobi 2015. Given the impact that bargaining as well as arguing strategies have plausibly had on the course of the negotiations, I appraise how processes of persuasion have shaped these preliminary outcomes and discuss the likely further course of negotiations.

Beyond assessing instances of persuasion and their impact on negotiation outcomes, this chapter will identify the practices of strategic arguing that have been decisive in these instances of persuasion and discuss factors that facilitated their success. Müller, Risse, and colleagues (Ulbert, Risse, & Müller, 2004) examined properties of the arguing process that contribute to the effectiveness of arguments. They found, first, that the credibility of speakers is of great importance. That credibility depends on their claim to cognitive or moral authority and/or on their perceived impartial position as well as on the consistency of their argumentation (Ulbert & Risse, 2005, pp. 359–60; Ulbert, Risse, & Müller, 2004, pp. 29–30; see also Crawford, 2002, 36, 112). Second, an argument will be more effective if it resonates with the audience's previous beliefs. Müller, Risse, and colleagues identified three strategies for generating resonance: drawing analogies to other negotiations, referring to existing principles, and framing the issue to resonate with existing beliefs (Ulbert & Risse, 2005, pp. 361–2; Ulbert, Risse, & Müller, 2004, pp. 30–2; see also Crawford, 2002, pp. 36, 113–17). Third, Müller, Risse, and collaborators suspected that uncertainty on behalf of the listeners would make them more open to persuasion. They could, however, not empirically prove this last hypothesis (Ulbert, Risse, & Müller, 2004, pp. 32–3).

Instances of Persuasion in the Negotiations about Cotton

The proponents of the sectoral initiative on cotton managed to persuade WTO representatives and the other members of the organization that cotton was an important issue that warranted special attention and an express solution. DG Supachai highlighted the importance of the issue at the start of the negotiations in Cancún (ICTSD, 2003a; WTO, 2003x). The draft for the Cancún ministerial declaration, issued by conference chairperson Derbez, proposed that members "recognize the importance of cotton for the development of a number of developing countries and understand the need for urgent action to address trade distortions in these markets" (WTO, 2003z, § 27). The July 2004 package, which was agreed upon by members, similarly stated: "The General Council recognizes the importance of cotton for a certain number of countries and its vital importance for developing countries, especially LDCs. It will be addressed ambitiously, expeditiously, and specifically, within the agriculture negotiations" (WTO, 2004d).

Observers saw this as a "major victory" for the sponsors of the initiative (Heinisch, 2006, p. 268). A special negotiation body, the SCC, was established for cotton (WTO, 2005a, 2005j). Even the US emphasized that it understood "the critical role cotton plays in the economic and social development of the African region" (WTO, 2005k, Annexe 2). DG Lamy adopted the C4's framing of the cotton issue as a "litmus test" for the development content of the Doha Round and believed there would be "no round without cotton on board" (WTO, 2007a). Given that cotton is one agricultural good among many and that subsidies are a general problem, it is quite an accomplishment for the C4 to have established the cotton issue as a specific and prominent issue in the Doha Round negotiations.

Is the prominence of the cotton issue a result of persuasion? Actors did not explicitly state that they had been convinced by the C4, but WTO representatives and members changed not only their position but also the framing they used when speaking about the topic. They accepted that cotton was an important issue. At the same time, they began to frame cotton as an issue of liberalization and development and to speak of it as a test case for the development promise of the round. According to Müller, Risse, and colleagues, this indicates persuasion. While opinions diverged regarding the appropriate solution, the significance of the issue was never called into question, not even by the US. Since the C4 commands little bargaining power, an explanation that this was a result of bargaining is not convincing. The moral weight of the C4's argumentation, which other actors could not publicly deny, applied greater pressure on other members than the threat of four small LDCs to block consensus. The WTO membership's acknowledgment that cotton was an issue of special importance can thus be attributed to persuasion.

But while the membership acknowledged the importance of the cotton issue as argued by the C4, the US managed to persuade WTO representatives and members that a more complex solution than the one proposed by the C4 was necessary. The idea that African cotton-producing countries needed development aid and economic diversification was adopted in chairperson Derbez's draft for the Cancún ministerial declaration (WTO, 2003z, § 27). At the Regional Workshop on Cotton organized by the WTO secretariat, the invited members, supported by officials from the WTO and other IGOs, participated in the identification of problems facing the West African cotton sector – problems that went far beyond the issue of subsidies (WTO, 2004b, § 7). The division of the cotton issue into a trade aspect and a development aspect was sanctioned by the membership as a whole in the July 2004 package (WTO, 2004d, § 1.b). Within the Consultative Framework for the coordination of bilateral and multilateral aid established by the July package (WTO, 2004h), members met regularly to discuss the development aspect of the cotton issue. The C4 itself participated in the widening of the solution within the Regional Workshop on Cotton and the Consultative Framework process.

While other members adopted the argumentation of the US regarding development deficits in the West African cotton sectors along with the position that a more complex solution was needed, and while they stuck to this consistently, the statements of the C4 were somewhat inconsistent. On the one hand, some statements made by the C4 very clearly reflected the argumentation of the US:

> The representative of Burkina Faso hoped that the absence of speakers on the issue of the development aspects of cotton did not mean that there was a lack of interest, particularly since, as had been stated by the Chairman, Members needed to establish some coherence between the trade and the development aspects of cotton. Burkina Faso therefore insisted on the fact that that aspect was also important, since there was no point in finding a solution to the trade issue if there was nothing to offer on the development side. In particular, Burkina Faso urged the development partners present at the meeting to continue to make every effort to ensure that the development dimension was also treated as an important aspect at every stage of the negotiations. (WTO, 2006n, § 18)

> In terms of domestic reforms of the cotton sector and related reforms in African countries, the Minister [Koné of Burkina Faso, speaking as C4 coordinator] confirmed that the requirement for those reforms was generally understood across the Continent. (WTO, 2011c, § 11)

On the other hand, the C4 repeatedly protested the prominence of the development issue and reminded members that in its view, the elimination of subsidies was the central issue:

> We are faced with a proliferation of conferences on "development aspects" ... These conferences seem to steer the attention of the African cotton-producing countries away from their real concerns by addressing issues such as competitiveness and research, when in fact the reforms undertaken by these countries have made the cotton sector one of the most competitive in the world, with the lowest production costs and fiber of an undisputed quality. (WTO, 2005d, § 3)

It can be concluded that the C4 were not thoroughly convinced that the development aspect of the cotton issue was as important as the trade aspect. The C4 acknowledged the development aspect nevertheless, due to its rhetorical entrapment in the development discourse as well as its interest in development aid. The offer of development aid can be viewed as a side payment and thus as a bargaining move by the US. However, the C4 not only accepted development aid but also agreed to undertake reforms in its cotton sectors – reforms perceived as painful (WTO, 2011c, § 11). This can only be explained by the force of the US argumentation.

Another success of the US was that it succeeded in linking the cotton issue to the overall agricultural negotiations in the July 2004 package (WTO, 2004d, Annexe A) and prevented any specific decision on the trade aspect of the cotton issue before modalities for agriculture were agreed to. The US provided reasons for linking the cotton issue to the overall agricultural negotiations; even so, it seems that bargaining power, not persuasion, is the most likely explanation for this. Other countries did not "sign onto" the US argumentation in this regard but merely accepted the fact that it had been agreed that cotton subsidies would be discussed within the agricultural negotiations. The C4 remarked that it had "accepted, in a spirit of compromise, that the issue be examined within the framework of the negotiations on agriculture" (WTO, 2005d, § 2). But even the US would not have been able to secure this result had it not created the development aspect, which enabled it to show engagement even while refusing to discuss the issue of cotton subsidies until after the completion of agriculture modalities. The WTO members had acknowledged the importance of the cotton issue; now they had to be seen doing something about it. Strategic arguing thus played a role, if only in providing a legitimization for bargaining moves.

The US refused to negotiate, yet discussion about the trade aspect of the cotton issue did take place. The C4 succeeded in gaining support among the WTO membership. The African Group submitted its own proposal on cotton in April 2005 (WTO, 2005i), and the ACP Group, the LDC Group (WTO, 2003ab), the G20 (WTO, 2006d, § 4), and the Cairns Group (WTO, 2005q, § 17) all expressed their support for the C4's position. In Hong Kong in 2005, members agreed that cotton was to be liberalized more, and more quickly, than other agricultural products; this would involve an early elimination of export subsidies, an early implementation of DFQF market access for LDCs, and deeper and faster cuts in domestic support (WTO, 2005u, § 11). When the C4 presented a concrete proposal for a formula for reducing domestic support for cotton (WTO, 2006c), it was supported by the African Group as well as members of the G20 and the EU (WTO, 2006m, 2006n). The reduction formula and implementation periods proposed by the C4 were included without brackets in the December 2008 draft modalities by chairperson Falconer (WTO, 2008f, §§ 54–6). While Falconer's successor Walker later explained that the text – even though not bracketed – was "annotated, with the annotation stating that further work was needed in order to reach a multilateral consensus solution" (WTO, 2010b, § 20), the inclusion of the proposal by the C4 in the draft as the only option still constituted a great success. When members, after acknowledging the deadlock of the Doha Round in 2011, started to unravel the single undertaking, cotton remained high on the agenda. At the 2013 ministerial conference in Nairobi, members agreed to expressly eliminate export subsidies for cotton and to provide DFQF market access for LDCs' cotton exports (WTO, 2013c).

Those countries that supported the C4 consistently reaffirmed the C4's argumentation and positions in terms of a solution to the trade aspect. Persuasion can be assumed here. The US, however, showed no indication that it had been persuaded by the C4 in any way. The agreement of the US to the decisions taken in Hong Kong in 2005 and Nairobi in 2013 regarding the express elimination of export subsidies and the provision of DFQF access for cotton can be attributed to the fact that the US had already committed itself to eliminating its export subsidies on cotton as a consequence of the DSB ruling in the case of Brazil against the US (Lee, 2007, p. 143; WTO, 2004f, 2005f), West African countries exported no cotton to the US (Ledermann & Moseley, 2007, p. 44), and the respective ministerial conferences also produced decisions on these issues for the overall agricultural negotiations (WTO, 2005u, § 6, Annexe F; 2013b; 2013d).

The central issue, domestic support, has yet to be resolved. Members agreed in Hong Kong that domestic support in cotton should be reduced more, and more quickly, than for other agricultural goods: however, the ministerial declaration did not say by what margin. It is not to be expected that the language relating to domestic support of cotton, included in the December 2008 draft, will become part of an eventual agreement. Once negotiations on domestic support in agriculture begin in earnest, the modalities for cotton will have to be discussed anew, and the US will be using its bargaining power to make sure its cotton farmers will not be without support.

Did strategic arguing thus have an impact on the outcome of the negotiations on cotton? It certainly did. On the one hand, while the tangible results the C4 has reaped from its initiative so far are meagre, cotton would have gotten no special treatment whatsoever had it not been for the C4's Cotton Initiative and its arguments about the importance of the issue. On the other hand, had the US not invested considerable time and effort in constructing a counterargument, it might have been compelled to make larger concessions on the subsidies issues in order to avoid being blamed by other members and being shamed by NGOs involved in the cotton issue. The current state of play – a lot of attention and support for the cotton issue, some additional development aid, but only small changes in the rules on subsidies – is the result of arguing strategies as well as bargaining power.

How can the instances of persuasion that were identified be explained? The success of the C4's argumentation was based on a prudent combination: references to the discourses of liberal economics and of development. On top of this, the C4 framed cotton as a test case for the development promise of the round. Since its framing resonated with the beliefs of all members, including the US, in one way or the other, the C4 was able to change everyone's beliefs about the correct normative frame of reference. Cotton had previously been regarded as one agricultural good among many; now, with the Cotton Initiative, it was being perceived as a core development issue in the Doha Round. References to the development discourse also enabled the C4 to establish a position of moral authority in the provision of a motivation for action and the legitimation of its claims. Because cotton was a question of development, other actors were morally obligated to help the suffering West African cotton farmers and find a solution to the cotton issue.

With regard to its supporters, the C4 could build on the development framing of the cotton issue and its linkage to the development master frame of the Doha Round for coalitional outbidding: developing countries identified with the cotton issue as a test case for the development promise of the round and made it a demand of their own. Some developed countries, including the EU members, let themselves be convinced that the solution the C4 proposed for the trade aspect of the cotton issue was the only effective, fair, and practicable one. The C4 was thus able to change the situational preferences of these members.

Building on the resonance of its framing with shared norms and the Doha Round master frame, as well as the moral authority derived from the development discourse, the C4 was also able to rhetorically entrap the US. To avoid being blamed and shamed by other actors, the US needed to be seen doing something about the cotton issue. The C4's skilful performance of various practices of strategic arguing thus enabled it to engineer resonance and moral authority, and in this way it was able to persuade WTO representatives and members that cotton was an important issue that deserved special attention and an express solution.

The US constructed a counterargument that rested centrally on the construction of a different factual situation. Enlisting the support of other members, the WTO secretariat, and representatives of other IGOs, the US presented a host of additional facts that served to prove that other countries' subsidies were only one problem among many for West African cotton farmers; consequently, the solution had to be more complex than the simple abolition of subsidies. With the help of development experts in its own ranks and those of the IGOs and studies by research institutions, the US was able to establish a position of cognitive authority. The fact that its presentation of the factual situation was backed by IGOs and research institutions, perceived as relatively neutral, further strengthened its argumentation.

The US was able to change the factual beliefs that WTO representatives and members held about the situation. The problem of cotton thus came to be seen as lying not only in subsidies, as presented by the C4, but also in development issues. Actors accordingly changed their situational preferences and adopted the idea that the solution would have to encompass a trade and a development component. The C4 itself succumbed to this view to some degree, sometimes asking for development aid, sometimes emphasizing that the central problem was subsidies. It was hard for the C4 to resist the US's identification of a more complex solution, not only because of the cognitive authority established by the US but also because the US skilfully drew on the development discourse to rhetorically entrap the C4.

As the developing countries' deficiencies, their need for reforms, and their dependence on aid are central elements of the development discourse, the C4 was unable to stick to the initial definition of its interests and reject the development aspect of the solution identified by the US. By framing its more complex solution as means to better help the development of the C4, the US was able to produce resonance with the C4's previously held beliefs and to claim moral authority. The C4 could not refuse to participate in negotiations about the development aspect of the cotton issue, even when the US used these to sideline the trade aspect, which was central to the C4. The US's success in persuading WTO representatives and members of the solution it had identified – including to a degree the C4 – thus also depended on the skilful performance of a number of practices of strategic arguing. These enabled it to construct cognitive and moral authority as well as resonance.

Even though the US was surprised by the prominence the Cotton Initiative quickly acquired in Cancún, it always argued consistently and showed no signs of uncertainty. The C4 on the other hand did not argue entirely consistently, sometimes emphasizing the issue of competitiveness, sometimes its need for aid. It did show some uncertainty regarding the desirability of the development aspect of the negotiations.

Instances of Persuasion in the Debate about Sectoral Tariff Elimination in Industrial Goods

The first instance of persuasion that can be identified in the debate about sectoral tariff liberalization in NAMA is the formation of a united developing country position: that a sectoral component in the NAMA modalities would be acceptable only if sectorals were conceptualized as a supplementary and voluntary element. Before the proponents of sectorals had arrived at a common position or convinced anybody of anything, Kenya and India, the most prominent opponents, had already rallied the majority of developing countries around their position. The opponents frequently referred to the Indian submission (WTO, 2002g) and the arguments made therein. These countries did not constitute a formal group, yet their positions were very consistent. Nothing would suggest that Kenya and India engaged in bargaining about the issue with other developing countries. The facts indicate that the other developing countries that had not previously identified their interests regarding NAMA sectorals were convinced by the Indian arguments about the detrimental effects sectorals might have on developing countries. It can thus be attested that Kenya and India persuaded the majority of the developing countries of their position that sectorals had to be supplementary and voluntary.

During the ensuing negotiations, the opponents of sectorals convinced the other WTO members that participation in sectorals should be voluntary. The first draft for the NAMA modalities, issued by chairperson Girard in May 2003, reflected the position of the proponents of a sectoral component. It included a list of mandatory sectorals in sectors (WTO, 2003j, § 7) that had been identified as export interests of developing countries by the WTO secretariat (WTO, 2003ad, § 1.4). As a supplementary element, voluntary sectorals in additional sectors were suggested (WTO, 2003j, § 11; 2003ad, § 1.6). The opponents of sectorals would, however, soon turn the tables: The NAMA modalities attached to the Cancún draft ministerial declaration, issued by conference chairperson Derbez, spoke of the importance of "participation of all participants" (WTO, 2003z, Annexe B, § 6), but mandatory sectorals were no longer proscribed. The same NAMA modalities were acquiesced to by all WTO members as part of the July 2004 package (WTO, 2004d, Annexe B) with the annotation that further negotiations were required on participation in sectorals (WTO, 2004d, Annexe B, §1). The Hong Kong ministerial declaration, another decision by the membership, finally stipulated that "participation should be on a non-mandatory basis" (WTO, 2005u, § 16).

There are no indications that the opponents were actually able to convince any of the proponents of sectorals of their position. Norway referred to the Indian submission, saying that "India had in its document TN/MA/W/10 raised some of the concerns that Norway had associated with other approaches than a comprehensive tariff formula, such as request-and-offer and sectorial ones, basically reflecting the fact that these approaches favored the more powerful trading partners" (WTO, 2003c, § 1.25). Norway, however, had proposed to base sectorals on a critical mass concept from the start, emphasizing that "such an approach should not lead to an unbalanced result favoring major trading partners" (WTO, 2002c, § 8). Other proponents of sectorals had suggested mandatory participation, but in Hong Kong consented to voluntary sectorals. They did not themselves adopt the position that sectorals should be voluntary. Nor did they adopt the argumentation of the opponents. Persuasion in the narrower sense of true conviction cannot be assumed to have taken place. Arguing nevertheless played a role in terms of rhetorical entrapment: the opponents argued that sectoral tariff elimination was incompatible with less than full reciprocity. As less than full reciprocity was part of the Doha NAMA mandate, the proponents of sectorals could not deny that it had to be ensured. Some of the proponents of sectorals expressed displeasure about the centrality of the rule of less than full reciprocity in the NAMA negotiations:

> [The EU declared:] Ministers had indicated less than full reciprocity in the mandate, but it was going too far to make that aspect the hub of the mandate. (WTO, 2003ac, § 1.73)

> [The US stated:] On the issue of less than full reciprocity, the US had always taken the view that the objective of special and differential treatment was to assist developing countries integrate into the global economy. The question was whether this integration was hindered or hastened by maintaining high tariffs and tariff plateaus. (WTO, 2003n, § 1,82)

But none of them ever explicitly doubted that less than full reciprocity had to be taken into account in the NAMA negotiations, and none were able to explain how sectoral tariff elimination could include less than full reciprocity. They were thus rhetorically coerced to accept the voluntary nature of sectorals.

While the opponents of sectorals thus succeeded in establishing the voluntary nature of sectorals, the proponents were able to persuade WTO representatives and members, including the opponents, that voluntary sectorals were an important element of the negotiations and that they should be based on the concept of critical mass. "We recognize that a sectorial tariff component, aiming at elimination or harmonization is another key element to achieving the objectives of paragraph 16 of the Doha Ministerial Declaration," was the wording proposed in the Cancún draft ministerial declaration (WTO, 2003z, § 6) and adopted by members in the July 2004 package (WTO, 2004d, Annexe B, § 7). Referring to this paragraph in the July 2004 package, the Hong Kong ministerial declaration, which established the non-mandatory nature of sectorals, at the same time stated: "In furtherance of paragraph 7 of the NAMA Framework, we recognize that Members are pursuing sectoral initiatives. To this end, we instruct the Negotiating Group to review proposals with a view to identifying those which could garner sufficient participation to be realized" (WTO, 2005u, § 16).

The reference to "sufficient participation" has to be seen in the context of the critical mass approach around which the proponents of sectorals had united (WTO, 2004e, § 3.1). In his 2006 text "Towards NAMA Modalities," chairperson Stephenson attested wide agreement on the core issues of sectorals. It was mentioned that one element of the sectorial negotiations was the definition of critical mass (WTO, 2006l). The opponents had no objections to this. Some of them had themselves proposed to base sectoral negotiations on a critical mass approach (WTO, 2002h, § 1.29; 2003c, § 1.44). In 2007, the ACP Group, the African Group, the NAMA-11 Group, and the SVE Group acknowledged in a joint statement on the NAMA modalities that "voluntary sectoral negotiations ... can be important to address the diverse needs and negotiating objectives of various Members" (WTO, 2007c, § 7). Notwithstanding remaining concerns about the adverse effects on non-participating preference-receiving countries, the countries that had objected to mandatory sectorals explicitly recognized voluntary sectorals based on a critical mass approach as an important element of the modalities. It can thus be concluded that they had been persuaded that sectorals conceptualized this way meant no unacceptable harm to them and were important to other members.

In addition to these arguing strategies of the opponents and proponents, bargaining is likely to have played an important role in the compromise of voluntary sectorals based on critical mass. The question of sectorals was closely linked to the overall level of ambition in NAMA by the proponents, and this in turn was linked to the level of ambition in agriculture by the opponents. The July 2004 package and the Hong Kong ministerial declaration of 2005, which stipulated the non-mandatory nature of sectorals, contained frameworks for the modalities for negotiations in NAMA and agriculture that certainly reflected the effects not only of arguing strategies but also those of bargaining processes, in which members arrived at an overall balance of commitments. Even these processes were not free from the impact of persuasion, however. Only because Kenya and India had persuaded the majority of developing countries that sectorals could only be accepted as a supplementary and voluntary element was there a large bargaining coalition behind this issue.

The compromise of voluntary sectorals based on a critical mass approach did not prove to be a sustainable solution. Another debate ensued over how critical mass in specific sectors could be established. In the draft modalities issued by chairperson Stephenson before the 2008 mini-ministerial, a qualification was added regarding the non-mandatory nature of the sectorals: "However, for some Members, sectoral initiatives that reach a critical mass of participation will help to balance the overall results of the negotiation on non-agricultural market access" (WTO, 2008b, § 9). During the mini-ministerial, the US and the EU sought to link the participation of developing countries in sectorals to their access to flexibilities regarding the formula and to commit the big emerging economies to participation. Brazil, India, and China successfully resisted the inclusion of such proposals in the draft (ICTSD, 2008b; Ismail, 2009, p. 208). In the end, the entire paragraph on the purpose of the sectorals, including their non-mandatory character, was placed within brackets in the new version of the NAMA draft modalities, issued in December 2008 (WTO, 2008g, § 9). It can be concluded that neither party was able to persuade the other or sway it to agree to its proposal by other means.

Instances of persuasion are much rarer in the case of the NAMA sectorals debate than in the case of cotton. Nevertheless, it can be expected that those instances of persuasion that occurred will have an effect on the overall outcome of the negotiations. Persuasion among developing countries was instrumental in building a strong developing country front against mandatory sectorals. Had developing countries not had a clear and consistent position on this, they might not have been able to assert the non-mandatory nature of sectorals in bargaining processes. Another factor in this accomplishment was the argumentative application of the rule of less than full reciprocity to the question of sectorals. Since the non-mandatory character of sectorals is fixed by the Hong Kong ministerial declaration, it is unlikely that participation in sectorals will become mandatory in any final agreement. Most developing countries will thus likely not be required to participate in sectorals, and this is a result of arguing strategies as well as bargaining processes. If NAMA negotiations ever pick up again, however, developed countries will make sure their liberalization demands are met one way or another. It can be expected that if sectoral tariff elimination is part of an eventual NAMA deal, the developed country proponents of sectorals will insist on measures to ensure that critical mass is reached in the sectors most important to them, which will necessitate the participation of certain big and successful developing countries. Such a demand is enabled by the fact that the opponents of mandatory sectorals let themselves be persuaded that sectorals based on critical mass should constitute an element of the NAMA modalities. But it is most likely that bargaining will play an important role in the determination of specific members' participation in sectorals.

How can the instances of persuasion identified be explained, and what accounts for their relative scarcity compared to the case of cotton? As in the case of cotton, the proponents drew on the discourses of liberal economics and development in their framing. They argued that all members, but developing countries in particular, would profit from additional trade generated through liberalization. However, while a framing of development through liberalization resonated well with the previously held beliefs of the US and other developed countries, which were the central addressees of the C4's argumentation, the same was not true for the developing countries opposing sectorals. Many of them believed that liberalization processes had brought more harm than benefits in the past and were wary of opening their markets more than was good for them. The proponents presented research findings that pointed to the positive impact liberalization could have on developing country economies. But they did not engage in a grand exercise of analysing the situation and establishing cognitive authority, as the US had in the case of cotton. The proponents' attempt to construct moral authority in the provision of a motivation for action through their linking of sectorals to development through liberalization and the argument of South–South trade failed because the framing lacked resonance with most developing countries and because the proponents' own interests were more obvious than in the US construction of the development aspect of the cotton issue. The weak resonance of arguments further prevented successful coalitional outbidding, the legitimation of their demands for developing country participation in sectorals, and rhetorical entrapment of the opponents in this regard.

The only argumentative success of the proponents – their persuasion of the opponents to accept voluntary sectorals based on a critical mass approach as an element of the NAMA modalities – was based on their framing around liberalization and non-discrimination and the argument that tariff harmonization or elimination sectorals were the only effective way to multilaterally liberalize NAMA. The opponents accepted liberalization and non-discrimination as norms of the world trade regime. As long as they did not believe their development interests to be harmed, they would not and could not object to liberalization. Because of the centrality of liberalization norms in the world trade regime, general arguments against liberalization are excluded from debates in the WTO. Thus, after the proponents of sectorals gave up on mandatory participation, they succeeded in legitimating their claims and rhetorically entrapping their opponents to accept voluntary sectorals based on a critical mass approach. The proponents had changed the opponents' normative and factual beliefs about the situation: while the opponents had originally viewed voluntary sectorals as one possible element of modalities among others, they now accepted the proponents' claim that sectorals were necessary to realize the proponents' legitimate liberalization ambitions. And while they had not felt forced to accept even voluntary sectorals at the beginning, they now perceived their consent as necessary if they did not want be excluded from the debate as anti-liberal extremists.

The leading opponents managed to persuade the majority of developing countries of their position in the initial stages of the negotiations because their framing around development and fair reciprocity between developed and developing countries resonated with the other developing countries. As many developing countries were sceptical about further liberalization steps, the Indian arguments about the adverse consequences of sectorals on developing countries struck a chord with them. The argument that sectorals required an unfairly high amount of concessions from developing countries resonated with the shared narrative of developing countries, which was that the developed countries had taken advantage of them in the Uruguay Round. The opponents of sectorals were thus successful at legitimating their claims towards other developing countries as well as at coalitional outbidding. The leaders of the opponents had changed the other developing countries' situational preferences. While the majority of the developing countries did not, presumably, have a clear picture of their interests with regard to sectorals at the start of the NAMA negotiations, they came to believe – through the arguments of Kenya and India – that sectorals had to be viewed in terms of their development implications and reciprocity between developed and developing countries. Developing countries were convinced that sectorals would be both ineffective for their development and unfair because they were not compatible with less than full reciprocity.

The opponents' framing in terms of development and fair reciprocity between developed and developing countries did not resonate well, however, with the proponents of sectorals. The proponents of sectorals self-identified as free-traders and firmly believed that development was best achieved through liberalization. The argument that sectoral liberalization would have detrimental effects on the development of developing countries did not convince them. As they understood the world trade regime's development norm, less than full reciprocity was secondary to the liberalization of sectors of export interest to developing countries. Thus Canada declared:

> The DDA was about development and the road to development lay in more effective integration of all WTO Members into the world trading system through the active process of reform and liberalization of trade policies rather than leaving many high tariff rates and other barriers and distortions largely intact. (WTO, 2003ad, § 1.71)

> [A representative of the US stated that] she did not judge the development dimension of this negotiation solely by approaches which called for opt outs. The best way for developing countries to gain in this negotiation was to opt in to the maximum degree possible, to encourage active participation and stimulate South-South trade to the maximum degree possible as well as North-South trade. (WTO, 2003p, § 1.58)

The opponents were thus unable to establish moral authority in their provision of a motivation for action; nor were they able to legitimize their claims; nor were they able to rhetorically entrap the proponents on the basis of the argument that sectoral tariff elimination would not be good for development.

The most efficient part of the opponents' framing in terms of persuading the proponents was the reference to the commitment to less than full reciprocity in the negotiation history. They were able to change the proponents' beliefs about the right frame of reference insofar as they argued convincingly that the issue of sectorals had to be considered also in the light of less than full reciprocity. They were also able to establish that sectoral tariff elimination was incompatible with less than full reciprocity, in this way legitimizing their claim that sectorals had to be voluntary and rhetorically entrapping the proponents to cede this point. As the proponents did not want to be blamed for ignoring the WTO development norm and the Doha NAMA mandate, they had to accept a voluntary conceptualization of sectorals.

The proponents and opponents were only loose groups. Their arguing strategies could not be planned in the same way as those of the proponents of the Cotton Initiative, which was a small group working in close cooperation, or those of the US as a single country opposing it. Nevertheless, their argumentation was consistent. Some uncertainty presumably existed in most developing countries at the start of the negotiations, but after the groups of proponents and opponents had consolidated, both stuck to their positions.

The type of problem treated in each case does not provide an explanation for the fact that instances of persuasion are much less prevalent in the debate over NAMA sectorals than in the negotiations on cotton. Both cases constitute least-likely cases for arguing to prevail because they were dominated by distributive problems and had low uncertainty. The difference is that in the debate about sectoral tariff elimination in NAMA, none of the actors succeeded in establishing cognitive or moral authority. This was due to lesser engagement as well as lesser congruence of beliefs: actors did not invest the same time and energy in their arguing strategies as had been the case with cotton, and their arguments did not resonate with one another's previously held beliefs.

Among the conditions for effective specific arguments identified by Müller, Risse, and colleagues, it was the resonance of arguments with the existing beliefs of the listener and the perceived cognitive and moral authority of actors that proved decisive in the two case studies. The consistency of arguments and the uncertainty of listeners played only a small role in comparison. The perceived neutrality of speakers did not have an impact, as the major actors were all negotiating parties and none of them were perceived as neutral.

The factors that mattered were not given at the start of the negotiations. Actors designed their arguments to resonate with others' beliefs, and they actively constructed cognitive and moral authority. The skilful use of strategic arguing thus played an important role. Actors' ability to construct effective arguments and get others to agree, however, depends on certain sources of persuasive power. The next two chapters are concerned with two central categories of such sources. Chapter 6 focuses on discursive contexts and the institutional norms of the word trade regime. Chapter 7 is concerned with the institutional procedures of the WTO and unequal human resources.

6 Discursive Contexts and Institutional Norms

In the previous chapters, I have described practices of strategic arguing in WTO negotiations and analysed their use in two particular debates within the Doha Round. This chapter, together with the next, treats the conditions for the effective performance of these practices, that is, the sources of persuasive power. The first set of these conditions is constituted by the discursive contexts and related institutional norms that actors can draw upon in making their arguments (see figure 6.1). By delimiting the scope of what counts as rational and legitimate claims within multilateral trade negotiations and by creating different subject positions with different abilities to speak, these discursive and institutional contexts empower some actors more than others to make effective arguments.

Arguing always takes place in a social context. Habermas counts a "shared lifeworld" among the conditions for communicative action (Habermas, 1987, p. 119) and Müller, Risse, and colleagues in their empirical studies on the prevalence of arguing in world politics found that a high degree of institutionalization in terms of consensual norms was indeed an important factor in enabling arguing processes (Ulbert, Risse, & Müller, 2004, p. 23). As Schimmelfennig (2003, pp. 285–6) points out, a "common ethos" of shared values, norms, and standards for the validity of arguments is decisive for the effectiveness of strategic arguing just as it is for communicative action. The literature on arguing, however, does not problematize the shared norms against which arguing takes place.

Drawing on Foucault (1971, 1972), I argue that the discursive contexts and institutional norms of world trade politics exercise power over the actors involved and privilege some of them over others. According to Foucault, discursive formations (Foucault, 1972, pp. 116–17) constitute systems of rules that organize what can be said in a specific context at a

Figure 6.1 Discursive contexts and institutional norms as sources of persuasive power

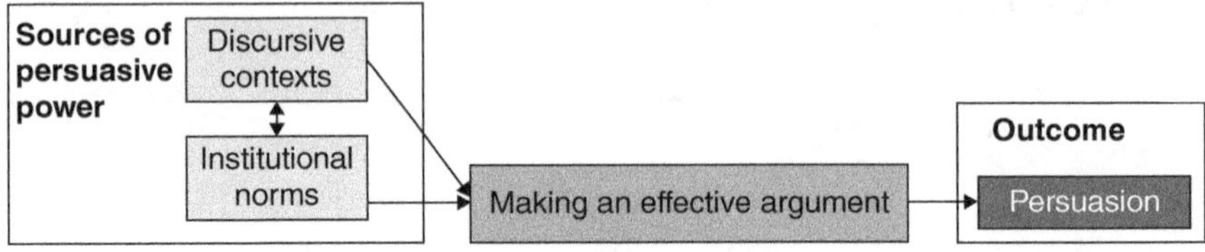

specific point in time (Kerchner & Schneider, 2006, p. 10). Some types of statements are excluded from the discourse by way of "prohibition" or by being defined as "mad" or "untrue." Those that may be made are organized in terms of being "commentaries" on major societal narratives, in terms of "authorship," and in terms of belonging to (scientific) "disciplines." Discursive formations also regulate who can say things. The properties a speaker has to fulfil are delimited by "rituals," "fellowships of discourse,, "doctrinal" schools, and inequality in the "social appropriation" of knowledge (Foucault, 1972, pp. 216–27). Likewise, the conditions for effective argumentation identified by Müller, Risse, and colleagues (Ulbert, Risse, & Müller, 2004) clearly denominate rules regarding what can be said (consistency of argumentation, resonance of arguments) and by whom (neutrality, moral and cognitive authority of the speaker). According to Foucault, however, the very identities of actors are produced by discourse (Foucault, 1972, pp. 50–5). "Discursive formations create subject positions that can – and must – be occupied by speaking individuals" (Downing, 2008, p. 49). Subjects are not given prior to or outside of discourse; rather, they are constituted as subjects through discourse, and in their very constitution they are "subjected" to the power structures inherent in discourse.

The power of discourses is a productive power (Foucault, 1978b, p. 35). Discursive formations must be conceptualized less as delimiting the range of what can be said and more as enabling actors to speak in the first place. The power of discourses is a "power to." For outside of discursive formations no meaningful communication is possible at all (Holzscheiter, 2005, p. 735). What is more, discursive power is not a power one actor exercises over another. In Foucault's conception, power has a decentralized, network-like character. It is composed of countless asymmetric but flexible relations that add up to strategies or "dispositifs," which have a common purpose but no single author (Foucault, 1978a, pp. 119–20). Nevertheless, discourses constitute inequalities among actors. Certain subjects are empowered to make certain statements, others are not. From this, actors can generate persuasive power, a form of compulsory "power over" other actors.

For a long time, Foucault insisted that discourses consisted of sub-jectless texts. In the last phase of his writings, marked by the second and third volumes of *The History of Sexuality* (Foucault, 1990, 1992), however, he reintroduced the subject as the locus of the (re)production of (discursive) practices, and, with this, according to Reckwitz (2000), developed a truly practice-theoretic approach.

> In his new conception, Foucault assumes that orders of knowledge do not reproduce outside of the "subjects" but are used by actors, which can be localized as bodies, in their everyday practices – discursive and non-discursive ones. The orders of knowledge guide the bodily-mental actors to specific interpretations, to an understanding of themselves and their environment. Thus, they enable them to constitute themselves as "self-interpreting animals" (Charles Taylor) and as agents, who control their own bodies to begin with. The orders of knowledge are part of routinized "practices" in so far as they are implemented by the bodily-mental actors in specific patterns of routinized and action-guiding ascriptions of mean-ing. The problematic proposition of the autonomy of systems of meaning in discourse outside of the mental sphere is replaced by the "practice-theoretical" idea that the actors bodily behaving and interpreting their environment constitute necessary bearers of these formations of knowl-edge and beyond that of a double structure of forms of action and orders of knowledge. (Reckwitz, 2000, p. 294, my translation)

Such a practice-theoretical interpretation of Foucault enables us to capture the agency inherent in actors' constant (re)interpretation of dis-courses. Discursive formations structure actors' options for speaking but do not completely determine them. They always require interpre-tation and thus leave room for agency. This becomes apparent as well in Müller, Risse, and colleagues' observation that it is not so much the existence of norms *per se* that enables effective arguing processes, but rather the occurrence of "norm entrepreneurs," who frame issues with reference to given norms (Ulbert, Risse, & Müller, 2004, pp. 22–3).

What is more, discursive formations are historic structures: they are supra-subjective but not universal (Foucault, 1972, pp. 73–5, 117). Dis-courses are sites of constant struggle between different social forces, which try to shape them according to their preferences (Foucault, 1972, p. 216). In this, institutional norms constitute a consolidated form of discourse. They preserve the discourses prevailing at the time of their establishment. As discourses change, eventually, institutional norms change as well. But this takes time and effort by reformist powers (Goldstein & Keohane, 1993, pp. 20–4).

In the two case studies in this book, three discursive formations and the related norms of the world trade regime play central roles for the arguing strategies of WTO members. The first is the concept of sovereign equality and the trade regime's reciprocity norm. The second comprises liberal economic thinking and the WTO's institutional norms of liberalization and non-discrimination. The third is constituted by the development discourse, which has entered the trade regime in the form of a development norm. In the following, I describe these three discursive contexts, their historic development, and their impact on trade politics. I then examine particular elements and interlinkages of them, which are currently the object of discursive struggles within the WTO, as can also be shown in examples from the case studies. These are the operationalization of reciprocity between unequal partners, the use of the term "emerging economies," and the hierarchy between the liberalization norm and the development norm.

Sovereign Equality and Reciprocity

The concept of state sovereignty is fundamental to the modern understanding of international law and politics. While authors have questioned its validity in the face of de facto existing hierarchies between states (Donnelly, 2006; Krasner, 1999, 2001; Lake, 2003) and the transnational forces of globalization (Archibugi, Held, & Köhler, 1998; Held, 1995; Sassen, 1996; Slaughter, 2004; Strange, 1996), the practice and analysis of global politics by and large is still firmly anchored in the idea of sovereign states facing one another in international relations. In their sovereignty, all states are equal (Kingsbury, 1998, p. 600). This sovereign equality is the basis for their representation in international institutions and negotiations. Article 2 of the UN Charter, spelling out the principles of international cooperation in the post-war era, begins by stating: "The Organization is based on the principle of the sovereign equality of all its Members" (UN, 1945).

State sovereignty is a social construction (Lake, 2003, p. 308). States' internal and external sovereignty depends on their populations' belief in the legitimacy of state power and on recognition by other states. While sovereignty is never absolute, in essence it is given as long as people believe it to be given. Sovereign equality is part of this constructed social reality of state sovereignty. States' actual powers differ, but as long as other states recognize them as equals – to a certain degree – this makes them equals. The discourse of sovereign equality creates only a single uniform subject position for states and thus endows all states with equal powers. Generally, this empowers smaller and poorer states to interact as equals with their larger and richer counterparts. With regard to obligations, however, the concept of sovereign equality also presents a great challenge for those smaller and poorer states.

In the WTO, the principle of sovereign equality manifests itself not only in the formally equal voting rights of member countries but also in the expectation that liberalization commitments will be reciprocal. Finlayson and Zacher (1981, pp. 574–8) identify reciprocity as one of the substantial norms of the world trade regime. GATT Article XXVIII bis on "Tariff Negotiations," added in 1955 (GATT, 1986), stipulates that negotiations are to be conducted on a "reciprocal and mutually advantageous basis." In the mindset of negotiators, reciprocity plays an important role (Eagleton-Pierce, 2013, pp. 56–7). The general expectation is that a member benefiting from the lowering of another member's trade barriers should reciprocate with a concession of equal worth. The very talk of "concessions" makes it obvious that liberalization steps are viewed as bargaining chips (Finlayson & Zacher, 1981, p. 576). It has even become practice to grant "credit for autonomous liberalization" (WTO, 2003j, § 5n2).

During the first GATT rounds, tariff concessions were exchanged in series of bilateral negotiations. Here reciprocity was relatively straightforward. With the introduction of general tariff-cutting formulas in the 1960s, and even more so with the extension of the trade regime to non-tariff barriers and trade-related economic policies, it has become much more difficult to determine what reciprocity means. This, however, has not led negotiators to give up on the notion; rather, what has happened is that they now spend considerable time arguing about what constitutes a fair balance of concessions and who has to "give" more (Finlayson & Zacher, 1981, p. 577). As Robert Keohane (1986, pp. 25–6) notes, the form that reciprocity takes in the world trade regime is a combination of elements of "diffuse reciprocity" (MFN-rule, formula approach to tariff reductions) and "specific reciprocity" (bargaining about equality of concessions).

The size of a concession a country is able to offer depends on the size of its market and the volume of trade it has with negotiation partners (Finlayson & Zacher, 1981, p. 576). As a consequence, reciprocal concessions place a much higher burden of political-economic restructuring on small and/or poor countries than on their larger and richer trading partners (Steinberg, 2002, p. 347). Reciprocity, therefore, is a norm that advantages large over small and developed over developing countries.

The case study on the Doha Round negotiations over sectoral tariff liberalization in NAMA provides ample examples of negotiators referring to the reciprocity norm. The proponents presented sectoral tariff harmonization or elimination as a means to re-establish reciprocity among members with different levels of NAMA tariffs; the opponents argued that the Doha Round needed to correct imbalances in the concessions made during the Uruguay Round (see chapter 4). As will be discussed below, the central bone of contention, however, was what constituted a fair amount of reciprocity between developed and developing countries and how emerging economies should be categorized in this context.

Liberalization and Non-Discrimination

Liberal economic thinking constitutes the essential intellectual background of the world trade regime. The core tenet of liberal economics, pioneered by Adam Smith (1776), is that the "invisible hand" of the market will regulate the economy better than state intervention. Economic actors, left to themselves, will specialize in the products they produce best. Prices will be determined by demand and supply. Through these mechanisms, overall welfare will be increased. State intervention should accordingly be restricted to the provision of an institutional framework to ensure that the market functions correctly (Gilpin, 2001, pp. 46–76; Schirm, 2004, pp. 19–20). Following the same logic, liberal economists hold that international trade will enhance global welfare because of comparative advantages (Ricardo, 1817) and economies of scale (Krugman, 1979). Of course, differences and debates exist within the liberal economic school. Regarding specific problems, different actors may arrive at opposing policy recommendations. Fundamental assumptions such as a general belief in market forces and free trade, however, are shared by all liberal economists and constitute a discursive formation, which structures the way people think and talk about the world economy and trade politics.

How the discourse of liberal economics regulates what can be said in trade negotiations is nicely illustrated by a passage from one of my interviews. Asked about the fairness of WTO negotiations, the interviewee, a diplomat from an emerging economy mission to the WTO in Geneva, said: "All relevant, legitimate interests will be taken into account." "What would not be seen as legitimate?," I asked. "Tactical demands," he replied, "somebody raising demands in an area they don't have an interest in ... You have to be a little thick skinned. This takes place quite a lot." "Why would they do that?," I inquired. "Because they want to be spoilers," he said, "then Cuba can rant about capitalism, they wish to make an impression. Why would you include them if they just do speeches? That's something that won't survive long in the WTO."[1] As this diplomat's account illustrates, arguments that question fundamental assumptions of liberal economic theory – assumptions such as the capitalist organization of the global economy – are excluded from the discourse as unreasonable and illegitimate.

Within the bounds of reasonable positions, the discourse of liberal economics creates two subject positions: free-traders, who subscribe to liberal economic trade policy, and protectionists, who follow more restricted trade policies. Protectionism, of course, has a negative connotation in this discourse. Those who follow liberal economic trade policies and are eager to open up markets will find it much easier to legitimize their claims than those who have adopted different trade policies and are seeking to protect their domestic markets. To some degree, the spearheaders of liberalization are imbued with the moral authority that Müller, Risse, and colleagues have identified as a condition for effective arguments (Ulbert, Risse, & Müller, 2004). Trade policy is not simply an ideological matter, however. Domestic political mechanisms are such that countries usually seek free trade in areas in which they are competitive and expect their producers to gain from trade, while at the same time adopting a more protectionist stance in areas where they are not competitive and their producers fear being marginalized (Oatley, 2008, pp. 60, 78–83). The discourse of liberal economics thus empowers those who are competitive in many areas and disempowers those who are competitive in few or no areas.

The discourse of liberal economics prevails today; however, a closer look at the norms of the trade regime and their historical roots brings to light a more complex picture. Ruggie (1982) has described the postwar economic order, reflected in the GATT, as one of "embedded liberalism." It has combined liberal international rules with Keynesian domestic government interventionism. As Ruggie points out, "the common tendency to view the postwar regimes as liberal regimes, but with lots of cheating taking place on the domestic side, fails to capture the full complexity of the embedded liberalism compromise" (Ruggie, 1982, p. 398). The GATT contains norms of liberalization and non-discrimination, which are based in liberal economics, but it also includes a safeguard norm that allows states – under certain conditions – to protect their industries from destructive market forces (Finlayson & Zacher, 1981). This combination generates contradictions, but Ruggie (1982, p. 415; 1997) argues that those contradictions are precisely what has made a liberal economic world order feasible in the post-war years. As Lang (2006) emphasizes, the vision of embedded liberalism imbued the post-war trade regime with a legitimate social purpose, one that rested on specific assumptions about state/market relations and the distribution of authority between the national and international levels.

Regarding liberal norms, in the immediate post-war era the non-discrimination norm, which manifests itself in the MFN-rule (GATT, 1947, Article I.1), was considered "the crucial GATT norm" (Finlayson and Zacher, 1981, p. 566). Intent on preventing protectionist spirals like the one that amplified the economic crisis of the 1930s, the US placed great emphasis on multilateral rules. As the international order stabilized and Europe recovered from the war, the liberalization norm grew in importance. It is embodied in the GATT's preamble, in which the signatories commit to a "substantial reduction of tariffs and other barriers to trade and ... the elimination of discriminatory treatment in international commerce" (GATT, 1947). Its more specific rules include the prohibition of quantitative trade restrictions (GATT, 1947, Article XI), the national treatment provision (GATT, 1947, Article III), and the goal of progressive tariff reductions (added in 1955) (GATT, 1986, Article XXVIII bis). Over the course of the GATT years, tariffs were cut substantially – at least in the sectors of interest to the big trading powers – and members started to tackle non-tariff barriers. Nevertheless, in 1981 Finlayson and Zacher still held that "the scope of this commitment [to trade barrier reduction] and its importance vis-à-vis other regime norms are unclear" (Finlayson & Zacher, 1981, p. 574).

Then, with the triumph of neoliberalism in the 1980s (Harvey, 2005; Morton, 2003; Simmons, Dobbin, & Garrett, 2006), liberalization became the central norm of the trade regime (Chorev, 2005; Lang, 2011). In 1994, by way of the Uruguay Round Agreements on Textiles and Clothing (ATC) and on Agriculture (AoA), two sectors of goods trade that had previously been excluded from liberalization were brought under (more or less) normal GATT rules; in addition, further liberalization steps in agriculture were placed on the agenda of the newly founded WTO (Hoekman & Kostecki, 2009, pp. 306–10). Moreover, the GATS conceptualized services as a tradable good and started multilateral negotiations over the liberalization of this sector (Drake & Nicolaides, 1992; Hoekman & Kostecki, 2009, pp. 333–64). The TRIPS Agreement introduced standards for intellectual property rights protection to the trade regime. Under the GATS, the TRIPS, and many other Uruguay Round provisions, the trade regime shifted away from dealing with "at the border" barriers to trade such as quantitative restrictions and tariffs towards addressing "behind the border" measures such as regulations concerning investment, the establishment of businesses, intellectual property rights, and product standards (Barton et al., 2006, pp. 125–6; Winslett, 2016). Some of these new rules require countries to refrain from certain forms of regulation (e.g., local content requirements for investments) that are regarded as trade barriers; some also require them to introduce regulations (e.g., for the protection of intellectual property rights) intended to ensure fair international competition (Hoekman & Kostecki, 2009, pp. 370, 583), with *fair* being understood in neoliberal terms, as levelling the playing field. In addition, the WTO possesses a dispute settlement mechanism that is more effective than the one the GATT was endowed with (Hoekman & Kostecki, 2009, pp. 87–92), thus enhancing the new organization's ability to enforce its liberal rules (Chorev, 2005).

Lang (2011) holds that the turn towards neoliberal ideas and the increasing legalization of the trade regime have together resulted in a minimalist understanding of global economic governance according to which the WTO is tasked with preventing states from unduly intervening in markets and with facilitating bargaining over reciprocal liberalization commitments, but – in contrast to the era of embedded liberalism – no longer serves a broader, collectively defined social purpose. These developments can, however, also be understood as manifestations of a new collective understanding of the trade regime's social purpose, which rests on different ideas about the relations between markets, states, and international regulation. Under the WTO, the ability of states to intervene in markets has become more strictly disciplined. This implies a stronger role not only for markets but also for international regulation (Chorev, 2005). Cho (2015, 2018) therefore claims that the trade regime has evolved from a contractual exchange of market access concessions into a community with shared norms.

Ford (2003) further argues that legalization and the disembedding of trade liberalization from the welfare state policies of the Global North have together provided the trade regime with a more genuinely collective understanding of its social purpose. Under the embedded liberalism compromise, developing countries were ascribed the role of "the protectionist other." Only when they adopted neoliberal ideas and liberalized their economies did they acquire a "trading self" and some influence in world trade politics. This assessment, however, overlooks the fact that equal treatment does not necessarily result in an equality of outcomes. As Conti (2010) shows, the legalization of the trade regime has provided developing countries with new ways to assert themselves against the dominant powers but has also created new challenges in terms of mustering the necessary legal expertise. Within the framework of the discourse of liberal economics, a country's position is enhanced by the adoption of liberal trade policies. As discussed earlier, however, such a trade policy is not equally suitable for all. It is well suited for developed countries with many competitive industries but not for small developing countries that are unable to compete in most sectors of the world market. The centrality the liberalization norm has acquired in the WTO is reflected in the observation that both the proponents of the Cotton Initiative (the C4) and the advocates of NAMA sectorals drew heavily on the discourse of liberal economics when framing their proposals (as we saw in chapters 3 and 4). In the case of the C4, a group of small LDCs was able to draw persuasive power from the discourse of liberal economics (see chapter 5). However, this was an extraordinary case. In some sectors, like cotton, small developing countries are competitive and could profit from free trade. But there are many more sectors where they cannot compete with developed and emerging economies, and the dominant discourse of liberal economics makes it difficult for them to articulate their needs.

Development

The discursive formation of development has been analysed in detail by critical scholars of development as well as by post-development theorists (Escobar, 1995; Rahnema & Bawtree, 1997; Sachs, 1992). They have deconstructed a number of assumptions that underpin any talk about development and that reproduce power relations between those called developed and those called developing countries.

The first assumption made by the development discourse is that there is a universal path of economic and social advancement along which all countries progress (Kößler, 1998, pp. 11–58; Rist, 2008). The developed countries have already achieved the highest stage along this path and thus serve as examples the developing countries should aspire to follow. A second assumption is that poverty, hunger, health deficits, and social problems in developing countries are a result of their underdevelopment, which in turn is rooted in their backwardness. It follows that they must modernize and grow their economies in order to develop. Related reforms, according to a third assumption, have to be planned by the state and/or development agencies. Development experts, coming from developed countries or having been educated there, are viewed as more competent than locals in identifying the necessary steps. Since underdevelopment is associated with suffering, a high priority is attached to the goal of development. A final assumption is that reform may increase suffering in the beginning but that these negative side effects have to be accepted for the sake of long-term development (Ziai, 2004a, pp. 136–45; 2004b).

Rist (2008, pp. 47–79) details how the contemporary concept of development evolved over the course of the twentieth century so as to legitimate the ongoing hegemony of the Global North over the Global South and its resources in the context of decolonialization. He locates the founding moment of the development discourse in the January 1949 inaugural address of US President Harry Truman, during which he declared: "We must embark on a bold new program for making the benefits of our scientific advances and industrial progress available for the improvement and growth of underdeveloped areas" (US Government Printing Office, 1964, p. 114). As Helleiner (2014a, 2014b, 2018) points out, the idea of development as both a national objective and a field of international cooperation has older and more global roots. Already after the First World War, for instance, the Chinese politician and scholar Sun Yat-sen proposed strategies for developing China; he also called for the creation of an International Development Organization. Rist's account of Truman's speech as the turning point for "a new way of conceiving international relations" (Rist, 2008, p. 72) seems a little exaggerated, given the larger historical process of conceptual evolution he himself describes. Also, it is certainly true that various actors from the Global South have contributed to the development discourse and have perceived development as a path their countries should follow. This, however, does not invalidate post-development scholars' analysis of the development discourse as erecting a hierarchy of societies that legitimizes the predominance of the Global North.

The development discourse encompasses two fundamental subject positions: developed countries and developing countries. Over time, several other specific subject positions have been constructed within the category of developing countries: the poorest have been labelled LDCs, whereas the most successful have been labelled emerging economies – a term that suggests they may reach the level of the developed countries in the near future.

The subject position of developing countries is defined by their deficiency, their suffering, and their reliance on external aid. On the one hand, it empowers them to present anything that is good for their economic growth as serving the higher goal of development. Framing an issue in terms of development imbues actors with moral authority (Ulbert, Risse, & Müller, 2004) and raises the prospects that their argument will be effective. Because developing countries are considered incompetent to raise themselves out of underdevelopment, developed countries are morally obliged to assist the developing countries in their development. Yet at the same time, developing countries are disempowered to judge for themselves what is best for their development. Development experts, socialized in developed countries, hold cognitive authority (Ulbert, Risse, & Müller, 2004) over development. Besides holding that cognitive authority, developed countries can draw on the moral authority associated with development, provided that they frame their suggestions in terms of development advice.

Overall, the development discourse empowers developed countries more than developing countries. When developing and developed countries interact in a situation of development cooperation, power relations become even more entrenched, as the recipients of development aid depend directly on the benevolence of the donors, which means that the latter can dictate the terms. Add to this that development aid, be it in the form of financial support or technical assistance, amounts to a form of charity or asymmetric gift exchange, which only reinforces and legitimizes relations of inequality and dependence (Eagleton-Pierce, 2013, pp. 57–9).

Contrary to some depictions in the literature, development concerns already played an important role in the post–Second World War discussions about norms and institutions for the international economic order. At the 1944 Bretton Woods conference, which set the parameters for the founding of the IMF and the World Bank, more than half of the delegations were actually from the Global South. Latin American countries, in particular, made significant contributions to the debate, demanding international assistance for their state-led industrialization and development plans. The US under the Roosevelt administration largely supported the Latin American position, and the US proposal for post-war financial institutions, written by senior Treasury Department official Harry Dexter White (the White Plan), included ambitious provisions for addressing development concerns; these were based on the model of US–Latin American cooperation initiatives in the preceding years (Helleiner, 2014a, pp. 9–19).

The US State Department, headed at the time by Cordell Hull, which represented the US in the negotiations over the planned International Trade Organization (ITO), was much less supportive of development concerns; even so, representatives from the Global South managed to insert substantial development provisions into the Havana Charter. The ITO, however, never came into existence because the US Congress failed to ratify it. The GATT, which became the foundation of the post-war trade regime instead, was a much more narrowly defined agreement that focused on the liberalization of trade and paid very little attention to the development concerns of the Global South

(Hoekman & Kostecki, 2009, p. 535; Steffek, 2006, pp. 37–52). US support for development considerations in international finance also waned quickly after Roosevelt died and Truman took over the presidency in 1945 (Helleiner, 2014a, pp. 260–4).

Despite these developments, Helleiner (2014a, pp. 10–11) claims that developmentalist interventionism as practised in the Global South and measures for global redistribution constituted part of the original idea for an embedded liberalism compromise just as much as the Keynesianist interventionism practised in the Global North. As Steffek (2006, pp. 52–3) points out, however, the core of the embedded liberalism compromise – the idea of embedding a free market at the international level in social policy at the national level – stands in opposition to the idea of redistributive measures at the international level. This marginalizes the interests of developing countries, which do not have the financial means to compensate those negatively affected by trade liberalization through social policy; it also fails to address global inequalities (see also Lang, 2006, pp. 99–101).

Of the twenty-three GATT founding members, at least eleven were developing countries. The exact number is debatable because the categorization of some states such as Australia, Canada, New Zealand, and South Africa was unclear at the time (Lamp, 2017, pp. 482, 493–5; Wilkinson & Scott, 2008, p. 478). Moreover, some of the contracting parties from the Global South were not yet fully independent at the time of the ITO and GATT negotiations. India, for instance, was represented at the Bretton Woods conference by a delegation that included Indian as well as British officials (Helleiner, 2014a, p. 14). In addition, colonial powers made commitments on behalf of territories that were still under their rule, which meant that large parts of the Global South were affected by GATT rules even though they were not counted as contracting parties (Trommer, 2011, pp. 21–4).

The GATT was dominated by the interests of the Global North, and the newly independent countries eyed this "rich men's club" with a good deal of suspicion (Steffek, 2006, pp. 59–60). Three of the original contracting parties from the Global South – China, Lebanon, and Syria – left the institution during 1950 and 1951 (Rolland, 2012, pp. 67–8). By the mid-1950s, only a handful of developing countries had joined the GATT but almost all of the major developed countries, with the result that the North–South balance in the membership shifted in favour of the North (Hudec, 2011, p. 39). In the UN, though, developing countries had acquired the majority by 1960, and they placed development issues at the top of that organization's agenda (O'Brien & Williams, 2016, p. 237). One result was the founding of UNCTAD in 1964; another was the founding of the Group of

77, which pledged to promote South–South cooperation and advance the shared interests of developing countries in global economic governance.

The overall situation exerted considerable pressure on the GATT to address the development concerns of the Global South. It wasn't until 1963, when a great number of newly independent African countries joined, that developing countries gained a clear majority in the GATT; however, UNCTAD challenged the GATT's authority in trade matters (Hudec, 2011, pp. 51–2; Jupille, Mattli, & Snidal, 2013, pp. 141–2; Rolland, 2012, p. 69). Against this background, a campaign initiated by developing countries to reform the GATT rules in 1965 achieved the addition of a Part IV on Trade and Development to the GATT. While this addition did not include any binding commitments placed on the developed countries, it amounted to important recognition of the special status of developing countries in the regime (Hoekman & Kostecki, 2009, pp. 536–7; Hudec, 2011, p. 66). Article XXXVI:8 exempted developing countries from (full) reciprocity, and Article XXXVII committed developed countries to accord high priority to the elimination of trade barriers placed on products of particular export interest to developing countries "to the fullest extent possible" (GATT, 1986).

At the second UNCTAD conference in 1968, a General System of Preferences (GSP) was created, which was supposed to give developing countries preferential market access to developed country markets. The GATT parties approved the GSP in a waiver in 1971 (Steffek, 2006, p. 96). The GATT Tokyo Round adopted an additional agreement on Differential and More Favourable Treatment, Reciprocity and Fuller Participation of Developing Countries (GATT, 1979). This so-called Enabling Clause provided a permanent exemption from the MFN rule for non-reciprocal FTAs under the GSP and preferential trade agreements between developing countries. It restated the exemption of developing countries from full reciprocity and established the notion of special and differential treatment. More far-reaching demands for a New International Economic Order, voiced by the G77 during the 1970s, however, did not gain traction (O'Brien & Williams, 2016, pp. 237–8). Writing in 1981, Finlayson and Zacher described the development norms as a "subsidiary norm" of the world trade regime. "The major trading states appear willing to make only limited sacrifices to promote the trade interests of the developing countries," they observed (Finlayson & Zacher, 1981, p. 582). With the debt crises in the 1980s, developing countries were forced back onto the defensive. Instead of challenging the international economic order, they had to accept IMF and World Bank conditions in order to obtain credits (O'Brien & Williams, 2016, p. 239). Meanwhile, the number of developing country GATT members and with it their percentage share in the institution continued to grow. In the first half of the 1990s, accessions spiked as the opportunity for countries that had entered the GATT as colonies to become independent members under a simplified procedure expired (Copelovitch & Ohls, 2012, pp. 83–4). By the end of the Uruguay Round, developing countries accounted for more than 80 per cent of GATT members (Jupille, Mattli, & Snidal, 2013, p. 136). This and the simple fact that development had been established as a GATT norm during the 1960s and 1970s led to an ongoing normalization of development issues in the trade regime. There always were debates about how to best address development concerns, but that they were to be addressed was less and less of an open question.

Over time the development norm has thus become an important regime norm. The preamble to the WTO Agreement (1994) mentions sustainable development and the integration of developing countries into the world market among the goals of the organization. Additional accessions, including by China in 2001, have further increased the political weight of developing countries in the WTO. The first negotiating round of the WTO has been titled the Doha Development Agenda. The Doha Declaration launching the round declared:

> International trade can play a major role in the promotion of economic development and the alleviation of poverty. We recognize the need for all our peoples to benefit from the increased opportunities and welfare gains that the multilateral trading system generates. The majority of WTO members are developing countries. We seek to place their needs and interests at the heart of the Work Program adopted in this Declaration. (WTO, 2001b, § 2)

This was a strategic move aimed at winning the support of developing countries for a new liberalization round (Wilkinson, 2006, p. 119). That said, the development master frame of the Doha Round (Eagleton-Pierce, 2012, p. 316) has in fact shaped expectations and influenced negotiation strategies. When China, India, and Brazil, as a result of their rapid economic growth, rose to become important players during the Doha Round, they defined themselves as speaking for the developing world and insisted that the WTO deliver on the development promise of the Doha Round.

The growing influence of developing countries in the WTO is also reflected in the selection of Directors General. The position of GATT/WTO DG had long been filled by a European, and developing countries increasingly criticized this practice during the late GATT and early WTO years (Jones, 2010, p. 24). The first WTO DG from the Global South was Supachai Panitchpakdi of Thailand (2002–5). Supachai lobbied for the office in 1999 and initially appeared to be the candidate with the most support. The US favoured another candidate, the New Zealander Mike Moore, and strove to build a majority in his favour. The selection process turned into a North–South confrontation that was finally resolved in a compromise: each candidate would serve for a fixed three-year term, with Moore going first and Supachai taking over in 2002 (Blustein, 2009, pp. 60–4; Jawara & Kwa, 2004, pp. 186–91). Because of this, Supachai wasn't in a strong position when he assumed office. To the disappointment of many developing countries, he constantly needed to secure the support of the major trading powers (Jawara & Kwa, 2004, pp. 232–4). Generally, his leadership was perceived as rather weak (White, 2015, pp. 292–5).

After Supachai, Pascal Lamy of France served as DG for two consecutive four-year terms. In 2013, Lamy was succeeded by a Brazilian, Roberto Azevêdo. The career diplomat, who had represented Brazil at the WTO since 2008, prevailed over the Mexican Herminio Blanco. While both the final candidates were from Latin America, Blanco was widely perceived as the "rich country" candidate. An advocate of free-market values, he was backed by the US and large parts of the EU, as well as Japan and South Korea. Azevêdo, who was associated with the Brazilian Doha Round initiative against developed countries' agricultural subsidies, was perceived as the "developing country" candidate and had the support of the majority of emerging and developing countries (Bourcier, 2013; ICTSD, 2013b; McClanahan, 2013). As DG, Azevêdo would take a much more proactive stance than his predecessor, Supachai. Nevertheless, he was able to maintain the image of an honest broker. The conclusion of the Bali Package in 2013, which was hailed as the first negotiation output since the WTO's founding, has been credited at least in part to Azevêdo's mediating skills and personal commitment (Wilkinson, Hannah, & Scott, 2014, pp. 1037–8). His influence on North–South politics, however, was mostly confined to the procedural front (see chapter 7).

Azevêdo secured a second term in 2017, but stepped down a year before it ended, saying that he wanted to ensure a smooth transition ahead of the next ministerial conference (WTO, 2020b). During the succession process, Ngozi Okonjo-Iweala of Nigeria and Yoo Myung-hee of South Korea emerged as the top candidates. Okonjo-Iweala won the support of the majority of WTO members, but the Trump administration blocked her election (Elliott, 2020). After Joe Biden took over the presidency, however, Myung-hee renounced her candidacy and the US declared their support for Okonjo-Iweala (White et al., 2021), who became the first African and the first woman to lead the WTO in March 2021.

Okonjo-Iweala is a development economist with twenty-five years of experience at the World Bank and was previously chair of the board of Gavi, the Vaccine Alliance. In 2020 she was appointed the African Union (AU) Special Envoy to mobilize international financial support for the fight against COVID-19 as well as WHO's Special Envoy for the Access to COVID-19 Tools Accelerator (WTO, 2022h). As DG of the WTO, she has urged members to take steps to improve equitable access to COVID-19 vaccines, making this a priority (WTO, 2021a, 2021b), while more generally emphasizing the centrality of development issues (WTO, 2021d). "Trade is an instrument for development, it's not an end in itself," she said in her opening address to the ministerial conference in Geneva in 2022, adding that "tapping into international markets for value-added goods and services has been history's most proven path towards development." She emphasized the need for special and differential treatment but added that "it would be great if members that don't need S&DT because they are on the right track make clear they won't avail of it, so that flexibilities can go to those who need them" (WTO, 2022l). Based on this, she can be expected to stress development issues but in a way that is more compatible with the positions of the Global North than with classical notions of developmentalism.

In both the case studies in this book, developing as well as developed countries drew on the development discourse for their argumentation (see chapters 3 and 4). This was a successful defensive strategy for the developing countries when it came to sectoral tariff elimination in NAMA; it also played an important role in the widespread acknowledgment of the offensive interests voiced by four LDCs with regard to cotton. The developed country proponents of NAMA sectorals did not succeed in presenting sectoral tariff elimination as a development issue. In the case of cotton, however, the US, finding itself playing defence, was able to exploit assumptions about the deficiencies of developing countries inherent in the development discourse as well as the cognitive authority those assumptions provided to developed country experts (see chapter 5). As can be seen from these examples, the development discourse contains elements that can boost the strategic arguments of both developing and developed countries. The problem for developing countries, however, is that developed countries set the standards for development and thus remain the cognitive authorities on development questions.

The Problem of Reciprocity between Unequal Partners

As noted earlier, developing countries were formally exempted from the expectation of full reciprocity once Part IV on development was added to the GATT in 1965. Article XXXVI:8 states that "the developed contracting parties do not expect reciprocity for commitments made by them in trade negotiations to reduce or remove tariffs and other barriers to the trade of less-developed contracting parties" (GATT, 1986, Article XXXVI:8). The enabling clause of 1979 allowed non-reciprocal trade agreements within the framework of the UNCTAD GSP and clarified the concept of less than full reciprocity in WTO negotiations. This meant that developing countries would not be required to make "concessions that are inconsistent with … [their] development, financial and trade needs." Furthermore, developed countries would exercise special restraint in seeking any commitments from LDCs (GATT, 1979, §§ 5–6). Distinct tariff-cutting formulas and reduced levels of required liberalization for developing countries have since become common practice in GATT/WTO negotiations.

The concept of less than full reciprocity is situated at the intersection of the reciprocity and development norms and thus the discourses of sovereign equality and development. It creates two subject positions: that of full participants in the liberalization process (developed countries), and that of less than full participants (developing countries). This empowers developing countries to demand greater concessions from the developed countries than they are willing to make themselves. At the same time, though, it disempowers them from participating in the negotiations as equal partners. Over the course of the GATT's history, developed countries making reciprocal concessions among themselves have liberalized the sectors of interest to them. Under the MFN rule, tariff cuts were extended to all GATT members. The sectors in which developing countries have export interests, namely agriculture and textiles, have, however, remained highly protected (Finlayson & Zacher, 1981, pp. 572–4; Wilkinson, 2006, pp. 47–74). Because they could not offer reciprocal concessions (Finlayson & Zacher, 1981, p. 576) and were perceived as free-riders, developing countries were not taken seriously as negotiating partners (Hudec, 2011, pp. 68, 78).

The economic power of developing countries has grown, with the result that the Doha Round faces a new discursive struggle over what constitutes fair reciprocity between developed and developing countries and whether emerging economies constitute a special case in this regard. The debate over developing country participation in NAMA sectorals – an important factor in the breakdown of negotiations in 2008 – is a case in point.

As detailed earlier (see chapter 4), the US and other developed countries demanded that developing countries participate in sectoral tariff elimination or harmonization initiatives in NAMA in order to re-establish reciprocity between developed countries, which already had very low NAMA tariffs, and developing countries, which had retained much higher tariffs. Developing country opponents of NAMA sectorals, however, pointed to the Doha NAMA mandate, which stipulated that "the negotiations shall take fully into account the special needs and interests of developing and least-developed country participants, including through less than full reciprocity in reduction commitments" (WTO, 2001b, §16). Given that developing countries had higher tariffs, they argued that tariff elimination or harmonization would demand larger concessions from them, which would turn the principle of less than full reciprocity upside down. This reference to the rule of less than full reciprocity was key to their success in locking in the agreement that participation in sectorals would be voluntary.

Beyond the question of sectorals, there were debates about what exactly constituted less than full reciprocity. Developing countries held the view that any tariff reductions they undertook would have to be smaller than those of the developed countries; developed countries countered by focusing on the levels of tariffs after reductions. Since the bound NAMA tariffs of developing countries were much higher, they would remain higher than those of the developed countries even if they undertook deeper cuts. Thus, NGMA chairperson Jóhannesson reported in 2005:

> One benchmark which has been the subject of differences of opinion has been that of "less than full reciprocity in reduction commitments" and how it should be measured. Some developing Members are of the view that this means less than average percentage cuts i.e. as translated through a higher coefficient in the formula, than those undertaken by developed country Members. However, the latter have indicated that there are other measurements of less than full reciprocity in reduction commitments including the final rates after the formula cut which in their markets would be less than in developing country markets. (WTO, 2005s, § 7)

Furthermore, developing countries focused on the "less than full" aspect of less than full reciprocity, whereas developed countries highlighted that the concept still included reciprocity. This is clear from the words Mauritius chose to use when it claimed that "non reciprocity [*sic*] was one of the principles of the WTO" (WTO, 2003ac, § 1.29); by contrast, the US maintained that the NGMA should "demonstrate flexibility as it remained faithful to the important concept of reciprocity" (WTO, 2002h, § 1.12).

The standing of the rule, including the definition of less than full reciprocity, has important repercussions for standards of fairness and ultimately the distribution of costs and benefits in the outcomes of trade negotiations. A closely related discursive struggle is ongoing regarding whether emerging economies shall receive a particular treatment in this context.

Emerging Economies – a Contested Term

In the debate over NAMA sectorals, the US and other developed countries targeted emerging economies in particular. Given their growing economic power and impressive growth rates, the US argued, big emerging economies like China, India, and Brazil could no longer expect to be treated the same as other developing countries. They should be required to enter into reciprocal commitments and participate in sectoral tariff elimination initiatives. The concerned countries responded that despite their growing GDPs, they were still developing countries, facing typical problems such as high income inequality, a large subsistence sector, and a dearth of infrastructure. They insisted on receiving special and differential treatment like other developing countries (see chapter 4).

A discursive struggle ensued over the term "emerging economies." Formally, the WTO only distinguishes between developed countries, developing countries, and LDCs. The injection of the term "emerging economy" into the WTO discourse amounted to an attempt to establish a new subject category that carried with it specific powers and obligations. The countries under threat of being placed under that rubric were aware of its dangers and consequently rejected it: "There is no word called emerging countries or emerging developing countries in the WTO terminology, but it is a word which is largely the word used by the US and its think tanks,"[2] a representative of an emerging economy said. Another diplomat, who worked for a large developing country that was sometimes included in the category of emerging economies, elaborated:

> If you consider that all the denomination of BRICs was the creation not even of a government, was of an analyst in the financial sector, Wall Street, and maybe without even considering the impact that the denomination would have. I think that, yes, we are clearly worried that this could not be more than an artificial category that could not be representative, this sort of emerging new powers. Whichever you want to say, you will use a different adjective attached to the group. But it makes no sense to us. We don't want that, no, we're opposed to that.[3]

Contestation of the term "emerging economies" is connected to a more general disagreement over how "developing country" should be defined. The emerging economies uphold a political definition, one that is rooted in past experiences of exploitation and Third World solidarity; meanwhile, the established powers push for a definition based on economic criteria (Weinhardt & Geck, 2019, pp. 140–2). In the debate over WTO reform, which has been ongoing since 2018, the US has argued that the WTO practice of self-declaration has to be replaced by objective criteria for granting developing country status (Weinhardt & Schöfer, 2022, p. 11). In particular, the US has demanded that countries that meet one of the following criteria be excluded from the developing country category: member of the OECD; member of the G20; classified as high-income country by the World Bank; or accounts for 0.5 per cent or more of global merchandise trade (WTO, 2019e). Concerned countries have responded by presenting extensive economic data to prove that they continue to face development challenges (WTO, 2019b), while also emphasizing that special and differential treatment is a corrective for historic discrimination (Weinhardt, 2020, p. 399).

This discursive struggle demonstrates the implications of categorizations, which constitute actors as subjects with specific identities and abilities. Eagleton-Pierce talks about "the power of symbolic naming" (Eagleton-Pierce, 2013, p. 65). Only since the introduction of terms like emerging economies or BRICs has it become possible to distinguish them as a separate group that should be treated in a separate way. Language has practical consequences.

The discursive struggle over the status of emerging economies affects not only the countries subsumed under this label but also other developing countries. Because the US and other developed countries do not want to grant special and differential treatment to China and other emerging economies but have so far been unable to exclude them from that category, they have become unwilling to agree to any substantial special and differential treatment provisions. The only exception to this involves the special provisions for LDCs. This development is unfavourable for those developing countries that neither share the economic power of the emerging economies nor profit from special and differential treatment for LDCs (Weinhardt, 2020; Weinhardt & Geck, 2019; Weinhardt & Schöfer, 2022).

Weinhardt and Schöfer (2022) argue that the trend towards fragmentation of the developing country category into smaller subcategories is contributing to a broader trend toward "unmaking the North–South distinction" as a core ordering principle in international relations. While that may in fact happen in the longer term, what we observe in WTO negotiations at the moment is a contest over how the developing country category is to be applied rather than over the general validity

(Deitelhoff & Zimmermann, 2020) of categorizing countries according to their development status.

Development versus Liberalization as Central Regime Norm

The final discursive struggle to be treated here is the question of whether the liberalization norm takes precedence over the development norm or the other way around. In contrast to the other two discursive struggles discussed so far, this one not only concerns the interpretation and application of specific regime norms but also addresses the more fundamental question of the norms' hierarchy. It thus constitutes the most important discursive contention within WTO negotiations at present. To fully understand the debate, one has to take into account the different meanings that can be attached to the concept of development in trade politics. During the 1960s and 1970s, when special and differential treatment provisions were introduced into the GATT, dependency theory dominated the discourse of developing countries. This theory of economic development, which has its roots in Latin America (Cardoso & Faletto, 1979; Prebisch, 1950), holds that the underdevelopment of countries in the Global South is caused not by the backwardness of their economic, political, or cultural structures but by an exploitative global division of labour that began under colonial rule and that continues to shape trade relations between the Global South and the Global North. The Global South is on the periphery of the global economy and is being exploited as a source of raw materials and cheap labour so as to enable the generation of an economic surplus and technological development in the capitalist centre, which is in the Global North. This analysis informed the import-substitution policies that many developing countries followed during the 1960s and 1970s, as well as the demands of the G77 and the politics of UNCTAD, whose first director, Prebisch, is counted among the central authors of dependency theory (Margulis, 2017). Ideas about development-oriented international trade rules centred around exemptions from liberalization requirements and preferential access to markets in the Global North. The goal was to redress the asymmetric global division of labour, which implied changes in the economies not only of the Global South but also of the Global North (Hoekman & Kostecki, 2009, pp. 535–6; Weinhardt & Geck, 2019, p. 135).

With the rise of neoliberalism in the 1980s, however, a very different understanding of the reasons and remedies for economic underdevelopment took hold (Alessandrini, 2010, pp. 71–81; Toye, 1987). Neoliberal scholars claim that national economic policies, not world market structures, are to blame when countries in the Global South fail to catch up with the Global North. They oppose market interventions at the national and the international levels. Instead of import substitution and industrial policies, they advocate for trade liberalization, privatization, and deregulation. With regard to international trade governance, preferential market access and exemptions from liberalization commitments are considered inadequate measures to foster development. The global trade regime needs to support developing countries in liberalizing their own markets and becoming competitive in an open world market. Assistance with addressing capacity and supply side constraints, coupled with prolonged implementation periods, has become an important new type of special and differential treatment that follows this line of thinking (Weinhardt & Geck, 2019, pp. 136–7). Most developing countries have adopted export-oriented trade policies, and many have undertaken unilateral liberalization (Hoekman & Kostecki, 2009, p. 539). This has been partly due to ideational changes; however, pressure exerted by the Global North and the Structural Adjustment Policies instituted by the IMF and World Bank in the 1980s debt crisis have played an important role as well (Alessandrini, 2010, pp. 93–102).

These historical developments notwithstanding, the trade policies and negotiation positions of developing countries have always contained both protectionist and liberal elements (Scott, 2010; Wilkinson & Scott, 2008), as have those of the developed world. While neoliberalism can still be considered the orthodox position in trade politics (Eagleton-Pierce, 2013, pp. 67–8; Weinhardt & Geck, 2019, p. 137), since the 2000s developing countries have increasingly questioned the connected ideals of deregulation and export-oriented economic development. In the WTO, this has led to demands for policy space (Eagleton-Pierce, 2013, p. 69; Hannah & Scott, 2017) but also to more fundamental debates about the relationship between the trade regime's development norm and its liberalization norm and the hierarchy that relationship entails.

From the perspective of neoliberalism, the development norm and the liberalization norm are in perfect harmony, for trade liberalization is an important development measure. If one assumes that state-driven development policies, selective protectionism, and/or international rules to correct unfavourable structures in the world economy are necessary to enable development in the Global South, however, the two norms come into conflict (Weinhardt & Geck, 2019, pp. 136–7). According to this view, the development norm at least constitutes a contradictory but necessary complement to the liberalization norm, playing a role similar to that of the safeguard norm within the embedded liberalism compromise. In a more extreme take, the development norm is incompatible with the liberalization norm. In any case, the hierarchy between the two norms becomes an issue.

Lee (2012, pp. 94–5) has argued that a discursive turn in global economic governance at the beginning of the twenty-first century, manifested most clearly in the UN Millennium Development Goals, has "placed development firmly at the top of the agenda of various global governance regimes" (Lee, 2012, p. 95). In the WTO, this discursive turn was reflected in the designation of the Doha Round as a development round. Lee holds that the development norm has assumed a central position in the world trade regime, next to or even above the liberalization norm:

> Having signalled that the current Doha Round would place the needs of the developing countries at the centre of the work program, the legitimacy of the WTO system of global governance, as well as the reputation of the powerful states that dominate the regime, now rests on a meaningful development outcome. Previously, the legitimacy of the global governance of trade rested on its remarkable success at reducing tariffs and generating growth in global trade. Few contest the effectiveness of global trade governance in achieving this, but trade liberalization as an end in itself is no longer sufficient. Since the emergence of the discourse of development, the success of the WTO now rests on its ability to govern trade in a more equitable and fair way to create development of the poorest countries in the international system and reduce poverty among the poor communities in the world. (Lee, 2012, p. 95)

Lee argues that this development turn in the WTO has enabled the success of the Cotton Initiative. My analysis (see chapter 3) supports this argument insofar as references to the development discourse and the linkage of the cotton issue to the development master framing of the Doha Round were essential for the effective strategic arguing of the C4. However, the success of the Cotton Initiative is also based on its prudent combination of references to the development discourse and references to the discourse of liberal economics. The C4 managed to present its case in such a way that the WTO norms of liberalization and development were mutually reinforcing. The US, in its counter-argumentation, presented a different picture of the factual situation, and this resulted in a focus on development rather than liberalization. However, the US did not contest the general idea that liberalization would have a positive effect on development. The question of whether the development norm or the liberalization norm was the central norm of the world trade regime did not arise.

The situation was different in the case of NAMA sectorals. Here, too, the proponents framed the issue with reference to the discourses of both liberal economics and development, but the discourse of liberal economics clearly dominated their argumentation. The opponents contested the positive linkage between liberalization and development and argued that the development norm should take precedence over the liberalization norm. Kenya declared with regard to the NAMA modalities: "At the centre of the modalities should be the goal of enabling and facilitating the industrial development of developing countries. Liberalization should only be seen as a possible means towards this goal" (WTO, 2003p, § 1.26). Developing countries thus no longer accepted the liberalization norm as the central norm of the world trade regime and sought to put the development norm in its place.

This attempted rearrangement of the norms of the world trade regime was, however, rejected by the developed country proponents of NAMA sectorals. "It was necessary to recall the overall purpose and objectives of the WTO and DDA[:] ... the substantial reduction of tariffs and other barriers to trade and ... the elimination of discriminatory treatment in international trade relations," (WTO, 2003ad, § 1.107) New Zealand asserted.

In my assessment, therefore, the development turn in global economic governance has not yet led to a consensual elevation of the development norm above the liberalization norm, but it has certainly strengthened the development norm. It has also helped ignite the discursive struggle regarding which of the two norms should take precedence, a struggle currently being waged between developed and developing countries. Even though, as discussed earlier, the development discourse does have disempowering effects for developing countries, most of them see the rise of the development norm in the WTO as a chance to draw more attention to their interests.

As this chapter has shown, prevailing discourses and related regime norms have an important effect on the persuasive power of different actors. The discourse of sovereign equality generally empowers weaker states, but in the context of the WTO's reciprocity norm, it also creates inequitable obligations for smaller and poorer members. The rule of less than full reciprocity is a mixed blessing for developing countries. The discourse of liberal economics and the WTO's liberalization norm mainly empower large, developed countries with liberal trade policies and many internationally competitive industries. The development discourse and the respective WTO norm are more ambiguous, empowering developing countries to demand special treatment but denying them acknowledgment as competent judges of their own situation.

Overall, persuasive power resides mostly with those actors that are also otherwise powerful.

The discursive struggles that have shaped recent WTO negotiations are all related to the status of developing countries and the development norm within the trade regime. The debates over what constitutes a fair amount of reciprocity between developed and developing countries and how emerging economies should be categorized in this context bend in the direction of curtailing any special rights that developing countries enjoy in the regime, at least for some of them. The increasing prominence of the development norm and new debates about its relationship to the liberalization norm, however, might give developing countries more argumentative leverage in the future.

7 Institutional Procedures and Unequal Human Resources

The discursive contexts and institutional norms described in chapter 6 are one key source of WTO members' unequal power to persuade. Other important reasons why countries diverge in terms of their capacity to make effective arguments relate to how negotiations are organized as well as to governments' unequal human resources (see figure 7.1). The challenges that small and developing countries face in WTO negotiations are already well documented in the literature (Apecu Laker, 2014; Barton et al., 2006, p. 172; Blackhurst, Lyakurwa, & Oyejide, 2000; Hoekman & Kostecki, 2009, pp. 61–2; Jawara & Kwa, 2004, pp. 21–2; Jones, Deere Birkbeck, & Woods, 2010; Kapoor, 2004, p. 529; Michalopoulos, 2001, 2014; Wilkinson, 2006). This chapter discusses how the factors just mentioned affect the distribution of persuasive power. The tendency among WTO members to hold closed, small-group meetings and the presence of small contingents in Geneva (i.e., small countries can't afford to send larger ones) are only the tip of the iceberg. Human resource constraints also affect officials in national capitals, domestic stakeholders, and local academia. They make countries struggle to develop well-founded negotiation objectives and effective arguing strategies.

The chapter opens with a discussion of the WTO's negotiation procedures. It will be shown that exclusive informal practices limit the impact of inclusive formal rules and that members do not all enjoy the same opportunities to weigh in. Then I cover capacity constraints and, drawing on my own interview material as well as the literature, show how effective arguing depends on human resources, which in turn depend on economic power. I end the chapter by describing a number of practices that less well-equipped countries have developed to improve their sources of persuasive power, such as setting priorities, heightening engagement, pooling resources with other members, and utilizing external support.

Figure 7.1 Institutional procedures and unequal human resources as sources of persuasive power

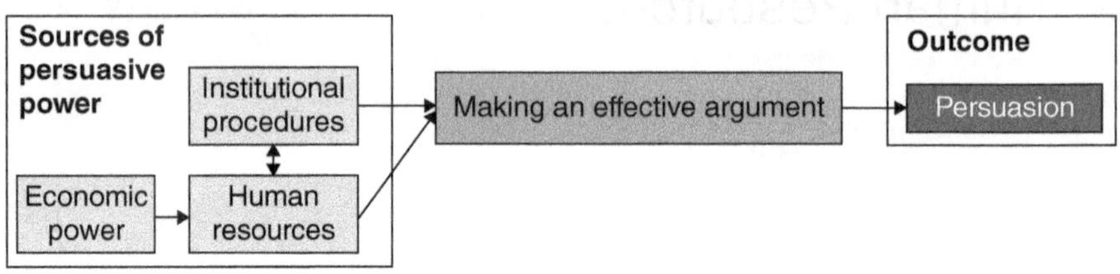

Inclusion and Exclusion in the Negotiating Procedures

Since the GATT days, the negotiation procedures of the trade regime have been shaped by the interplay of two contradictory normative ideas. Finlayson and Zacher have termed them the *multilateralism* norm and the *major interest* norm:

> Multilateralism signifies the willingness of governments to participate in rule-making conferences and to allow multilateral surveillance of, and even a degree of control over, their trade policy. It symbolizes regime members' acceptance of the proposition that they have a legitimate interest in each other's policies and behaviour. What we call the major interest norm, on the other hand, stems from a contrasting belief that participation in certain aspects of decision making ought to be restricted to those most affected or most influential, or both, in respect of the issue being dealt with. That a tension exists between the two procedural norms is obvious. (Finlayson & Zacher, 1981, pp. 585–6)

The GATT's first negotiation rounds were organized around the "principal supplier rule." Bilateral negotiations over tariff reductions were conducted between importing countries and their principal suppliers. Concessions were given on an MFN basis. Secondary suppliers, who profited from the concessions, were then expected to offer reciprocal concessions to the importing country. They were, however, not allowed to participate in the initial negotiation of the concessions. As Finlayson and Zacher observe, this procedure clearly reflected the major interest norm, with the balancing of concessions between the importing country and secondary suppliers at the end of the round being the only multilateral element. Small developing countries had no large import markets to open up and were not the principal suppliers of any product, and the result was that they were effectively excluded from the negotiations (Finlayson & Zacher, 1981, pp. 590–1).

As a consequence, many developing countries lost interest in participating in the GATT negotiations (Wilkinson & Scott, 2008, p. 488). More and more countries were joining the GATT, yet the percentage of members that exchanged concessions declined from negotiation round to negotiation round. All countries that were members participated in the first Geneva Round (1947, twenty-three members) and the Annecy Round (1949, thirty-three members). The Torquay Round (1950–1) saw the first decline – only twenty-nine of thirty-three members exchanged concessions. During the second Geneva Round (1956), the Dillon Round (1960–1), the Kennedy Round (1964–7), and the Tokyo Round (1973–9), only about half the members made concessions. Because new members were continuously being added, the number of those participating in the negotiations was still growing. By the end of the Tokyo Round, the GATT had eighty-four members, forty-four of which made concessions (Wilkinson, 2017, p. 1138).

The growing number of participants and the rising percentage of those opting out of the negotiations led members to look for alternatives to the bilateral request-and-offer approach. Besides this, the growing importance of non-tariff barriers and regulatory issues required a different negotiation method. In the Kennedy Round, members first used a linear tariff-cutting formula (Wilkinson & Scott, 2008, p. 497). The Tokyo Round saw another formula approach and a first attempt at binding all members in a single undertaking. Conflicts between developed and developing countries, however, led to the abandonment of the single undertaking and the adoption instead of several plurilateral accords on sectoral issues and non-tariff barriers (Rolland, 2012, p. 220; Wilkinson, 2017, p. 1138). The final GATT round, the Uruguay Round (1986–94), reverted to a request-and-offer approach but implemented the single undertaking, requiring all – now 123 – members to accept the entire package of negotiation outcomes. The WTO Doha Round, finally, sought to combine linear tariff-cutting formulas with a single undertaking (Rolland, 2012, pp. 220–5).

With these changes, the multilateralism norm has gained more influence over negotiation procedures (Finlayson & Zacher, 1981, p. 591). The Doha Round is supposed to produce an agreement on new rules and liberalization steps negotiated by all members in a multilateral process. There are other mechanisms, however, that ensure that important decisions will still be hashed out between the most powerful players.

Formal WTO decision-making procedures are based on inclusive multilateral principles. Not just the ministerial conference but *all* WTO bodies consist of the membership as a whole. No delegation of authority to a representative body is envisaged (Hoekman & Kostecki, 2009,

p. 61). Decision-making is governed by the consensus principle, which is enshrined in article IX:1 of the WTO Agreement (WTO, 1994): "The WTO shall continue the practice of decision making by consensus followed under GATT 1947." The agreement provides for voting "where a decision cannot be arrived at by consensus." For the purpose of voting, in line with the idea of sovereign equality, each country has one vote. However, except for waivers and accessions (Barton et al., 2006, p. 49), members have not resorted to voting since the foundation of the WTO, instead taking all decisions by consensus. Consensus is defined in Article XI:1 of the WTO agreement as a situation in which "no Member, present at the meeting when the decision is taken, formally objects to the proposed decision." In principle, therefore, each member has veto power over WTO decisions. These formal procedures provide all member countries with the same opportunities to participate.

However, decision-making does not actually take place in the formal bodies of the WTO. Arriving at a consensus decision in a committee of the whole of an organization that now counts 164 members (WTO, 2022e) is nearly impossible. The necessary consensus is thus constructed through informal decision-making. In contrast to the official decision-making procedures, the informal ones are characterized by practices of exclusion and delegation. The process is often characterized as consisting of concentric circles (Blackhurst, 1998, p. 49; Barton et al., 2006, p. 52).

Most successful initiatives originate with one of the two major trading powers, the US and the EU (Steinberg, 2002). When these two coordinate, their power is immense, but there have been few joint positions during the Doha Round (Elsig, 2006, p. 25). The inner circle of discussion used to be the Quad, comprising the US, the EU, Japan, and Canada (Jones, 2010, p. 87; Kwa, 2003, p. 36). In recent years, shifts in the distribution of economic power and the changing engagement of different members have led to some rearrangements of the inner circle of informal WTO decision-making (Jones, 2010, p. 87). After the Cancún ministerial, the agriculture negotiations of the WTO came to be dominated by the Five Interested Parties (FIPs), the US, the EU, Australia, Brazil, and India (Clapp, 2007, pp. 45–6; Wilkinson & Lee, 2007, p. 6). In the following years, all high-level talks included the US, the EU, Brazil, and India. Those four met with Australia and Japan (G6) in Geneva in 2006 (ICTSD, 2006), among themselves (G4) in Potsdam, Germany, in 2007 (ICTSD, 2007), and with Australia, Japan, and China (G7) in Geneva in 2008 (ICTSD, 2008d). Most recently, during the run-up to the ministerial conference in 2022 in Geneva, the informal core group that worked out a compromise proposal for an intellectual property response to COVID-19 and that consisted of the US, the EU, India, and South Africa has been referred to as the Quad (WTO, 2022j). Regardless of the exact composition of the inner circle, it serves to establish a compromise among the most important parties prior to more inclusive discussions.

Within the further circles of the decision-making procedure, talks are held with other members whose position on the subject is deemed important. Often, countries invited to such talks are expected to function as representatives of a group or category of members, whether or not the other members formally elected the country as a spokesperson (Kwa, 2003, pp. 19–20). The infamous Green Room meetings form one of the outer rings of the process. Their name refers to a (formerly) green-painted conference room within the WTO building in which the DG used to call meetings of twenty to forty countries. Generally, meetings of about thirty members at the level of heads of delegations (ambassadors or ministers, depending on the context) are referred to as Green Room meetings. They take place in other venues – at ministerial conferences, for example – and may be called by the chairpersons of the General Council or a ministerial conference besides the DG. What is agreed to in a Green Room meeting is presented to the membership as a whole as a draft decision and usually accepted without major amendments (Elsig, 2006, p. 23; Jones, 2010, p. 87; Steinberg, 2002, p. 355). Prior drafts are often provided by the DG or the chairpersons of the General Council, the ministerial conference, and issue-specific negotiation bodies in order to facilitate discussions (Odell, 2005, pp. 436–40; Steinberg, 2002, pp. 355–6).

Green Room meetings were first introduced during the Tokyo Round. The growing GATT membership and the declining hegemony of the US as well as the increasing complexity of the negotiation topics and the attempt to negotiate a single undertaking required new means to structure the consensus building process. The same trends, however, have led to an rising critique of Green Room meetings and negotiations in concentric circles. The continued growth of the GATT/WTO-membership and the increasing multipolarity of economic power have together made it difficult for Green Rooms to represent the full diversity of interests. Within the Green Room, decision-making has become complicated by the ever-increasing complexity of the issues, the single undertaking principle, and the legalization of the trade regime (Barton et al., 2006, 51–2, 166; Jones, 2010, 93–5).

Developing countries, in particular, began to view the Green Room process as unfair. As their percentage of the GATT/WTO membership rose, they felt starkly underrepresented in the Green Room. At the same time, the impact that Green Room decisions had on them increased considerably with the consolidation of the single-undertaking principle. Many perceived the Uruguay Round outcome as an uneven bargain that had been forced upon developing countries through the Green Room process (Jones, 2010, p. 95). Criticism of the process reached a peak after the failed WTO ministerial in Seattle in 1999 (Jones, 2010, p. 97; Odell, 2005, p. 434). During the conference, protesters blocking delegates' paths made it still harder for smaller delegations to attend meetings (Wilkinson, 2006, pp. 114–15). The conference chair, US Trade Representative Barshefsky, was criticized for being partisan and for devoting too little effort to consensus building (Odell, 2005, p. 432). As it became apparent that no outcome was in the cards, Barshefsky called a last-minute Green Room meeting in order to forge a consensus. A number of developing country delegates attempted to enter the room but were denied access by security guards (Jones, 2010, p. 37; Rolland, 2012, p. 92).

After Seattle, the General Council held a consultation on internal transparency and effective participation (Hoekman & Kostecki, 2009, p. 653; Rolland, 2012, pp. 92–3). Some efforts were later made to make negotiations more inclusive and transparent. More informal working groups with a variable membership were convened, informal meetings were opened to all, and regular briefings were provided about the results of small-group meetings (Hoekman & Kostecki, 2009, p. 653; Kwa, 2003, p. 19; Odell, 2005, pp. 434–5). At the same time, however, new exclusionary procedures were established. In the run-up to the Doha ministerial of 2001, a select group of members met for several so-called mini-ministerials. While some token representatives of smaller developing countries were invited and an informal system of group representation evolved, other member countries that expressed interest in participating were turned away (Jawara & Kwa, 2004, pp. 13–16, 56–65; Kwa, 2003, pp. 19–20; Odell, 2005, p. 435; Wilkinson, 2006, p. 119). The Chair of the General Council, Harbinson, drafted an outcome text that was criticized for not representing the interests of the whole membership (Broinowski & Wilkinson, 2006, p. 121; Odell, 2005, p. 438). At the ministerial itself, members complained about the way the facilitators for the main negotiation topics had been chosen, a lack of information about the place and timing of meetings, the extent of bargaining taking place in exclusionary informal settings, and how the Green Room participants had been selected (Wilkinson, 2006, p. 121).

In 2002, the Like-Minded Group (LMG), a coalition of developing countries that had initially formed around the goal of preventing new issues such as labour standards from being included in the first WTO negotiation round, submitted a proposal for regulating the organization of negotiations at ministerial meetings as well as the preparatory process to the General Council. They suggested a number of things: The General Council should organize the preparatory process and appoint chairpersons and facilitators. Draft decisions should reflect all positions in an equal and transparent manner and only be forwarded to the ministerial conference as a decision of the General Council. All informal meetings should be open-ended and open to all interested members. Meetings should be announced and negotiation documents provided early enough for all members to consider them. During ministerial meetings, there should be regular meetings of a committee of the whole, during which facilitators report on the progress made in the different working groups (WTO, 2022i). The proposal was supported by most developing countries and even by some developed countries, but in the end it did not win the support of the General Council. Opponents argued its proposals were too rigid (Jawara & Kwa, 2004, pp. 136–7; Jones, 2010, p. 39).

Odell (2005, pp. 435, 446) observes that delegations' complaints about being excluded from meetings and a lack of international transparency declined after 1999. Still, there had been no fundamental changes in decision-making procedures. The ministerial conference in 2003 in Cancún was characterized by Green Room discussions, an opaque process for choosing facilitators, and draft texts put together first by the chair of the General Council, Pérez de Castillo, in cooperation with DG Supachai, and later by the conference chair, the Mexican minister Derbez. All of these drafts strongly reflected US and EU positions, which infuriated many developing country representatives (Jawara & Kwa, 2004, pp. xliii–xlvi; Jones, 2010, pp. 97–8; Odell, 2005, pp. 439–40; Wilkinson, 2006, pp. 126–7). The striking new development in Cancún, however, was the unprecedented strength of Global South coalitions. The traditional trading powers were unable to force their preferred outcome on the other members, and the meeting collapsed (Narlikar & Tussie, 2004; Narlikar & Wilkinson, 2004).

As mentioned earlier, this brought about some rearrangement of the inner circle. However, it did not change the general principle of negotiating in concentric circles (Blustein, 2009, pp. 182–3). The General Council Meeting in July 2004, during which members agreed on modalities for the negotiations in agriculture and NAMA, as well as the ministerial meeting in 2005 in Hong Kong, were characterized by exclusionary small-group meetings, with chairs presenting drafts according to their own judgment (Blustein, 2009, pp. 190–2; Wilkinson, 2006, pp. 132–7). When the Doha Round ran into serious trouble after

Hong Kong, DG Lamy sought to break the impasse by convening meetings of an inner circle of four to seven countries and Green Rooms in Geneva in 2006 and 2008, in addition to a mini-ministerial in Potsdam 2007 (Blustein, 2009, pp. 223–76).

In 2013, when the Doha Round negotiations were revived after several years of deadlock, newly elected DG Azevêdo placed great emphasis on ensuring that small-group meetings were held in a transparent manner and that the process was as inclusive as possible. The negotiations at the ministerial meeting in Bali largely consisted of the typical bilateral and small-group consultations. Azevêdo and the Indonesian minister Wirjawan, who chaired the conference, however, made sure to conduct the discussions on the basis of a mandate they had secured from the opening informal Heads of Delegations (HoD) meeting. Azevêdo consulted a great number of delegations and ensured that the draft text was based on a bottom-up process (Wilkinson, Hannah, & Scott, 2014, p. 1038)

The ministerial conference in 2015 in Nairobi saw a refined version of this approach. During broad-based informal consultations, dialogue among representatives of opposing positions was encouraged. Quite deliberately, the least contentious issues were addressed first in order to create a critical mass of agreement; only then were more divisive issues taken up. Kenyan minister Mohamed, who chaired the meeting and led the bilateral consultations, enjoyed great credibility as a neutral facilitator. In the final hours of the conference, however, small-group meetings among the inner circle still played a role (Wilkinson, Hannah, & Scott, 2016, pp. 247–50).

In the lead-up to the ministerial conference in 2017 in Buenos Aires, Azevêdo announced that there would be no closed-door Green Room meetings but that he might hold consultations with members. Issue-specific meetings open to all were held, and each day concluded with an informal HoD meeting, where members were briefed about progress on the various topics (ICTSD, 2017b, p. 2). But there were still some complaints about opaque and exclusive processes: the Argentinian Chair of the ministerial meeting, Malcorra, had selected the facilitators without consulting the membership (Kanth, 2017a), and Kenyan minister Mohamed, who this time served as the facilitator of the agriculture talks, had called a small-group meeting between the US, the EU, China, India, Brazil, and Australia in order to resolve divergent positions within the inner circle (Kanth, 2017b).

While the informal negotiation procedures became more inclusive and transparent during Azevêdo's term in office, it needs to be noted that the WTO had dismissed the idea of the single undertaking and moved back to issue-specific and often plurilateral agreements. This weakened the multilateralism norm (Hannah, Scott, & Wilkinson, 2018). Besides this, the details of the informal negotiation procedures remained at the discretion of DGs and chairs. Azevêdo, in his former capacity as chief Brazilian trade negotiator, had been involved in the coordination of the G20, a heterogeneous group of developing countries that relied on the emerging economies to keep the smaller members on board. Perhaps reflecting this experience, as DG he put great effort into making sure all members felt included in the negotiations. Succeeding DGs, even if they hail from the Global South, might set different priorities.

DG Okonjo-Iweala's track record regarding the transparency and inclusiveness of negotiation procedures is so far mixed. The negotiations leading up to the first ministerial meeting during her tenure, in 2022 in Geneva, featured small groups, but these were organized in a transparent manner. When the Chair of the General Council, Castillo, oversaw the drafting of the outcome document, he convened a small group for that task, albeit one that included all group coordinators and that had been chosen to be representative of the WTO membership. He regularly reported to the entire membership in informal General Council meetings (WTO, 2021c). To resolve an impasse in the discussion about a TRIPS waiver, DG Okonjo-Iweala together with Deputy Director-General Gonzalez facilitated negotiations among the US, the EU, India, and South Africa, from which the draft text for the Ministerial Declaration on the TRIPS Agreement evolved. The draft was presented to the TRIPS Council and discussed in further small-group consultations before the ministerial (WTO, 2022j).

The ministerial conference itself featured open-ended thematic sessions as well as HoD meetings at the end of each day, just like the 2017 meeting in Buenos Aires (WTO, 2022b). Yet informal, small-group negotiations played an important role. At an HoD meeting in July to review the results of the conference, around forty countries complained that they had not been able to attend meetings because they had not received invitations or access badges. DG Okonjo-Iweala seemed not to take this critique seriously (Kanth, 2022). After the conference had been extended first for one, then for another day, with negotiations continuing throughout the night, members were presented with the final texts during an informal HoD meeting at 4 a.m. on 17 June. Some of the central decisions were presented only verbally, and members who had not been involved in the small-group discussions had no time to review the details, as the HoD meeting was followed immediately by the closing ceremony, during which the decisions were officially declared consensus (Mohamadieh, 2022).

Despite the fact that some emerging economies have managed to move into the inner decision-making circle and efforts have been made to make the whole process more transparent and inclusive, WTO decision-making procedures must still be characterized as excluding many members, especially smaller developing countries. This amounts to an institutionalized practice of excluding others from the debate (see pp. 42–6), whereby the established powers keep developing country positions from becoming dominant and ensure their continued control of the trade regime (Eagleton-Pierce, 2013, p. 71). Actors that have no access to important negotiating forums obviously cannot exercise persuasive power. The problems facing small developing countries do not end here, however. Their persuasive power is also curtailed by human resource constraints, and in some respects – as will be explained below – those constraints interact with the hurdles created by the decision-making process.

Differences in Human Resources

The WTO's headquarters in Geneva is the site of ongoing meetings and negotiations. The General Council, which between ministerial conferences constitutes the highest decision-making body, holds sessions once or twice a month. It also meets in its role as DSB and Trade Review Body. Then there are the Councils for Trade in Goods, Trade in Services, and Trade-Related Aspects of Intellectual Property Rights, which oversee the functioning of the GATT, GATS, and TRIPS. In addition to all these, there are around thirty committees, subcommittees, working parties, and working groups that have been established for specific issues or functions (WTO, 2022f). The negotiations for the Doha Round are organized by the Trade Negotiations Committee (TNC), which has established as subsidiary bodies special sessions of a number of permanent WTO bodies as well as negotiation groups on specific issues (Abbott, 2007, p. 321; WTO, 2022c). The official meetings of these bodies are complemented by a still larger number of unofficial meetings.

At the beginning of the Doha Round, the number of important WTO meetings per week was estimated to be forty-five or fifty (UK House of Commons, 2006, p. 96). For the year 2009, Apecu Laker (2014, p. 20) counted 322 formal and 237 informal multilateral and plurilateral meetings, which were accompanied by 6,536 private meetings. This amounts to 147 meetings a week. Even in 2012 – a time when Doha Round negotiations were deadlocked and therefore no multilateral negotiations were going on – diplomats estimated the number of scheduled meetings per week to be around sixty, not counting informal gatherings and consultations between delegations (Michalopoulos, 2014, p. 189).

To be able to participate in all these meetings, most member countries have established permanent missions to the WTO in Geneva. Only for especially important meetings are capital-based officials flown in. Meetings are differentiated according to the seniority of the representatives taking part. During ministerial conferences and sometimes other high-level encounters, talks are held at the ministerial level. There are also talks at the level of senior officials (i.e., high-ranking capital-based officials from the ministries). Talks at the ambassadorial level involve the heads of the countries' permanent missions in Geneva. All of these are rather infrequent, however, and are referred to as meetings at a "political level." Most WTO meetings are "technical level" talks among lower-ranking members of the missions in Geneva.

In the first years of the WTO, developing countries were starkly underrepresented in Geneva. In 2000, Michalopoulos (2001, p. 156) found that twenty-seven of the ninety-nine developing country members had no mission in Geneva; another twenty-four were represented by missions in Brussels or elsewhere in Europe, and three others by capital-based officials. In contrast, all developed and transition economies had permanent representatives to the WTO in Geneva. The average number of WTO representatives developing countries listed in the WTO Directory in 2000 was 4.1, compared to 7.3 for developed countries (Michalopoulos, 2001, p. 157). Due to the accession of a number of small European countries, which maintain relatively small missions in Geneva, the average number of delegates from developed countries declined to 6.0 in 2012. The average number of WTO representatives from developing countries increased to 4.9. Fourteen developing country members, however, did not have a permanent mission in Geneva (Michalopoulos, 2014, pp. 188–9). Nine WTO members, most of them small island states, continued to be represented from outside Geneva in 2019 (WTO, 2019a). The WTO Directory in 2020 contained an average number of 6.6 delegates for developed countries and 5.7 for developing countries (WTO, 2020a)[1].

Differences in the average staff numbers of developed and developing country members have thus been reduced, but large differences continue between individual countries. In 2020 the EU mission employed seventeen diplomats and the twenty-seven EU member-states an additional 123 (five on average). Other developed countries had an average of twelve delegates per mission, and the US had twenty-two. Some of the big developing countries also had sizeable delegations in Geneva. With thirty diplomats, the Chinese mission was the largest of all. The Brazilian mission employed seventeen diplomats and the Indian mission eight. At the other end of the spectrum, twenty-nine of the

164 WTO members had only one or two representatives to the WTO. This included 22 per cent of LDCs, 15 per cent of non-LDC developing countries, and 18 per cent of transition economies. Also, 22 per cent of the EU member-countries had only one or two representatives of their own, but here the small numbers were offset by the larger ones of the EU mission. None of the non-EU developed countries had fewer than five representatives (WTO, 2020a).[2]

Comparable numbers of delegates listed as WTO representatives can hide disparities that arise from the differences in their portfolios. The diplomats the large players list as representatives in the WTO directory usually work on the WTO only, whereas it is not uncommon for the representatives of small developing countries to cover other IGOs in Geneva and, in some cases, Europe in general as well. Thus, many countries are unable to attend all meetings of WTO bodies, let alone adequately prepare for them (Apecu Laker, 2014, pp. 16–20; Michalopoulos, 2001; 2014, p. 189).

A similar problem exists with regard to ministerial conferences. These usually last four or five days. During this time, many formal and informal meetings are held in parallel. When things get difficult, negotiations go on throughout the night. Large developed countries attend these conferences with delegations of one hundred people or more, including ministers, government officials, and parliamentarians as well as industry and civil society representatives. In contrast, the delegations of small developing countries often comprise only a single-digit number of people. To the ministerial meeting in Cancún in 2003, for instance, the US brought a delegation of 212, the EU institutions (Commission and Council) sent 100, and the delegations of the EU member-states another 564. China's delegation had 54 people, India's 59, and Brazil's 34. Most developing countries sent 10 to 15 people. Sixteen delegations, however, had three people or fewer (WTO, 2003y). As with the mission staff in Geneva, differences between developed and developing countries have been somewhat reduced since then. Differences within the group of developing countries have, however, widened. To the ministerial meeting in Buenos Aires in 2017, the US only sent 74 representatives. The EU institutions had a delegation of 129 people, and the member-states, despite having almost doubled in number since 2003, no more than 414 people in addition. China had a delegation of 76 people, India, 29, and Brazil, 85. Twenty-seven member countries sent delegations of three people or fewer, and four member countries did not attend the ministerial at all.[3]

Their inability to participate in all the meetings in Geneva as well as at ministerial conferences causes problems for smaller WTO members, because they will be ill informed about what is going on in the negotiations. This deprives the representatives of small developing countries of the opportunity to influence the discussion and voice objections at an early stage. Because consensus is defined as the absence of formal objections, members that do not object during the discussion of a draft at a formal meeting, either since they are not well enough informed or because they are absent, may later be confronted with the argument that they have acquiesced to the draft (Barton et al., 2006, p. 62). Those in charge of organizing WTO negotiations often pay little attention to the capacity constraints of small developing countries. Developing country representatives have contended at times that the major players have set schedules tightly on purpose in order to keep them from studying new proposals in detail (Kwa, 2003, 28, 40–1). This is where differences in human resources interact with exclusionary institutional procedures.

Moreover, the problems that limited human resources pose for effective strategic arguing are not limited to insufficient capacities for reading proposals and attending meetings; they run much deeper. Considerable human resources and expertise are required to determine negotiation objectives, analyse proposals, understand the positions of other members, and craft effective arguing strategies.

First of all, representatives need to identify their country's interests in the respective negotiations. For this, they need detailed knowledge of their own and other members' economies, trade flows, and trade policies. Several of my interviewees indicated that it was crucial for them to have a clear idea of their countries' interests. As becomes obvious from two interviewees' descriptions of the process, identifying these interests is no easy task:

> In specific sectors you look at the figures in terms of where does your trade go, not only now, but you look at the trends, you look at the trends in global trade … And then you look in terms of specific products or sectors, where these exports are, and then you look at what kind of tariffs are we facing? So, this is now an opportunity to do something about it.[4]

Diplomats from LDCs often lack the capacity to properly perform this task:

> I think the greatest challenge facing the LDCs is that we do not have sufficient capacity to basically formulate our own positions, formulate our future plans. We don't know which way we want to go, we don't know about our own potentials. So in this are massive, I mean huge, handicaps, which restricts us.[5]

Second, diplomats need knowledge of the technical language of trade agreements, existing agreements, traditional interpretations of terms, and past WTO dispute settlement decisions in order to judge what the wording of an agreement might imply for them. But even when diplomats have detailed economic data available and possess good institutional knowledge, it is difficult for them to assess what the exact distribution of the costs and benefits of a proposed agreement will be. Computer simulations, which project the gains different countries would reap from an agreement in dollar terms, are therefore an important instrument for WTO members (Scott, 2008). Again, diplomats from LDCs often do not have the capacities necessary for performing these tasks adequately:

> When we have had to make assessments, all these issues, we wouldn't even know whether certain kind of issues are our interest. So we would even have difficulty in assessing whether certain things are our own interest.[6]

This bars them from engaging in the negotiations and making effective arguments.

> So, it's either in the meeting you tend to just be defensive without any backing of data or information, you get my point, or you just keep quiet, because you don't know what to say. You don't have the information and sometimes only realize afterwards that actually whatever has been decided or was being discussed is not even to your interest or [will] not help you in any [way].[7]

Finally, country representatives require knowledge about the state of the negotiations, other countries' interests and negotiation positions, the proposals on the table, and existing coalitions and informal accords among other members in order to design an effective arguing strategy. "That's what this whole city trades in … information," one interviewee explained. "Who knows what's going on?"[8] Another explained: "There is also a very important part, which is sort of gathering information on other members' positions and what is behind them, so that we understand also better what their interests are, how we can basically find solutions which are addressing everybody's interests."[9]

Access to this sort of knowledge is so important because the successful performance of all the practices of strategic arguing (described in chapter 2) hinges on them. In order to frame an issue skilfully, actors need information on which discourses will resonate with others,

which issue linkages will be productive, and which parts of the negotiation history support their cause. The presentation of facts is closely
linked to access to authoritative knowledge about the factual situation, be it in the form of statistics, academic studies, or computer simulations. To identify a solution, actors depend on knowledge of their
own and others' interests and of institutional norms of fairness. To
provide a motivation for action, diplomats need to have insights into
others' interests and normative beliefs. The same is true for the practices of getting others to agree, which build on the aforementioned
practices of constructing an argument (the legitimation of claims, coalitional outbidding, rhetorical entrapment, and veiled threats), and
even for the practices of preventing others from making an effective
argument (the exclusion of other actors from the debate, and stalling). The skilful application of all practices of strategic arguing relies
on professional expertise and information about one's own interests
and others' positions as well as the factual situation and institutional
context.

In a study on the constraints faced by small developing countries in
WTO negotiations, Jones and colleagues found that

> information availability and analytical capacity is a significant problem
> across small states – a challenge closely related to human resource con-
> straints. Most small states have access to national trade data, but rarely
> have economic impact assessments or analytical capacity to properly
> assess the trade-offs of different trade policy options. Even where small
> states have access to vast amounts of information, they face substantial
> human resource–related challenges in analysing this information and
> turning it into concrete negotiating positions. (Jones, Deere Birkbeck, &
> Woods, 2010, p. 15)

In the interviews I conducted, developing country representatives
and even a diplomat from a medium-sized developed country indicated that their time for preparing negotiation positions was insufficient: "You know other countries just have three or five people to think
about and analyse and research and provide all these statistics about
a particular issue. You are not doing. I had ten minutes to write these
talking points, because I had eight other things to do."[10]

Jones and colleagues (2010, p. 15) emphasize that it is not just the
small number of staff but a lack of adequate training as well that troubles small developing country missions.

But the differences in Geneva personnel are only the most visible
indicator of unequal capacities. The ability of members to acquire

knowledge also depends on the capacities of the relevant ministries at home, the domestic stakeholder process, and the existence of research institutions in the country. Jones and colleagues highlight weak oversight of negotiators from national capitals (Jones, Deere Birkbeck, & Woods, 2010, p. 15) as well as weaknesses in consultative processes that would harness support and information from the domestic private sector and civil society in small developing countries (Jones, Deere Birkbeck, & Woods, 2010, p. 34). During the interviews, several developing country diplomats reported that scarce instructions from their capitals, a lack of input from domestic stakeholders, and missing domestic research institutions impaired their ability to identify their country's interests, assess the impact of proposed agreements, and develop a negotiating strategy.

Representatives from LDCs, in particular, indicated that they received no adequate instructions from their capitals:

> To make matters worse is that we, at least I can speak on behalf of the LDCs, we generally all have a weakness in terms of coordination between capital and Geneva. So, and that is made even much more worse because the person in Geneva is also overwhelmed and they don't get input from capital at the right time, if at all you get feedback. If at all you even get feedback, it's not at the right time.[11]

> There are countries, delegations who get line-by-line instructions on the negotiation text, and there are countries who send their delegates and they have to depend on their own understanding and their own judgment to negotiate. And that is the case for most of the LDCs, that we do not receive instructions. It is the capacity constraint. We don't have that kind of institution back home, which can provide us with the necessary support, the research, the analysis, that [inaudible]. We don't have that. Whereas you have entire organizations sitting behind, perhaps, I mean, you think about USTR! I should not be comparing with the US trade department but even if you look at India, they have the capacity, they have the think tanks working on each and every issue, so they have had the positions all fed to the missions here. But in most cases when we go in to negotiate, we just have to rely on our experiences, our judgment, our understanding of the issues. So that makes quite a lot of difference, you see.[12]

Representatives of larger and more advanced developing countries generally reported that they received some helpful instructions from their capitals, but much was still left to their discretion:

> Although legally speaking [capital of the of country of the interviewee],
> they decide. But the nature of our unit and, I expect, other units in the de-
> veloping countries are relatively, what they call it, proactive, have a big say,
> a bigger say in the process … [Capital of the country of the interviewee]
> would only have the broad outlines on what to do, on what the interests
> are. But when it comes to strategy, I suspect, that what happens since the
> beginning, we have this liberty or, you know, big rooms of manoeuvre what
> to do, well, as long as the bottom line of our interest has been served.[13]

Interviewees also highlighted the importance of input from domestic stakeholders and research institutions. The capacities of civil society are limited in most developing countries, and consultative processes are poorly developed. Few research institutions and think tanks exist. Several developing country diplomats expressed that they needed more input from the private sector, civil society, and research institutions in their countries:

> The stakeholder processes, inter agencies, we try as much as possible to con-
> tribute that they come up with a position, but the process has always been
> very, very critical in terms of bringing them together … Most … countries,
> particularly developed countries, they have most of their analyses done by
> NGOs, research organizations, so they can always have something at their
> fingertips they're able to use as a basis to either support or to go against a
> particular proposal. We lack that kind of capacity to be able to do that.[14]

One diplomat from an emerging economy indicated that the stakeholder consultation process his country had established for the Doha Round greatly improved his delegation's ability to acquire knowledge:

> One essential element that we had in this round that we were lacking in
> the past is a quite good process of domestic consultation with the stake-
> holders. I mean, a good trade policy starts at home. I mean, who are your
> key exporters? Your key importers? What are the sectors that are com-
> plicated? What are the government agencies that have been brought on
> board? What are the other stakeholders? Different views, bring everybody
> together, explain the situation, and from there onwards you would count
> with domestic [inaudible] or what you want to do. If you don't count with
> that you can't even start.[15]

In addition to all this, capacity constraints limit countries' ability to build up institutional memory and to ensure effective learning by new personnel. As most countries only post individual diplomats to Geneva for three or four years, this is an important issue. Developed country representatives[16] explained that they had been trained on the job and learned from their colleagues and superiors in Geneva. In small developing country missions, newcomers to Geneva have very few, if any, experienced fellow diplomats to learn from.

All in all, limited human resources in Geneva and the capitals as well as weak consultation processes and a lack of domestic research institutions seriously impede the ability of small, developing countries to engage successfully in practices of strategic arguing. This undercuts their persuasive power, as diplomats are well aware:

> Obviously, nations which have more resources, much better understanding, much more continuity in the negotiation, they always get in that sense, yes, they get upper hand vis-à-vis smaller countries with lesser resources, with lesser number of people who have the understanding, the lesser involvement with the stakeholders back in the nation, the lesser debate or discussion within the country.[17]

Access to expertise and information depends on the capacities of a country's government, civil society, and academia. It requires financial, human, and institutional resources, all of which are linked to economic power. Mission staffs in Geneva cost money, and so do qualified professionals in ministries back in the capital. Engaging experts and consultants is expensive, and so is commissioning studies. Small and/or developing countries often lack the necessary financial resources for all this. In a study on small developing countries by Jones and collaborators, the lack of financial resources was identified as a major constraint in adequately staffing Geneva missions (Jones, Deere Birkbeck, & Woods, 2010, p. 20). Diplomats interviewed for this book made remarks to the same effect.

More fundamentally, however, the availability of qualified people, the range and capacities of civil society organizations, and the existence of research institutions and think tanks are all linked to a country's population size and economic development. Countries with smaller populations and at lower levels of development are thus disadvantaged when it comes to acquiring the expertise and information necessary for the skilful performance of practices of strategic arguing in the WTO context. The power to persuade depends on material resources connected to economic power, and those resources are distributed unevenly between large and small states as well as between developed and developing countries.

Figure 7.2 Practices of improving sources of persuasive power

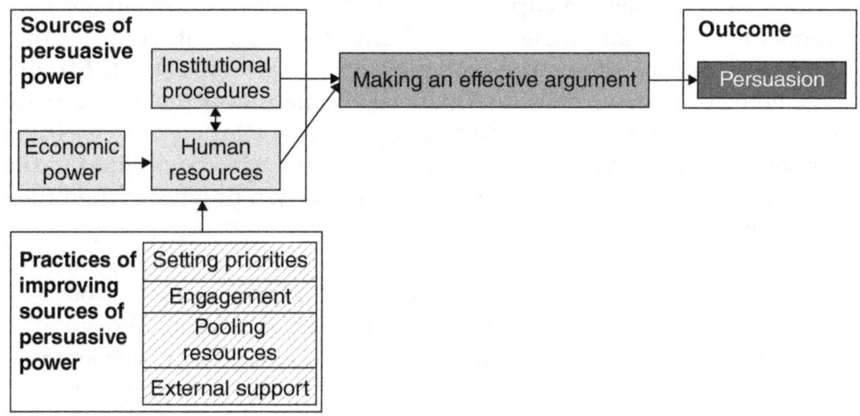

Practices of Dealing with Resource Constraints

Small and developing country members of the WTO have developed a number of practices to address the problems arising from their limited human resources. These practices are their means to improve their sources of persuasive power (see figure 7.2).

The most basic strategy to deal with capacity constraints is priority setting. Small developing countries do not have the resources to acquire the necessary information and participate in all areas of the negotiations, so they pick a limited number of issues of importance to them and focus on those. In the interviews, several representatives from small developing countries indicated that this was how they approached the Doha Round negotiations. By concentrating their resources on one or a few issues, even small developing countries are able to develop well-informed positions and make effective arguments. The obvious downside of this strategy is that other issues have to be neglected.

Another practice for heightening persuasive power, often employed by smaller players alongside priority setting, is strong engagement. That is, they engage in the negotiations on an issue by making submissions, speaking at meetings, reiterating claims, meeting opponents, and addressing the DG; in doing so, they improve their expertise on the issue through experience and exchange with other actors. Countries that have already gained a reputation as engaged and competent negotiators can further increase their experience if they serve as group coordinators or chair negotiating bodies. Coordinating coalitions can even lead to a temporary increase in capacity, as the WTO offers sponsorship programs for additional officials in the Geneva missions of countries that coordinate groups of small developing countries[18] (WTO, 2022d). Engagement, of course, requires financial, human, and institutional resources. That is why engagement and priority setting usually go hand in hand in small developing countries. One interviewee pointed to the C4 as an example of the effectiveness of these two practices when they are combined:

> The Cotton Four is a good example: particular group of countries otherwise not very active in the WTO, but on this particular issue? Very vocal, have to be included and make up a huge fuss … I imagine the smaller the country and the fewer resources you have, the more focused you have to be about discriminating and saying, this is our one priority and we are going to throw all of the small resources that we have at this priority. For Chad, for Burkina Faso, and for Cameroon things like cotton, but also bananas, for instance, are particular issues where they are very, very present.[19]

Another practice for improving expertise and information as sources of persuasive power is the pooling of resources through coalitions or informal networks. Most of the stable developing country coalitions like the ACP Group, the African Group, the LDC Group, and the SVE Group have developed systems of rotating coordinatorship. The coordinating country is responsible for representing the group, organizing meetings, and preparing joint positions. The ACP Group has also established a secretariat in Geneva that supports the ACP missions. The ACP Group, the African Group, the LDC Group, and the SVE Group have developed a system of focal points for the central issues of the Doha Round. Group members that serve as focal points attend the respective meetings and report back to the group. This way, group members can pool their resources and theoretically follow the negotiations on all issues of interest to them.[20] Jones and colleagues (Jones, Deere Birkbeck, & Woods, 2010, p. 49) found that small developing countries viewed resource pooling as a significant benefit of coalition building.

The downside of this practice is that group members depend on the quality of the work and the neutrality of the coordinator and the focal points. One interviewee, whose country is a member of a group that practises the focal point system, reported that the capacity constraints of the individual missions troubled the system and that group members could not really rely on the focal points.

Well, asked if it's a good strategy, I mean, that's the only way probably you can do it, because if you try to follow everything, you are not going to be effective at all. My personal observation is that it's probably the best option right now, but I don't think even that is really that effective ... You are at the mercy of the seriousness of a person. If somebody is not serious about attending meetings, they do their own personal things, you are at their mercy. But generally, what has been the case has been not necessarily that the focal points don't want to attend meetings, but they are just overwhelmed. And if they are sent for other different meetings [by their national superiors], UNCTAD, WIPO, ILO, they have to go there.[21]

Besides this, coordinators or focal points may inject their *own* interests into group positions. This problem is even more pronounced when issue-specific coalitions include developing countries with unequal levels of power. These coalitions typically do not have rotating coordinators; instead, they are led more informally by some of their more powerful members. The smaller members profit from expertise provided by the group leaders and from information on small-circle meetings,[22] but the information conveyed by the group leaders is naturally coloured by their own interests.

Geneva delegates working on the same issues may also develop informal networks for sharing information. "Groups of colleagues who deal with a particular issue in a placid circumstance become kind of a little community amongst themselves."[23] People who are part of these groups will inform one another when they are going to make important statements, and they circulate copies of their statements via email after meetings, which is very helpful, as official minutes usually come out only months later. These contacts are also mobilized when a delegate needs information about ongoing negotiations that is not available to all members. Colleagues help one another out as much as possible. But inclusion in these informal networks depends on involvement in the negotiations, so this practice is not an option for those in most need of resource pooling – indeed, it works to their detriment:

My relationship with my different colleagues from different countries depends hugely on how active that country is, how much I see them, how much they come to meetings, how much I interact with them in a meeting and outside a meeting. So yes, I mean, when I say, kind of the colleagues who deal with a particular issue become a little community, what I really mean is that the colleagues who are most active in that issue become their own little community amongst themselves, which I imagine could actually be quite difficult if you were Bangladesh for example.[24]

Last but not least, WTO members with limited expertise and little capacity to acquire information resort to external support from the WTO secretariat, other IGOs like UNCTAD and South Centre, and international NGOs and think tanks (Jones, Deere Birkbeck, & Woods, 2010, pp. 26–7; Lee, 2012, p. 97; Scott, 2008). External support ranges from the consultation of research publications by think tanks to tailored support by external organizations.

"Of course we usually get help from NGOs, who do some analytical work for us," said one LDC representative I interviewed.[25] A diplomat from a large, non-LDC developing country similarly reported: "We outsource, we rely and we look for the studies that [are] made by think tanks, by other, you know, those [inaudible] international study, transnational writings that deals with that."[26] Several authors have reported that NGOs such as Oxfam and the IDEAS Centre played a prominent role in establishing the Cotton Initiative (see pp. 51–5) (Eagleton-Pierce, 2012, p. 320; Lee, 2012, p. 97).

But this practice also has its drawbacks. It takes more effort to evaluate think tank studies and coordinate with international NGOs than to have analysis and support provided by one's own government.[27] Besides that, the information and studies gathered by this means often are not tailored to the negotiator's country (Jones, Deere Birkbeck, & Woods, 2010, p. 28). As well, if analyses of a country's economy or simulations of the impacts of proposed agreements are performed by external actors, it will not always be at the discretion of the country concerned to decide whether the results will be published. This is a disadvantage, for the publication of such studies may compromise a country's negotiating strategy by revealing its bottom lines.[28] Finally, there is the question of impartiality. IGOs, NGOs, and think tanks have their own agendas, and the knowledge they provide will reflect this (Jones, Deere Birkbeck, & Woods, 2010, p. 28; Scott, 2008, p. 95). State actors are aware of this and draw on several sources, if possible, to gain a more holistic picture: "When we'd have to see the extreme critics to certain moves or proposal from developed members, then we know that South Centre is the way to go … but then we do want more neutral think tank, then we could go further to the ICTSD [International Centre for Trade and Sustainable Development] et cetera, then we can judge from their different positions on what to do."[29]

To summarize, small developing countries have developed a number of practices to compensate for their limited human resources. Setting priorities, engaging in selected negotiations, pooling resources, and mobilizing external support make it somewhat easier for them to attain the expertise and information necessary to identify their countries' interests, analyse others' proposals, and devise effective arguing strategies. All of these practices, however, have drawbacks, and none can fully compensate for the advantages that larger and more developed WTO members have, given their greater human, financial, and institutional resources. As with the discursive contexts and institutional norms, WTO procedures and the distribution of human resources give large, developed economies the power to persuade.

8 Who Has the Power to Persuade?

The central purpose of this book is to analyse the distribution of persuasive power among WTO members. In this final chapter, I return to the question of who has the power to persuade.

As detailed in chapter 1, existing research on arguing in international politics is heavily influenced by a Habermasian understanding of arguing as communicative action (Habermas, 1984, 1987). This type of arguing is characterized by an understanding-oriented interaction orientation and the assumption of an ideal speech situation. Actors presume that all have equal access to the debate, that relations of power are suspended, and that the only force that counts is the force of the better argument (Habermas, 1983, pp. 99–102). Accordingly, they engage in an open-ended debate and are ready to be convinced by others' arguments (Habermas, 1984, pp. 285–6).

From this perspective, the distribution of persuasive power is not a pressing concern. For communicative action is, by definition, not about exercising power or forcing your opinion onto other actors or making them do something they would not otherwise do. It is about exchanging arguments and finding a reasoned consensus. If certain actors are better at arguing, it does not empower them over others. To the contrary, those who are less able to devise arguments profit from the superior rationality of the outcome, which they could not have arrived at by themselves.

In this book, however, I am not concerned with communicative action, but with strategic arguing. As explained in chapter 1, strategic arguing is a form of social interaction in which actors raise empirical or normative claims that can be challenged in the light of their propositional truth, normative rightness, and truthfulness, as is characteristic of the speech act type of arguing (Elster, 1999–2000; Habermas, 1984, p. 307), but they do this in order to convince others of their positions and reach predefined goals, as is characteristic of the interaction orientation of strategic action (Habermas, 1984, pp. 285–6). In contrast to communicative action, strategic arguing does not presuppose that actors are oriented towards understanding, or an ideal speech situation in which relations of power are suspended.

From this perspective, arguing is a way to exercise power and get one's way in negotiations. This is where the question of whether some actors have superior abilities to persuade, and what these are grounded in, becomes relevant. Against this background, it is problematic when Habermas scholars claim that everybody is equal in arguing and that arguing can thus be expected to empower weaker actors – a claim that Risse (2000) makes in an influential article about arguing in international politics: "Assuming that the materially more powerful actors do not necessarily have the better arguments, an arguing situation should disproportionately empower the weaker actors who have less material resources at their disposal" (Risse, 2000, pp. 18–19).

There is some truth to his observation that "we have probably witnessed processes of argumentative persuasion ... when materially less powerful actors such as small states or non-state actors carry the day" (Risse, 2000, p. 19). Materially less powerful actors that manage to influence outcomes to their benefit most likely have drawn on ideational resources, and that usually involves arguing. But the reverse is not true: arguing does not disproportionally empower weaker actors – rather, the contrary is true. At fault is Risse's assumption that "materially more powerful actors do not necessarily have the better arguments" (Risse, 2000, p. 18). The analysis of WTO negotiations undertaken in this book has shown that indeed, very often they do.

As I will explain in more detail, large developed countries with many competitive industries and a liberal trade policy are most likely to carry the day in arguing processes in global trade governance. This means actors that are powerful in material terms also possess the greatest persuasive power. However, the link between economic and persuasive power is not absolute and immutable. In the second section of this chapter, I address a number of qualifications. First, the development discourse and the corresponding development norm of the world trade regime to some extent also empower developing countries above developed countries. Second, the combination of factors empowers not one monolithic group of countries, but several overlapping groups. This makes the picture complex and dynamic. Third, actors can overcome disadvantages to some degree through practices such as prioritization and resource pooling as well as through well-designed negotiation strategies. They can further challenge prevailing discourses and initiate institutional reforms. In a final section, I discuss how these insights about persuasive power complement theories about bargaining power as well as the generalizability of my findings beyond the WTO negotiations analysed in this book and avenues for further research.

Materially More Powerful Actors Often Have the Better Arguments

To start with, materially powerful actors are advantaged by the fact that the real-life settings of WTO negotiations do not conform to the ideal-speech situation. As described in chapter 7, WTO negotiations are characterized by exclusionary and often opaque informal processes. Formally, decisions are made by consensus and each member country has veto power. However, consensus is fabricated in a process of concentric circles (Blackhurst, 1998, p. 49; Barton et al., 2006, p. 52): the fundamental parameters of agreements are set by a small group of the most important trading nations. Only after this are proposals discussed with other members. During the further process, minor changes are made to bring smaller and poorer members on board, but they have little influence over the basics. Using the practice of excluding others from the debate (see chapter 2), the countries that economically dominate world trade shape the direction of global trade governance. Even more fundamentally, access to the debate is restricted to member governments, although multinational corporations exert considerable influence "in the 'shadows' of WTO deliberations" (Kapoor, 2004, p. 530). Civil society organizations, especially more critical ones, by contrast, have a hard time making themselves heard. The first condition of Habermas's ideal speech situation, equal access to the debate, is therefore not fulfilled. Rich, developed countries and powerful economic actors dominate the discussion and exclude small, developing countries and critical civil society organizations. The same is true for the other conditions of the ideal speech situation: relations of power are not suspended and negotiations are not restricted to rational argumentation. Bargaining and power politics play an important role.

And even within arguing processes, in situations where WTO members exchange rational arguments on an ostensibly level playing field, power differences play a role. Country representatives use rational arguments to legitimize their positions, win others for their coalition, rhetorically entrap their opponents, make veiled threats (see chapter 2), and ultimately secure negotiation outcomes that conform to their country's predefined interests. But WTO members are not equally endowed with the resources that enable actors to make effective arguments and convince others. They do not have the same power to persuade, and often it is the materially more powerful actors that have more persuasive power. There are two main reasons for this.

First, the discourses and institutional norms that provide the context in which trade negotiations take place empower some actors more than others. The discourses of liberal economics, sovereign equality, and, increasingly, development dominate the discursive context of WTO negotiations and shape the norms of the world trade regime. As analysed in detail in chapter 6, these discourses largely privilege actors that are materially powerful.

The discourse of liberal economics and the liberalization norm, which is usually considered central to the world trade regime, empower those countries that have liberal trade policies and that are willing to open up their own markets in exchange for new export opportunities in other countries. But trade policy is not simply a matter of intellectual choice. Countries are remarkably similar in that they favour open trade in sectors where their industries are competitive and seek to protect domestic markets in sectors where their industries are not. A liberal trade policy is thus something that only those countries that have internationally competitive industries in many sectors can afford. Thus, materially more powerful actors are empowered by the discursive setting.

The picture is more ambiguous with regard to the discourses of sovereign equality and development. In that it constitutes nation-states as sovereign entities with equal rights and obligations, the discourse of sovereign equality does have a fundamentally equalizing effect on all actors that fall within this category. With regard to obligations such as liberalization concessions, this does not do justice to smaller and poorer nations with smaller domestic markets and hence less to offer in terms of concessions. The problems small and developing countries have encountered with the trade regime's reciprocity norm over the course of the GATT/WTO history demonstrate this. Like the liberalization norm, the reciprocity norm advantages actors that are materially powerful.

The development discourse entitles the developing country subjects it creates to ask for compassion and aid from other international actors, thus providing them with a kind of moral authority. As post-development theory (Escobar, 1995; Rahnema & Bawtree, 1997; Rist, 2008; Sachs, 1992; Ziai, 2004a) has shown, however, countries labelled "developing" are constructed as inferior, backward, and unable to judge for themselves what their needs are and what their course of action should be. The term entitles countries labelled "developed" to continue dominating the Global South after decolonization, to subdue developing countries' voices, to tell them which policies to adopt, and to exploit their natural resources and inhabitants. Under the guise of development aid or cooperation, materially powerful countries gain the moral and cognitive authority to exert power over poorer countries. This is also evident in the way developed countries apply the development discourse and the related development norm, which plays an ever greater role in the multilateral trade regime, to achieve their own negotiation objectives. Even here, in the end, it is mostly the materially powerful actors that are enabled by the discursive context and institutional norms to make effective arguments.

As the case of the Cotton Initiative illustrates, it is especially difficult for developing countries to make offensive claims. Even though the four small LDCs, which make up the C4, presented an argument for abolishing cotton subsidies that aligned perfectly with the discourses not only of development but also of liberal economics, the US found ways to prevent serious discussion about its domestic support of cotton. An important element in US strategy was the claim that the subsidies rich countries paid to their cotton farmers was only one problem among many that West African cotton farmers faced. Therefore, a more complex solution, including development aid and domestic reform, was needed. This argumentation, which enabled the US to sideline the C4's demand for the abolition of cotton subsidies and stall discussions about the issue, was enabled by the structure of the development discourse, which gives cognitive authority over development questions to developed country experts and reduces developing countries to the subordinate role of aid recipients. If developing countries make demands that go against the interests of developed countries, they can always claim that they know better what the developing countries need, pinpoint some domestic problems, and offer aid instead of real concessions.

In the other series of negotiations analysed in this book, the debate over sectoral tariff elimination in NAMA, developing countries had to play defence. Here, the development discourse served them better. By pointing to the WTO rule about less than full reciprocity, they were able to fend off the developed country proponents' attempts to make participation in sectorals mandatory for all WTO members. Defensive claims are generally more easily supported by the development discourse because they align with the image of developing countries as deficient and needy. Developed countries, however, still managed to establish voluntary sectorals as an essential element of the NAMA modalities, and with the concept of critical mass they brought demands for the participation at least of the more advanced developing countries in through the back door. Their framing of sectoral tariff elimination as necessary for the liberalization of NAMA prevented developing countries from rejecting sectorals altogether.

Taken together, the two cases demonstrate how the discursive contexts and institutional norms of the world trade regime make it difficult for small and developing countries to argue effectively for their interests. The reason why does not lie in the absence of an ideal speech situation. Developing countries were able to participate in the debate, and actors engaged in arguing, although bargaining at times also took place. The factors described above – the ones that advantaged materially powerful actors – were located within the process of rational argumentation. Those factors are rooted in the fact that the shared lifeworld (Habermas, 1987, 119ff) of trade negotiators is not neutral but rather is shaped by discursive formations (Foucault, 1972) that regulate what can be said by whom, create different subject positions, and empower some more than others. As these discourses are institutionalized in the norms of the trade regime, "the power of norms and the norms of the powerful interact" (Jaeger, 1996, pp. 326–7, my translation), further entrenching the superior persuasive power of large developed countries with many competitive industries and liberal trade policies.

The second reason why materially more powerful actors often have the better arguments is that they have more of the financial, human, and institutional resources needed to devise effective arguing strategies. Trade politics is a complex matter. As we saw in chapter 7, countries require considerable human resources in order to identify their interests, analyse the effects that new market openings or regulations would have on their trade, understand other members' objectives, and craft successful arguing strategies. But the staffing of members' permanent missions in Geneva and the size of the delegations they send to ministerial meetings vary greatly. Diplomats representing developing countries often do not even have the capacity to read all the proposals and attend all the meetings. And this is only the most visible part of the problem. Developing country representatives often do not receive the same level of training as their counterparts in developed countries, and they often receive scant instructions from their capitals. The resources of their countries are limited on a fundamental level: in quantity and quality of academic institutions and think tanks, large developed countries far exceed them in capacity to churn out economic analyses and policy advice. Stakeholder consultation processes are less developed and leave governments and diplomats with less input from business and civil society (Apecu Laker, 2014; Barton et al., 2006, p. 172; Blackhurst, Lyakurwa, & Oyejide, 2000; Hoekman & Kostecki, 2009, pp. 61–2; Jawara & Kwa, 2004, pp. 21–2; Jones, Deere Birkbeck, & Woods, 2010; Kapoor, 2004, p. 529; Michalopoulos, 2001, 2014; Wilkinson, 2006). In sum, small developing countries often lack the time and expertise to truly understand what they are negotiating about, to know with certainty what their interests are, and to design effective arguing strategies. All of this compromises their power to persuade.

With the Cotton Initiative, the cognitive authority the US managed to establish over the problems of the C4 was strengthened not only by the role the development discourse assigns to developed country experts but also by the superior ability of the US to mobilize scientific expertise and the analytical support of IGOs. In an elaborate process of analysis and discussion, they identified a host of domestic problems in the West African cotton sectors such as technological backwardness, poor infrastructure, and ineffective institutions. These problems supposedly constituted proof that US subsidies were of minor importance. The C4 did not have the capacity and institutional support to counter all these ostensibly factual arguments (see chapter 3).

Capacity constraints are obviously linked to material resources. Adequately staffing permanent missions in Geneva and sending large delegations to ministerial meetings costs money. The more fundamental differences in the institutional and human resources of countries are a function of the size of their populations and the level of their economic development. Like the discursive context and the institutional norms of the trade regime, these differences in analytical and strategic capacities endow materially more powerful actors with greater persuasive power. And again, these differences persist even in situations where institutional arrangements approximate an ideal speech situation. Differences in the power to persuade stemming from unequal human resources empower some actors over others, even when the only force available is the force of the better argument. For materially more powerful actors do have an easier time coming up with convincing arguments.

The Link between Economic and Persuasive Power Is Not Set in Stone

From the preceding, one might conclude that persuasive power is an epiphenomenon of material power. That would make its analysis and hence this book quite superfluous. But that is not the case. Discursive formations and institutional norms often privilege materially powerful actors, but not always. Material resources make it easier to develop good arguments, but this is not automatic. Persuasive power is a specific kind of compulsory power (Barnett & Duvall, 2005b) that is linked to but not determined by other forms of power. Often it aggravates the existing differences between rich and poor, large and small countries. And even in these situations it is a specific, additional factor, which should be taken into account. Moreover, there are times when persuasive power works in the opposite direction.

With respect to WTO negotiations, the thesis that materially more powerful actors have the better arguments needs to be qualified in at least three regards. First, relevant discursive formations do not just empower the materially better off. While liberal economics has long been regarded as the central discourse underpinning world trade governance, the development discourse has steadily gained in influence. As explained earlier, that discourse has its pitfalls for developing countries, but there are still many examples of countries identified as developing successfully drawing on that discourse in order to demand special rights and more favourable treatment. Institutional provisions established under the GATT (1965, 1979) give developing countries the legal backing to ask for exemptions from liberalization commitments as well as preferential market access. While tangible results have always been limited, especially with regard to market access, and while neoliberal ideas about development and economic policy have, since the Uruguay Round, confounded the way these provisions are understood (Weinhardt & Geck, 2019), they still give developing countries a discursive opening and bestow moral authority on their demands. The fact that the first negotiation round of the WTO was named the Doha Development Round gave development arguments extra force (Lee, 2012).

As mentioned, my case studies of the Cotton Initiative and the debate over sectoral tariff elimination in NAMA offer evidence of how the development discourse can empower developing countries in their arguing strategies. Drawing on the WTO rule of less than full reciprocity, developing countries opposing sectoral tariff elimination were able to force the proponents to accept that participation in such sectorals could not be made mandatory. The C4 managed to make the single commodity of cotton a top issue of the Doha Round by establishing it as a test case for the development promise of the round. The US was able at first to fend off the attack on its subsidy system, and it was actually the dispute settlement case brought by Brazil rather than the initiative by the C4 that eventually forced the US to make some alterations; that said, cotton would never have received so much attention had it not been for the C4's skilful argumentation, which combined references to the development discourse with a liberal economic framing. In both cases, the development discourse provided the basis for powerful coalitions of countries united by their common identity and position as developing countries.

Second, it is not a single monolithic group of countries that is empowered by the factors mentioned in the previous section. Even large developed countries are not competitive in all sectors, and their trade policies are not liberal in all aspects. Discursive context and institutional norms can turn against them too. Small but highly developed countries have their specific sources of persuasive power, and large but less developed countries have theirs. Small developing countries are disempowered in many regards but are often the ones best able to exploit the development discourse. Various combinations of enabling and disabling conditions make power relations complex and dynamic.

Third, human agency matters. To some degree, actors can overcome disadvantages. They can enhance their resources by setting priorities, actively engaging in selected issues, pooling resources with one another, and acquiring external support from NGOs and think tanks (see chapter 7). They can design arguing strategies that exploit whatever sources of persuasive power they can draw on and that downplay aspects where their stance is less strong. On a more fundamental level, they can challenge prevailing discourses and initiate institutional reforms. As described in chapter 6, there is currently a discursive struggle over whether the liberalization norm should take precedence over the development norm in the trade regime or the other way round. In the debate over NAMA sectorals, Kenya declared that liberalization should be viewed as only one possible means to further the economic development of developing countries, which in its eyes was the actual goal of the NAMA negotiations. If developing countries succeeded in advancing development so that it became the central norm of the trade regime, this would change the discursive context of WTO negotiations in a fundamental way. Another discursive struggle, which has been going on for a long time, concerns the relative weight of the major-interest norm, which privileges negotiations among the major trading powers, vis-à-vis the multilateralism norm, which demands the equal participation of all members. Some improvements regarding the inclusiveness and transparency of small-group meetings have actually been made.

Conclusions and Avenues for Further Research

As these findings demonstrate, persuasive power does a great deal to influence negotiation outcomes. An analysis based solely on theories about bargaining would not have been able to fully grasp and theoretically explain the subtle exercises of power entailed in the C4's establishment of cotton as a test case for the development promise of the Doha Round, the extensive efforts of the US to address the development aspects of cotton, or the developing countries' application of the rule of less than full reciprocity to sectoral tariff elimination initiatives in NAMA. These elements of the Doha Round negotiations over cotton and the sectoral initiatives in NAMA constitute tactics through which negotiators have manipulated the WTO membership's perceptions of the negotiation agenda and the range of possible outcomes or at least rhetorically entrapped their opponents into relinquishing certain claims. The insights about the distribution of persuasive power among WTO members detailed earlier complement findings about the distribution of bargaining power. Taken together, these two factors reveal the complex and dynamic power structure of international trade negotiations.

The practice-theoretic perspective (Adler & Pouliot, 2011a; Schatzki, Knorr-Cetina, & Savigny, 2001) on strategic arguing I have taken in this book implies that the preconditions for effective arguing depend on the social context. Different communities of practice (Wenger, 1998) might reproduce different practices of strategic arguing that require different kinds of resources. Thus, the results of this study cannot necessarily be assumed to hold for other contexts of international relations. They constitute a first foray into the empirical analysis of the power to persuade in world politics.

The within-case comparison (Gerring, 2007, p. 28) between the negotiations over the Cotton Initiative and the debate over sectoral tariff elimination in NAMA is a first step in comparing persuasive power across different contexts. However, further research will be required to determine which similarities and differences with regard to prevailing practices and the distribution of resources exist in other issue areas and institutional forums. While this study is limited to the interactions of state representatives within international negotiations, it would be interesting for further research to address the distribution of persuasive power among different types of actors such as global social movements, transnational NGOs, states, and IGOs.

In terms of Grounded Theory (Corbin & Strauss, 2008; Glaser & Strauss, 1967), what this book provides is a "substantive theory" about the power to persuade in WTO negotiations. It develops some theoretical propositions that need to be contrasted with the conditions, actions, and consequences of making effective arguments in a diverse set of other contexts in order to arrive at a more general – in Grounded Theory terms, more "formal" – theory about the power to persuade in international relations.

It would also be interesting to compare the findings on persuasive power in international relations to the insights of political theory research on inequality in citizens' ability to partake in deliberative democracy at the domestic or local level (Fraser, 1990; Fung, 2016; Kohn, 2000; Mansbridge, 1994; Sanders, 1997; Williams, 2000; Young, 1996,

2001, 2002). The factors identified in this field of research share remarkable similarities with those at work in WTO negotiations. First, there are differences in access, resources, and capabilities. Second, hegemonic discourses and predetermined policy frameworks constrict the debate.

Any research on – not only strategic – arguing should acknowledge that arguing processes are never devoid of power. Even where institutional arrangements create a situation that approximates an ideal speech situation and actors assume an understanding-oriented interaction orientation, discursive formations and differing resources provide actors with unequal powers to persuade. This is not to suggest that power differences are the most important thing about arguing and that there are no other interesting research questions. But if scholars assume that all are equal in arguing, and that processes of arguing disproportionally empower materially weak actors and are therefore morally superior to other forms of interaction, they misapprehend the empirical reality of arguing.

At the same time, persuasive power should be discussed in the context of theories of power. The influential typology of Barnett and Duval (2005a, 2005b) was meant to be a starting point for further research on the interactions between different forms of power (Barnett & Duvall, 2005b, p. 68). This book's analysis of persuasive power in WTO negotiations can contribute to that research agenda. The power to persuade is a form of compulsory power, meaning it is exercised in situations of interaction directly by one actor over the other. The actor who persuades gets the actor who is persuaded to do something they would not have otherwise done. The other three forms of power, which Barnett and Duvall distinguish, are all more indirect or structural: institutional power is at work in situations of interaction, too, but indirectly through institutional rules and procedures, not directly between one actor and the other. The productive power of discourses and the structural power inherent in asymmetric economic interdependencies are not exerted in interactions between given actors, but by discursive and material structures in the very constitution of actors. In contrast to compulsory power, the other three forms of power do not rely on the agency of an actor which exercises power but are more structural in nature.

What I find with regard to persuasive power in WTO negotiations is that it is closely linked to all three of the more structural forms of power. The productive power of discourses constitutes state actors with different identities, which provide them with unequal abilities to draw on the discursive formations prevailing in global trade politics when framing their arguments. The institutional power inherent in the norms and procedures of the world trade regime empowers some member-states more than others to participate in negotiations and to make demands that match their interests. The structural power of asymmetric international economic interdependence, finally, endows countries with different amounts of the financial, human, and domestic institutional resources necessary for identifying their own interests, understanding the content of the negotiations, and crafting effective arguing strategies.

I thus conceptualize productive, institutional, and structural power as systemic forms of power that shape the capabilities of actors to exert compulsory power. It would be interesting to compare the way persuasive power interacts with productive, institutional, and structural power with the way other forms of compulsory power do. Do all of them link to all three of the more structural forms of power? Do some of them depend more on one kind of systemic power and others on another kind? These kinds of questions could sharpen our understanding of power in international relations and beyond.

Notes

1. Strategic Arguing as a Means to Power

1 Interview with a diplomat working at a developed country's permanent mission to the WTO in Geneva, Geneva, 05.11.2010.

2 Interview with another diplomat working at a developed country's permanent mission to the WTO in Geneva, Geneva, 05.11.2010.

3 Schelling's definition of bargaining largely conforms to what Walton and McKersie (1965) call distributive bargaining. Only promises of side payments would fall into Walton and McKersie's other category of integrative bargaining. The distinction between distributive and integrative bargaining hinges on the conflictual or cooperative nature of actors' strategies. As Odell (Odell, 2000; 2010, p. 628) points out, this differs from the distinction between bargaining and arguing, which distinguishes between strategies that use any kind of sanctions (positive or negative) and strategies that use arguments.

4 BRICs is a label for Brazil, Russia, India and China devised by Goldman Sachs economist Jim O'Neill (2001), who identified these countries as the emerging economies of the coming decade.

5 As Reichertz (2011, pp. 279–80) points out, Grounded Theory is often understood as a purely inductive approach. Most Grounded Theory scholars, however, like Strauss (1987, p. 300), acknowledge that familiarity with a wide range of theoretical concepts fosters the ability to think about empirical phenomena in abstract terms. Glaser and Strauss (1967, p. 253), Strauss and Corbin (1998, pp. 46–52), and Corbin and Strauss (2008, pp. 32–42) encourage bringing empirical results into dialogue with existing theories during the research process. According to Strauss and Corbin (1998, pp. 43–8), the important thing is to stay open and faithful to the data. Empirical insights always take precedence over theories imported from other areas or arrived at through deduction, Glaser and Strauss (1967, p. 253) emphasize.

2. Practices of Strategic Arguing at the WTO

1   Interview with a diplomat working at a developed country's permanent mission to the WTO in Geneva, Geneva, 16.09.2010.
2   Interview with a diplomat working at a BRICs country's permanent mission to the WTO in Geneva, Geneva, 15.09.2010.
3   Interview with a diplomat working at an LDC's permanent mission to the WTO in Geneva, Geneva, 17.11.2010.
4   Interview with a diplomat working at a developed country's permanent mission to the WTO in Geneva, Geneva, 01.11.2010.
5   Interview with a diplomat working at an LDC's permanent mission to the WTO in Geneva, Geneva, 17.11.2010.
6   Interview with a diplomat working at a BRICs country's permanent mission to the WTO in Geneva, Geneva, 15.09.2010.
7   Interview with a diplomat working at an LDC's permanent mission to the WTO in Geneva, Geneva, 10.08.2010.
8   Interview with a diplomat working at a BRICs country's permanent mission to the WTO in Geneva, Geneva, 15.09.2010.
9   Interview with a diplomat working at a developing country's permanent mission to the WTO in Geneva, Geneva, 12.08.2010.
10   Interview with a diplomat working at a developed country's permanent mission to the WTO in Geneva, Geneva, 05.11.2010.
11   Interview with a diplomat working at a developed country's permanent mission to the WTO in Geneva, Geneva, 16.09.2010.
12   Interview with a diplomat working at a developing country's permanent mission to the WTO in Geneva, Geneva, 01.11.2010.
13   Interview with a diplomat working at an LDC's permanent mission to the WTO in Geneva, Geneva, 17.11.2010.
14   Interview with a diplomat working at a developed country's permanent mission to the WTO in Geneva, Geneva, 05.11.2010.
15   Interview with a diplomat working at a developing country's permanent mission to the WTO in Geneva, Geneva, 12.08.2010.
16   Interview with a diplomat working at an LDC's permanent mission to the WTO in Geneva, Geneva, 10.08.2010.
17   Interview with a diplomat working at a BRICs-country's permanent mission to the WTO in Geneva, Geneva, 03.11.2010.
18   Interview with a diplomat working at a developed country's permanent mission to the WTO in Geneva, Geneva, 05.11.2010.
19   Interview with a diplomat working at a BRICs country's permanent mission to the WTO in Geneva, Geneva, 15.11.2010.
20   Interview with diplomat working at a BRICs country's permanent mission to the WTO in Geneva, Geneva, 03.11.2010.

21 Interview with a diplomat working at a BRICs country's permanent mission to the WTO in Geneva, Geneva, 03.11.2010.
22 Interview with a diplomat working at a developing country's permanent mission to the WTO in Geneva, Geneva, 16.11.2010.
23 Interview with a diplomat working at an LDC's permanent mission to the WTO in Geneva, Geneva, 18.11.2010.

3. The Cotton Initiative and the Reaction of the US

1 See the annual reports of the ICAC on "Production and Trade Policies Affecting the Cotton Industry" (ICAC, 1999, 2001, 2002, 2003).
2 See the annual reports of ICAC (note above).
3 As mentioned on page 33, the Singapore issues were four new issues introduced at the ministerial conference in Singapore 1996. They included investment, competition policy, transparency in government procurement, and trade facilitation. Most developing countries objected to negotiations on these new issues, and in the July 2004 package all but trade facilitation were dropped from the Doha Round agenda.
4 Eagleton-Pierce (2012, p. 322; 2013, p. 98) concurs with Diouf from the ICTSD in seeing the demand for compensation as connected to the self-definition of the C4 as victims (and thus to the development discourse), but in my opinion the initial phrasing of the demand for a transitory measure as compensation for losses did not imply a self-identification as victims beyond the understanding that they had been victims of a breach of rules. The self-identification as victims and the use of the development discourse is, rather, connected to the provision of a motivation for action and the counter-framing by the US, as will be discussed in the following.
5 Because of the distinction between a trade aspect and a development aspect of the cotton issue, Eagleton-Pierce (2012, p. 323; 2013, p. 101) calls the US counter-frame a "trade and development" frame. I prefer to call it the uncompetitive victim frame, because this highlights the common ground as well as the crucial difference between the C4 and the US framing. Calling the US framing a trade and development frame, furthermore, doesn't fit well with the fact that the US concentrated on the development aspect and relegated the trade aspect to the stalling overall agricultural negotiations.

4. The Debate about Sectoral Tariff Elimination in Industrial Goods

1 Interview with a diplomat working at an emerging economy's permanent mission to the WTO in Geneva, Geneva, 03.11.2010.

6. Discursive Contexts and Institutional Norms

1 Interview with a diplomat working at an emerging economy's permanent mission to the WTO in Geneva, Geneva, 03.11.2010.
2 Interview with a diplomat working at an emerging economy's permanent mission to the WTO in Geneva, Geneva, 15.09.2010.
3 Interview with a diplomat working at a developing country's permanent mission to the WTO in Geneva, Geneva, 16.11.2010.

7. Institutional Procedures and Unequal Human Resources

1 Countries were categorized as developed, developing or transition economies according to UNCTAD (2020).
2 LDCs were identified on the basis of UN-OHRLLS (2018).
3 Delegation numbers are not publicly available, but were provided to the author by the WTO secretariat.
4 Interview with a diplomat working at a developed country's permanent mission to the WTO in Geneva, Geneva, 05.11.2010.
5 Interview with a diplomat working at an LDC's permanent mission to the WTO in Geneva, Geneva, 10.08.2010.
6 Interview with a developing country's permanent mission to the WTO in Geneva, Geneva, 12.08.2010.
7 Interview with a diplomat working at an LDC's permanent mission to the WTO in Geneva, Geneva, 17.11.2010.
8 Interview with a diplomat working at a developed country's permanent mission to the WTO in Geneva, Geneva, 16.09.2010.
9 Interview with a diplomat working at a developed country's permanent mission to the WTO in Geneva, Geneva, 05.11.2010.
10 Interview with a diplomat working at a developed country's permanent mission to the WTO in Geneva, Geneva, 16.09.2010.
11 Interview with a diplomat working at an LDC's permanent mission to the WTO in Geneva, Geneva, 17.11.2010.
12 Interview with a diplomat working at an LDC's permanent mission to the WTO in Geneva, Geneva, 10.08.2010.
13 Interview with a diplomat working at a developing country's permanent mission to the WTO in Geneva, Geneva, 12.08.2010.
14 Interview with a diplomat working at a developing country's permanent mission to the WTO in Geneva, Geneva, 01.11.2010.
15 Interview with a diplomat working at an emerging economy's permanent mission to the WTO in Geneva, Geneva, 03.11.2010.
16 Interviews with diplomats working at developed countries' permanent missions to the WTO in Geneva, Geneva, 16.09.2010 and 05.11.2010.

17 Interview with a diplomat working at an emerging economy's permanent mission to the WTO in Geneva, Geneva, 15.09.2010.
18 Interviews with diplomats working at LDCs' permanent missions to the WTO in Geneva, Geneva, 17.11.2010 and 18.11.2010.
19 Interview with a diplomat working at a developed country's mission to the WTO in Geneva, Geneva, 16.09.2010.
20 Interviews with diplomats working at LDC's permanent missions to the WTO in Geneva, Geneva, 17.11.2010 and 18.11.2010.
21 Interview with a diplomat working at an LDC's permanent mission to the WTO in Geneva, Geneva, 17.11.2010.
22 Interview with a diplomat working at an emerging economy's permanent mission to the WTO in Geneva, Geneva, 03.11.2010.
23 Interview with a diplomat working at a developed country's mission to the WTO in Geneva, Geneva, 16.09.2010.
24 Interview with a diplomat working at a developed country's mission to the WTO in Geneva, Geneva, 16.09.2010.
25 Interview with a diplomat working at an LDC's permanent mission to the WTO in Geneva, Geneva, 17.11.2010.
26 Interview with a diplomat working at a developing country's permanent mission to the WTO in Geneva, Geneva, 12.08.2010.
27 Interview with a diplomat working at a developing country's permanent mission to the WTO in Geneva, Geneva, 12.08.2010.
28 Interview with a diplomat working at a developing country's permanent mission to the WTO in Geneva, Geneva, 01.11.2010.
29 Interview with a diplomat working at a developing country's permanent mission to the WTO in Geneva, Geneva, 12.08.2010.

References

Abbott, R. (2007). The World Trade Organization. In N. Bayne & S. Woolcock (Eds.), *The new economic diplomacy: Decision-making and negotiation in international economic relations* (2nd ed., pp. 315–31). Ashgate.

Adler, E., & Pouliot, V. (Eds.). (2011a). *International practices*. Cambridge University Press.

Adler, E. & Pouliot, V. (2011b). International Practices. *International Theory, 3*(1), pp. 1–36. https://doi.org/10.1017/S175297191000031X.

Adler-Nissen, R., & Pouliot, V. (2014). Power in practice: Negotiating the international intervention in Libya. *European Journal of International Relations, 20*(4), pp. 889–911. https://doi.org/10.1177/1354066113512702.

Akyüz, Y. (2005). *The WTO negotiations on industrial tariffs: What is at stake for developing countries?* Penang (TWN Trade and Development Series 24).

Alessandrini, D. (2010). *Developing countries and the multilateral trade regime: The failure and promise of the WTO's development mission*. Hart.

Amsden, A.H. (2005). Promoting industry under WTO law. In K.P. Gallagher (Ed.), *Putting development first: the importance of policy space in the WTO and IFIs.* (pp. 216–32). Zed Books.

Apecu Laker, J. (2014). *The African participation at the World Trade Organization: Legal and institutional aspects: 1995–2010*. Nijhoff.

Archibugi, D., Held, D., & Köhler, M. (Eds.). (1998). *Reimagining political community: Studies in cosmopolitan democracy*. Polity Press.

Badiane, O., et al. (2002). *Cotton sector strategies in West and Central Africa*. Washington, D.C. (World Bank Policy Research Working Paper 2867). http://elibrary.worldbank.org/doi/book/10.1596/1813-9450-2867-A.

Barnes, B. (2001). Practice as Collective Action. In T.R. Schatzki, K. Knorr-Cetina, & E. von Savigny (Eds.), *The practice turn in contemporary theory* (pp. 25–6). Routledge.

Barnes, M. (2002). Bringing difference into deliberation? Disabled people, survivors, and local governance. *Policy and Politics, 30*(3), 319–31. https://doi.org/10.1332/030557302760094694.

Barnett, M., & Duvall, R. (eds.) (2005a). *Power in global governance*. Cambridge University Press.

Barnett, M., & Duvall, R. (2005b). Power in international politics. *International Organization, 59*(1), 39–75. https://doi.org/10.1017/S0020818305050010.

Barton, J., et al. (2006). *The evolution of the trade regime: Politics, law, and economics of the GATT and WTO*. Princeton University Press.

Benford, R.D., & Snow, D.A. (2000). Framing processes and social movements: An overview and assessment. *Annual Review of Sociology, 26*, 611–39. https://doi.org/10.1146/annurev.soc.26.1.611.

Blackhurst, R. (1998). The capacity of the WTO to fulfil its mandate. In A. O. Krueger (Ed.), *The WTO as an international organization* (pp. 31–58). University of Chicago Press.

Blackhurst, R., Lyakurwa, B., & Oyejide, A. (2000). Options for improving Africa's participation in the WTO. *The World Economy, 23*(4), 491–510. https://doi.org/10.1111/1467-9701.00286.

Blustein, P. (2009). *Misadventures of the most favoured nations: Clashing egos, inflated ambitions, and the great shambles of the world trade system*. Public Affairs.

Bourcier, N. (2013). Roberto Azevedo's WTO appointment gives Brazil a seat at the top table. *The Guardian*, 21 May. https://www.theguardian.com/world/2013/may/21/azevedo-head-world-trade-organisation.

Branco, M. (2014). New US farm bill can hurt Brazil's cotton trade. *Agência Brasil*, 10 February. http://agenciabrasil.ebc.com.br/en/economia/noticia/2014-02/new-us-farm-bill-can-hurt-brazils-cotton-trade.

Broinowski, A., & Wilkinson, J. (2006). *Haben die Vereinten Nationen eine Zukunft? Eine Vision in Gefahr*. Parthas.

Cardoso, F.H., & Faletto, E. (1979). *Dependency and development in Latin America*. University of California Press.

Chauffour, J.-P., & Maur, J.-C. (2010). *Beyond market access: The new normal of preferential trade agreements*. Washington, D.C. (World Bank Policy Research Working Paper 5454). http://documents1.worldbank.org/curated/en/6388914468326209179/pdf/WPS5454.pdf.

Checkel, J.T. (2001). Why comply? Social learning and European identity change. *International Organization, 55*(3), 553–88. https://doi.org/10.1162/00208180152507551.

Chin, G. (2009). Reforming the WTO: China, the Doha Round, and beyond. In A. Narlikar & B. Vickers (Eds.), *Leadership and change in the multilateral trading system* (pp. 121–47). Republic of Letters Publishing.

Cho, S. (2015). *The social foundations of world trade: Norms, community, and constitution*. Cambridge University Press.

Cho, S. (2018). Social constructivism and the social construction of world economic reality. In M. Hirsch & A.T.F. Lang (Eds.), *Research handbook on the sociology of international law*. Edward Elgar.

Chorev, N. (2005). The institutional project of neo-liberal globalism: The case of the WTO. *Theory and Society, 34*(3), 317–55. https://doi.org/10.1007/s11186-005-6301-9.

Clapp, J. (2007). WTO agriculture negotiations and the global South. In D. Lee & R. Wilkinson (Eds.), *The WTO after Hong Kong: Progress in, and prospects for, the Doha Development Agenda* (pp. 37–55). Routledge.

Conti, J.A. (2010). *Between law and diplomacy: The social contexts of disputing at the World Trade Organization.* Stanford University Press.

Copelovitch, M.S., & Ohls, D. (2012). Trade, institutions, and the timing of GATT/WTO accession in post-colonial states. *The Review of International Organizations, 7*(1), 81–107. https://doi.org/10.1007/s11558-011-9129-2.

Corbin, J.M., & Strauss, A.L. (2008). *Basics of qualitative research: Techniques and procedures for developing grounded theory* (3rd ed.). Sage.

Crawford, N.C. (2002). *Argument and Change in world politics: Ethics, decolonialization and humanitarian intervention.* Cambridge University Press.

Crawford, N.C. (2011). Homo politicus and argument (nearly) all the way down: Persuasion in politics. In C. Bjola. & M. Kornprobst (Eds.), *Arguing global governance: Agency, lifeworld, and shared reasoning* (pp. 19–51). Routledge.

Crystal, J. (2003). Bargaining in the negotiations over liberalizing trade in services: Power, reciprocity and learning. *Review of International Political Economy, 10*(3), 552–78. https://doi.org/10.1080/09692290308423.

Dahl, R. (1957). The concept of power. *Behavioral Science, 2*(3), 201–15. https://doi.org/10.1002/bs.3830020303.

D'Angelo, P. (2002). News framing as a multi-paradigmatic research program: A response to Entman. *Journal of Communication, 52*(4), 870–88. https://doi.org/10.1111/j.1460-2466.2002.tb02578.x.

Deitelhoff, N. (2006). *Überzeugung in der Politik: Grundzüge einer Diskurstheorie internationalen Regierens.* Suhrkamp.

Deitelhoff, N. (2007). Was vom Tage übrig blieb: Inseln der Überzeugung im vermachteten Alltagsgeschäft internationalen Regierens. In P. Niesen & B. Herborth (Eds.), *Anarchie der kommunikativen Freiheit: Jürgen Habermas und die Theorie der internationalen Politik.* (pp. 25–6). Suhrkamp.

Deitelhoff, N. (2009). The discursive process of legalization: Charting island of persuasion in the ICC case. *International Organization, 63*(1), 33–65. https://doi.org/10.1017/S002081830909002X.

Deitelhoff, N. (2017). Billiges Gerede und leeres Geschwätz? Was ist eigentlich geblieben von der zib-Debatte? *Zeitschrift für Internationale Beziehungen, 24*(1), 130–42. https://doi.org/10.5771/0946-7165-2017-1-130.

Deitelhoff, N. & Müller, H. (2005). Theoretical paradise: Empirically lost? Arguing with Habermas. *Review of International Studies, 31*(1), 167–79. https://doi.org/10.1017/S0260210505006364.

Deitelhoff, N., & Zimmermann, L. (2020). Things we lost in the fire: How different types of contestation affect the robustness of international norms. *International Studies Review*, 2(1), 51–76. https://doi.org/10.1093/isr/viy080.

Denzin, N.K. (1970). *The research act*. Aldine.

Dingwerth, K., & Weinhardt, C. (2019). Terms of trade: Introduction. In K. Dingwerth & C. Weinhardt (Eds.), *The language of world trade politics: Unpacking the terms of trade* (pp. 1–21). Routledge.

Donnelly, J. (2006). Sovereign inequalities and hierarchy in anarchy: American power and international society. *European Journal of International Relations*, 12(2), 139–70. https://doi.org/10.1177/1354066106064505.

Doty, R.L. (1997). Aporia: A critical exploration of the agent–structure problematique in International Relations theory. *European Journal of International Relations*, 3(3), 365–92. https://doi.org/10.1177/1354066197003003004.

Downing, L. (2008). *The Cambridge introduction to Michel Foucault*. Cambridge University Press.

Drake, W.J., & Nicolaides, K. (1992). Ideas, interests, and institutionalization: "Trade in Services" and the Uruguay Round. In P. M. Haas (Ed.), *Knowledge, power, and international policy coordination*. Special Issue of *International Organization*, 46(1), 37–100.

Dryzek, J.S., & Niemeyer, S. (2012). *Foundations and frontiers of deliberative governance*. Oxford University Press.

Eagleton-Pierce, M.D. (2013). *Symbolic power in the World Trade Organization*. Oxford University Press.

Eagleton-Pierce, M.D. (2019). Trade. In K. Dingwerth & C. Weinhardt (Eds.), *The language of world trade politics: Unpacking the terms of trade* (pp. 22–31). Routledge.

Eagleton-Pierce, M.D. (2012). The competing kings of cotton: (Re)framing the WTO African cotton initiative. *New Political Economy*, 17(3), 313–37. https://doi.org/10.1080/13563467.2011.577207.

Eckstein, H. (1975). Case study and theory in political science. In F.L. Greenstein & N.W. Polsby (Eds.), *Handbook of political science*, Vol. VII (pp. 79–138). Addison-Wesley.

Elliott, L. (2020). US blocking selection of Ngozi Okonjo-Iweala to be next head of WTO. *The Guardian*, 28 October. https://www.theguardian.com/world/2020/oct/28/us-blocking-selection-of-ngozi-okonjo-iweala-to-be-next-head-of-wto.

Elsig, M. (2006). *Different facets of power in decision making in the WTO*. (NCCR Trade Regulation Working Papers 2006/23). https://papers.ssrn.com/sol3/papers.cfm?abstract_id=1090146.

Elster, J. (1991). *Arguing and bargaining in two constituent assemblies: The Storrs Lectures*. Yale Law School.

Elster, J. (1999–2000). Arguing and bargaining in two constituent assemblies. *Journal of Constitutional Law*, 2(2), 345–421.

Escobar, A. (1995). *Encountering development: The making and unmaking of the Third World*. Princeton University Press.

FAO. (2022). *FAOSTAT: Food and agriculture data*. http://www.fao.org/faostat/en/#home.

Finlayson, J.A., & Zacher, M.A. (1981). The GATT and the regulation of trade barriers: Regime dynamics and functions. *International Organization, 35*(4), 561–602. https://doi.org/10.1017/S002081830003424X.

Flick, U. (2011). *Triangulation: Eine Einführung* (3rd ed.). VS Verlag für Sozialwissenschaften.

Ford, J. (2003). *A social theory of the WTO: Trading cultures*. Palgrave Macmillan.

Forman, S., & Seegar, D. (2006). New coalitions for global governance: The changing dynamics of multilateralism. *Global Governance, 12*(2), 205–25. https://doi.org/10.1163/19426720-01202007.

Foucault, M. (1971). *The order of things: An archaeology of the human sciences*. Pantheon.

Foucault, M. (1972). *The archaeology of knowledge; and, the discourse on language*. Pantheon.

Foucault, M. (1978a). Ein Spiel um die Psychoanalyse: Gespräch mit Angehörigen des Département de Psychanalyse der Universität Paris VIII in Vincennes. In M. Foucault (Ed.). *Dispositive der Macht: Über Sexualität, Wissen und Wahrheit* (pp. 118–75). Merve.

Foucault, M. (1978b). Wahrheit und Macht: Interview mit Michel Foucault von Allessandro Fontana und Pasquale Pasquino. In M. Foucault (Ed.), *Dispositive der Macht: Über Sexualität, Wissen, und Wahrheit* (pp. 22–54). Merve.

Foucault, M. (1990). *The history of sexuality*, Vol. 3: *The care of the self*. Penguin.

Foucault, M. (1992). *The history of sexuality*, Vol. 2: *The use of pleasure*. Penguin.

Fraser, N. (1990). Rethinking the public sphere: A contribution to the critique of actually existing democracy. *Social Text, 25/26*, 56–80. https://doi.org/10.2307/466240.

Fung, A. (2016). Deliberation before the revolution. *Political Theory, 33*(3), 397–419. https://doi.org/10.1177/0090591704271990.

G20. (2003). *G-20 ministerial communiqué, Cancún, 9 September 2003*. https://web.archive.org/web/20060521142945/http://www.g-20.mre.gov.br/conteudo/ministerials_Cancun01.htm.

Gao, H. (2011). China's ascent in global trade governance: From rule taker to rule shaker and maybe rule maker? in C. Deere Birkbeck (Ed.), *Making global trade governance work for development: Perspectives and priorities from developing countries* (pp. 153–80). Cambridge University Press.

GATT. (1947). *General agreement on tariffs and trade*. UN ECOSOC: E/PC/T/214 Add.1.Rev.1.

GATT. (1965). *L/2355. Protocol amending the GATT to introduce Part IV on trade and development*.

GATT. (1979). *L/4903. Differential and more favourable treatment, reciprocity, and fuller participation of developing countries.*

GATT. (1986). *Text of the general agreement: Including all amendments.* https://www.wto.org/english/docs_e/legal_e/gatt47_e.pdf.

Gerring, J. (2007). *Case study research: Principles and practices.* Cambridge University Press.

Gerring, J. (2008). Case selection for case-study analysis: Qualitative and quantitative techniques. In J.M. Box-Steffensmeier, H.E. Brady, & D. Collier (Eds.), *The Oxford handbook of political methodology* (645–83). Oxford University Press.

Gilpin, R. (2001). *Global political economy: Understanding the international economic order.* Princeton University Press.

Glaser, B.G., & Strauss, A.L. (1967). *The discovery of grounded theory: Strategies for qualitative research.* Aldine.

Goddard, S.E. (2006). Uncommon ground: Indivisible territory and the politics of legitimacy. *International Organization, 60*(1), 35–68. https://doi.org/10.1017/S0020818306060024.

Goffman, E. (1974). *Frame analysis. An essay in the organization of experience.* Harper Colophon.

Goldstein, J., & Keohane, R.O. (1993). Ideas and foreign policy: An analytical framework. In J. Goldstein & R.O. Keohane (Eds.), *Ideas and foreign policy: Beliefs, institutions, and political change* (pp. 3–30). Cornell University Press.

Goreux, L. (2004). *Prejudice caused by industrialized countries subsidies to cotton sectors in Western and Central Africa* (2nd ed.). World Bank. http://web.worldbank.org/archive/website00276E/WEB/PDF/2004_01_.PDF.

Gross, A. (2006). Can Sub-Saharan African countries defend their trade and development interests effectively in the WTO? The case of cotton. *The European Journal of Development Research, 18*(3), 368–86. https://doi.org/10.1080/09578810600893429.

Habermas, J. (1983). *Moralbewusstsein und kommunikatives Handeln.* Suhrkamp.

Habermas, J. (1984). *The theory of communicative action,* Vol. 1: *Reason and the rationalization of society.* Beacon Press.

Habermas, J. (1987). *The theory of communicative action,* Vol. 2: *Lifeworld and system: A critique of functionalist reason.* Beacon Press.

Habermas, J. (1996). *Between facts and norms: Contributions to a discourse theory of law and democracy.* MIT Press.

Hammouda, H.B., Karingi, S.N., & Jallab, M.S. (2007). Non-agricultural market access negotiations in the World Trade Organization: Modalities for a positive post–Hong Kong African agenda. *Journal of World Trade, 41*(1), 99–126. https://doi.org/10.54648/TRAD2007004.

Hannah, E., & Scott, J. (2017). From Palais de Nations to Centre William Rappard: Prebisch and UNCTAD as sources of ideas in the GATT/WTO. In M. Margulis (Ed.), *The global political economy of Raúl Prebisch* (pp. 116–33). Routledge.

Hannah, E., Scott, J., & Trommer, S. (2016). *Expert knowledge in global trade.* Routledge.

Hannah, E., Scott, J., & Wilkinson, R. (2018). The WTO in Buenos Aires: The outcome and its significance for the future of the multilateral trading system. *The World Economy, 41*(10), 2578–98. https://doi.org/10.1111/twec.12657.

Hanrieder, T. (2011). The false promise of the better argument. *International Theory, 3*(3), 390–415. https://doi.org/10.1017/S1752971911000182.

Harvey, D. (2005). *A brief history of neoliberalism.* Oxford University Press.

Heinisch, E.L. (2006). West Africa versus the United States on cotton subsidies: How, why, and what next? *The Journal of Modern African Studies, 44*(2), 251–274. https://doi.org/10.1017/S0022278X06001625.

Held, D. (1995). *Democracy and the global order: From the modern state to cosmopolitan governance.* Stanford University Press.

Helleiner, E. (2014a). *Forgotten foundations of Bretton Woods: International development and the making of the postwar order.* Cornell University Press.

Helleiner, E. (2014b). Southern pioneers of international development. *Global Governance, 20*(4), 375–88. https://doi.org/10.1163/19426720-02003004.

Helleiner, E. (2018). Sun Yat-sen as a pioneer of international development. *History of Political Economy, 50*(S1), 76–93. https://doi.org/10.1215/00182702-7033860.

Hendriks, C.M. (2009). Deliberative governance in the context of power. *Policy and Society, 28*(3), 173–84. https://doi.org/10.1016/j.polsoc.2009.08.004.

Hoekman, B.M., & Kostecki, M.M. (2009). *The political economy of the world trading system: The WTO and beyond* (3rd ed.). Oxford University Press.

Holzinger, K. (2001a). Kommunikationsmodi und Handlungstypen in den Internationalen Beziehungen: Anmerkungen zu einigen irreführenden Dichotomien. *Zeitschrift für Internationale Beziehungen, 8*(2), 243–86. https://doi.org/10.5771/0946-7165-2001-2-243.

Holzinger, K. (2001b). Verhandeln statt Argumentieren oder Verhandeln durch Argumentieren? Eine empirische Analyse auf der Basis der Sprechakttheorie. *Politische Vierteljahresschrift, 42*(3), 414–46. https://doi.org/10.1007/s11615-001-0073-2.

Holzinger, K. (2004). Bargaining through arguing: An empirical analysis based on speech act theory. *Political Communication, 21*(2), 195–22. https://doi.org/10.1080/10584600490443886.

Holzscheiter, A. (2005). Discourse as capability: Non-state actors' capital in global governance, *Millenium, 33*(3), 723–46. https://doi.org/10.1177/03058298050330030301.

Holzscheiter, A. (2010). *Children's rights in international politics: The transformative power of discourse.* Palgrave Macmillan.

Holzscheiter, A. (2014). Between communicative interaction and structures of signification: Discourse theory and analysis in International Relations. *International Studies Perspectives, 15,* 142–62. https://doi.org/10.1111/insp.12005.

Holzscheiter, A. (2017). Was vom arguing übrig blieb …: Der Nachhall der kommunikativen Wende in den Internationalen Beziehungen. *Zeitschrift für Internationale Beziehungen*, 24(1), 143–59. https://doi.org/10.5771/0946-7165-2017-1-143.

Hopewell, K. (2010). *A delicate dance: The rise of new developing country powers in the multilateral trading system*. Brisbane (Alliance for Governance Research and Analysis [AGORA] Working Paper).

Hopewell, K. (2016). *Breaking the WTO: How emerging powers disrupted the neoliberal project*. Stanford University Press.

Hopf, T. (2018). Change in international practices. *European Journal of International Relations*, 24(3), 687–711. https://doi.org/10.1177/1354066117718041.

Hudec, R.E. (2011). *Developing countries in the GATT legal system*. Cambridge University Press.

ICAC. (1999). *Working paper II: Government measures affecting cotton: Report from the secretariat to the 58th plenary meeting of the Cotton Advisory Committee in Charleston, South Carolina, USA in October 1999*.

ICAC. (2001–4, 2010–19). *Production and trade policies affecting the cotton industry: [Reports] by the secretariat of the International Cotton Advisory Committee*. Washington, D.C.

ICAC. (2020–21). *Production and trade subsidies affecting the cotton industry: [Reports] by the secretariat of the International Cotton Advisory Committee*. Washington, D.C.

ICTSD. (2002a). New US farm bill upsets WTO partners, could hurt developing countries. *Bridges Weekly Trade News Digest*, 6(18).

ICTSD. (2002b). Dispute settlement I: Brazil – sugar & cotton, *Bridges Weekly Trade News Digest*, 6(33).

ICTSD. (2003a). Cotton – the "TRIPS and health" of Cancun? *Bridges Daily Updates*, WTO ministerial conference, Cancún, 2003(2).

ICTSD. (2003b). Will chair's AG text warm up frozen talks? *Bridges Daily Updates*, WTO ministerial conference, Cancún, 2003(3).

ICTSD. (2003c). New ministerial text to be issued today. *Bridges Daily Updates*, WTO ministerial conference, Cancún, 2003(4).

ICTSD. (2003d). Cancun collapse: Where there's no will there's no way. *Bridges Daily Updates*, WTO ministerial conference, Cancún, 2003(6).

ICTSD. (2006). Doha Round suspended indefinitely after G-6 talks collapse. *Bridges Weekly Trade News Digest*, 10(27).

ICTSD. (2007). G-4 talks in Potsdam break down, Doha Round's fate in the balance once again. *Bridges Weekly Trade News Digest*, 11(23).

ICTSD. (2008a). NAMA talks budge at last, but major differences persist. *Bridges Review*, 12(2).

ICTSD. (2008b). WTO News – "substantial convergence" but no consensus on NAMA. *Bridges Review*, 12(4).

ICTSD. (2008c). US farm bill passes with broad support, casting a pall on world trade talks. *Bridges Weekly Trade News Digest, 12*(19).

ICTSD. (2008d). Doha: Close, but not enough. *Bridges Weekly Trade News Digest, 12*(27).

ICTSD. (2008e). Revised NAMA text fails to bridge gaps on key issues. *Bridges Review, 12*(6).

ICTSD. (2009a). WTO confirms ministerial meeting for 30 Nov. – 2 Dec. *Bridges Weekly Trade News Digest, 13*(20).

ICTSD. (2009b). WTO ministerial conference opens in Geneva: Expect no surprises. *Bridges Daily Updates*, WTO ministerial conference, Geneva, 2009(1).

ICTSD. (2009c). Day 1: Ministers target 2010 for Doha conclusion, but gaps remain. *Bridges Daily Updates*, WTO ministerial conference, Geneva, 2009(2).

ICTSD. (2013a). *Cotton: Trends in global production, trade, and policy: Information note.*

ICTSD. (2013b). WTO members choose Brazil's Azevêdo as next Director-General. *Bridges Weekly, 17*(16), 1–3.

ICTSD. (2016). WTO farm talks chair welcomes negotiating "shift in gear." *Bridges, 20*(40).

ICTSD. (2017a). Harvesting outcomes or planting seeds for the future? *Bridges, 21*(40).

ICTSD. (2017b). Ministers arrive in Buenos Aires for high-level WTO meet, amid shifting landscape on trade politics and policy. *Bridges Daily Updates*, Buenos Aires, 2017(1).

IDEAS Centre. (2020). *The cotton project.* https://ideascentre.ch/the-cotton-project.

Imboden, N., & Nivet-Claeys, A.-S. (2008). Cotton and the LDCs in the WTO: Negotiations and litigation, two sides of the same coin. In E. Durán (Ed.), *The Doha era and beyond: The coming of age of developing countries in the multilateral trading system* (pp. 121–32). Cameron May.

Ismail, F. (2009). Reflections on the WTO July 2008 collapse. In A. Narlikar & B. Vickers (Eds.), *Leadership and change in the multilateral trading system.* (pp. 203–30). Republic of Letters.

Jaeger, H.-M. (1996). Konstruktionsfehler des Konstruktivismus in den Internationalen Beziehungen. *Zeitschrift für Internationale Beziehungen, 3*(2), 313–40.

Jawara, F., & Kwa, A. (2004). *Behind the scenes at the WTO: The real world of international trade negotiations: The lessons of Cancun.* Zed Books.

Jones, E., Deere Birkbeck, C. & Woods, N. (2010). *Manoeuvring at the margins: Constraints faced by small states in international trade negotiations.* Commonwealth Secretariat.

Jones, K.A. (2010). *The Doha blues: Institutional crisis and reform in the WTO.* Oxford University Press.

Jörke, D. (2013a). The power of reason in international negotiations: Notes on Risse, Müller, and Deitelhoff. *Critical Policy Studies, 7*(3), 350–63. https://doi.org/10.1080/19460171.2012.739784.

Jörke, D. (2013b). The productive power of argumentative illusions. *Critical Policy Studies, 7*(4), 463–6. https://doi.org/10.1080/19460171.2013.851316.

Jupille, J.H., Mattli, W. & Snidal, D. (2013). *Institutional choice and global commerce*. Cambridge University Press.

Kanth, D.R. (2017a). MC11 chair appoints "facilitators" without prior consensus of Members. *South-North Development Monitor* (8592). https://www.twn.my/title2/wto.info/2017/ti171210.htm.

Kanth, D.R. (2017b). DG promised open-ended meets, but "Green Rooms" galore at MC11. *South-North Development Monitor* (8594). https://www.twn.my/title2/wto.info/2017/ti171215.htm.

Kanth, D.R. (2022). WTO: DG's "push-back" against members' complaints on opaque process. *South-North Development Monitor* (9613). https://www.twn.my/title2/wto.info/2022/ti220703.htm.

Kapoor, I. (2004). Deliberative democracy and the WTO. *Review of International Political Economy, 11*(3), 522–41. https://doi.org/10.1080/0969229042000252882.

Keohane, R.O. (1986). Reciprocity in international relations. *International Organization, 40*(1), 1–27. https://doi.org/10.1017/S0020818300004458.

Kerchner, B., & Schneider, S. (2006). Endlich Ordnung in der Werkzeugkiste: Zum Potential der Foucaultschen Diskursanalyse für die Politikwissenschaft – Einleitung. In B. Kerchner & S. Schneider (Eds.), *Foucault: Diskursanalyse der Politik: Eine Einführung* (pp. 9–30). VS Verlag für Sozialwissenschaften / GWV Fachverlage GmbH.

Kingsbury, B. (1998). Sovereignty and inequality. *European Journal of International Law, 9*, 599–625. https://doi.org/10.1093/ejil/9.4.599.

Kohn, M. (2000). Language, power, and persuasion: Toward a critique of deliberative democracy. *Constellations, 7*(3), 408–29. https://doi.org/10.1111/1467-8675.00197.

Kößler, R. (1998). *Entwicklung*. Westphälisches Dampfboot.

Krasner, S.D. (1999). *Sovereignty: Organized hypocrisy*. Princeton University Press.

Krasner, S.D. (Ed.). (2001). *Problematic sovereignty: Contested rules and political possibilities*. Columbia University Press.

Krebs, R.R., & Jackson, P.T. (2007). Twisting tongues and twisting arms: The power of political rhetoric. *European Journal of International Relations, 13*(1), 35–66. https://doi.org/10.1177/1354066107074284.

Krugman, P.R. (1979). Increasing returns, monopolistic competition, and international trade. *Journal of International Economics, 9*(4), 469–79. https://doi.org/10.1016/0022-1996(79)90017-5.

Kwa, A. (2003). *Power politics in the WTO* (updated 2nd ed.). Focus on the Global South.

Laird, S., Fernandez de Cordoba, S. & Vanzetti, D. (2003). Market access proposals for non-agricultural products. In I. Mbirimi, B. Chilala, & R. Grynberg (Eds.), *From Doha to Cancún: Delivering a development round.* (Commonwealth economic paper series 57) (pp. 9–47). Commonwealth Secretariat.

Laird, S., Vanzetti, D., & Santiago Fernández de Córdoba. (2006). *Smoke and mirrors: Making sense of the WTO industrial tariff negotiations.* New York (Policy Issues in International Trade and Commodities Study Series 30).

Lake, D.A. (2003). The new sovereignty in international relations. *International Studies Review, 5*(2), 303–23. https://doi.org/10.1046/j.1079-1760.2003.00503001.x.

Lamp, N. (2017). The "development" discourse in multilateral trade lawmaking. *World Trade Review, 16*(3), 475–500. https://doi.org/10.1017/S1474745616000616.

Lang, A.T.F. (2006). Reconstructing embedded liberalism: John Gerard Ruggie and constructivist approaches to the study of the international trade regime. *Journal of International Economic Law, 9*(1), 81–116. https://doi.org/10.1093/jiel/jgi057.

Lang, A.T.F. (2011). *World trade law after neoliberalism: Reimagining the global economic order.* Oxford University Press.

Ledermann, S.T., & Moseley, W.G. (2007). The World Trade Organization's Doha Round and cotton: Continued peripheral status or a "historical breakthrough" for African farmers? *African Geographical Review, 26*(1), 37–58. https://doi.org/10.1080/19376812.2007.9756201.

Lee, D. (2007). The cotton club: The Africa Group in the Doha Development Agenda. In D. Lee & R. Wilkinson (Eds.), *The WTO after Hong Kong: Progress in, and prospects for, the Doha Development Agenda* (pp. 137–54). Routledge.

Lee, D. (2012). Global trade governance and the challenges of African activism in the Doha Development Agenda negotiations. *Global Society, 26*(1), 83–101. https://doi.org/10.1080/13600826.2011.629990.

Legrain, P. (2006). Why NAMA liberalization is good for developing countries. *World Economy, 29*(10), 1349–62. https://doi.org/10.1111/j.1467-9701.2006.00847.x.

MacDonald, S., & Meyer, L. (2018). *Long run trends and fluctuations in cotton prices* (Munich Personal RePEc Archive Paper 84484). https://mpra.ub.uni-muenchen.de/84484.

Mansbridge, J. (1994). Using power/fighting power. *Constellations, 1*(1), 53–73. https://doi.org/10.1111/j.1467-8675.1994.tb00004.x.

Margulis, M. (2017). Introduction. The global political economy of Raúl Prebisch. In M. Margulis (Ed.), *The global political economy of Raúl Prebisch* (pp. 1–23). Routledge.

Maur, J.-C. (2013). Deep integration in preferential trade agreements. In A. Lukauskas, R. M. Stern, & G. Zanini (Eds.), *Handbook of trade policy for development* (pp. 537–68). Oxford University Press.

Mayring, P. (1983). *Qualitative Inhaltsanalyse: Grundlagen u. Techniken*. Beltz.

Mayring, P. (2000). Qualitative content analysis. *Forum Qualitative Sozialforschung / Forum: Qualitative Social Research, 1*(2). http://www.qualitative-research .net/index.php/fqs/article/view/1089/2386.

McClanahan, P. (2013). Roberto Azevêdo to be named new World Trade Organisation chief. *The Guardian,* 8 May. https://www.theguardian.com /global-development/2013/may/08/roberto-azevedo-world-trade -organisation.

Mendelberg, T., & Oleske, J. (2000). Race and public deliberation. *Political Communication, 17,* 169–91. https://doi.org/10.1080/105846000198468.

Meuser, M., & Nagel, U. (2009). Das Experteninterview – konzeptionelle Grundlagen und methodische Anlage. In S. Pickel et al. (Eds.), *Methoden der vergleichenden Politik- und Sozialwissenschaft: Neue Entwicklungen und Anwendungen* (pp. 465–79). VS Verlag für Sozialwissenschaften / GWV Fachverlage GmbH.

Michalopoulos, C. (2001). *Developing countries in the WTO*. Palgrave.

Michalopoulos, C. (2014). *Emerging powers in the WTO: Developing countries and trade in the 21st century*. Palgrave Macmillan.

Mohamadieh, K. (2022). *Exclusionary unrepresentative processes behind the celebrated MC12 "Package"* (TWN Info Service on WTO and Trade Issues Jun22/25). https://www.twn.my/title2/wto.info/2022/ti220625.htm#_ednref17.

Morin, J.-F., & Gold, E.R. (2010). Consensus-seeking, distrust, and rhetorical entrapment: The WTO decision on access to medicines. *European Journal of International Relations, 16*(4), 563–87. https://doi.org/10.1177/1354066110366054.

Morton, A.D. (2003). Social forces in the struggle over hegemony: Neo-Gramscian perspectives in international political economy. *Rethinking Marxism, 15*(2), 153–79. https://doi.org/10.1080/0893569032000113514.

Müller, H. (1995). Spielen hilft nicht immer: Die Grenzen des Rational-Choice-Ansatzes und der Platz der Theorie des Kommunikativen Handeln in der Analyse internationaler Beziehungen. *Zeitschrift für Internationale Beziehungen, 2*(2), 371–91.

Müller, H. (2004). Arguing, bargaining, and all that: Communicative action, rationalist theory and the logic of appropriateness in international relations. *European Journal of International Relations, 10*(3), 395–435. https://doi .org/10.1177/1354066104045542.

Müller, M. (1996). Vom Dissensrisiko zur Ordnung der internationalen Staatenwelt: Zum Projekt einer normativ gehaltvollen Theorie der internationalen Beziehungen. *Zeitschrift für Internationale Beziehungen, 3*(2), 371–91.

Narlikar, A., & Tussie, D. (2004). The G20 at the Cancun ministerial: Developing countries and their evolving coalitions in the WTO. *The World Economy, 27*(7), pp. 947–66. https://doi.org/10.1111/j.1467-9701 .2004.00636.x.

Narlikar, A., & Wilkinson, R. (2004). Collapse at the WTO: A Cancun post-mortem. *Third World Quarterly, 25*(3), 447–60. https://doi.org/10.1080/0143 659042000191375.

Niesen, P. (2007). Anarchie der kommunikativen Freiheit - ein Problemaufriss. In P. Niesen & B. Herborth (Eds.), *Anarchie der kommunikativen Freiheit: Jürgen Habermas und die Theorie der internationalen Politik* (pp. 7–25). Suhrkamp.

Niesen, P., & Herborth, B. (Eds.). (2007). *Anarchie der kommunikativen Freiheit: Jürgen Habermas und die Theorie der internationalen Politik.* Suhrkamp.

Oatley, T. (2008). *International political economy: Interests and institutions in the global economy.* Pearson Longman.

O'Brien, R., & Williams, M. (2016). *Global political economy: Evolution and dynamics.* Palgrave Macmillan.

Odell, J.S. (2000). *Negotiating the world economy.* Cornell University Press.

Odell, J.S. (2005). Chairing a WTO negotiation. *Journal of International Economic Law, 8*(2), 425–48. https://doi.org/10.1093/jielaw/jgi028.

Odell, J.S. (Ed.). (2006). *Negotiating trade: Developing countries in the WTO and NAFTA.* Cambridge University Press.

Odell, J.S. (2010). Three islands of knowledge about negotiations in international organizations. *Journal of European Public Policy, 17*(5), 619–32. https://doi.org/10 .1080/13501761003748534.

Odell, J.S., & Sell, S.K. (2006). Reframing the issue: The WTO coalition on intellectual property and public health, 2001. In J.S. Odell (Ed.), *Negotiating trade: Developing countries in the WTO and NAFTA,* (pp. 85–114). Cambridge University Press.

Office of the USTR. (2008). *2008 trade policy agenda and 2007 annual report of the president of the United States on the trade agreements program.* http://www .ustr.gov/archive/Document_Library/Reports_Publications/2008/2008 _Trade_Policy_Agenda/Section_Index.html.

Office of the USTR (2009a). *Remarks by Ambassador Ron Kirk at Georgetown University Law Center: Trade and the economic agenda: Serving America's families and the global recovery.* 23 April 2009, Georgetown University Law Center, Washington, D.C. https://ustr.gov/about-us/policy-offices/press-office/speeches/transcripts /2009/april/remarks-ambassador-ron-kirk-georgetown-univers.

Office of the USTR. (2009b). *United States Trade Representative Ron Kirk, press briefing, May 13, 2009.* Headquarters of the WTO, Geneva, Switzerland. https:// ustr.gov/about-us/policy-offices/press-office/speeches/transcripts/2009 /may/ustr-ron-kirk-wto-press-briefing.

Office of the USTR. (2010). *Memorandum of understanding between the government of the United States of America and the government of the Federative Republic of Brazil regarding a fund for technical assistance and capacity building with respect to the cotton dispute (WT/DS267) in the World Trade Organization.* Punte del Este. https://ustr.gov/sites/default/files/20141001201606893.pdf.

O'Neill, J. (2001). *Building better global economic BRICs* (Global Economic Paper 66). http://www.goldmansachs.com/our-thinking/archive/building -better.html.

Oxfam. (2002). *Cultivating poverty: The impact of US cotton subsidies on Africa* (Oxfam Briefing Paper 30). https://www.oxfamamerica.org/explore /research-publications/cultivating-poverty.

Panagariya, A. (2002a). Developing countries at Doha: A political economy analysis. *World Economy, 25*(9), 1205–33. https://doi.org/10.1111/1467-9701 .00489.

Panagariya, A. (2002b). India at Doha: Retrospect and prospect. *Economic and Political Weekly, 37*(4), 279–84.

Pigman, G.A. (2009). US trade policy and the rise of the big emerging economies. In A. Narlikar, & B. Vickers (Eds.), *Leadership and change in the multilateral trading system* (pp. 45–71). Republic of Letters Publishing.

Potter, C., & Burney, J. (2002). Agricultural multifunctionality in the WTO – legitimate non-trade concern or disguised protectionism? *Journal of Rural Studies, 18*(1), 35–47. https://doi.org/10.1016/S0743-0167(01)00031-6.

Prebisch, R. (1950). *The economic development of Latin America and its principal problems*. Economic Commission for Latin America.

Rahnema, M., & Bawtree, V. (Eds.). (1997). *The post-development reader*. Zed Books.

Reckwitz, A. (2000). *Die Transformation der Kulturtheorie: Zur Entwicklung eines Theorieprogramms*. Velbrück Wissenschaft.

Reichertz, J. (2011). Abduktion: Die Logik der Entdeckung der Grounded Theory. In G. Mey & K. Mruck (Eds.), *Grounded theory reader* (2nd Ed., 279–97). VS Verlag für Sozialwissenschaften.

Ricardo, D. (1817). *On the principles of political economy and taxation*. John Murray.

Rice, C. (2006). *Transformational diplomacy*. US Department of State. 18 January. https://web.archive.org/web/20080708213151/http://www.state.gov /secretary/rm/2006/59306.htm.

Risse, T. (1999). International norms and domestic change: Arguing and communicative behavior in the human rights area. *Politics and Society, 27*(4), 529–59. https://doi.org/10.1177/0032329299027004004.

Risse, T. (2000). "Let's argue!": Communicative action in world politics. *International Organization, 54*(1), 1–39. https://doi.org/10.1162/002081800 551109.

Risse, T. (2013). Arguing about arguing: A comment. *Critical Policy Studies, 7*(3), 339–49. https://doi.org/10.1080/19460171.2013.831675

Risse, T., Jetschke, A., & Schmitz, H. (2002). *Die Macht der Menschenrechte: Internationale Normen, kommunikatives Handeln und politischer Wandel in den Ländern des Südens*. Nomos.

Risse, T., Ropp, S., & Sikkink, K. (Eds.). (1999). *The power of human rights: International norms and domestic change*. Cambridge University Press.

Rist, G. (2008). *The history of development: From Western origins to global faith*. 3rd Ed. Zed Books.

Rolland, S.E. (2012). *Development at the World Trade Organization*. Oxford University Press.

Ruggie, J.G. (1982). International regimes, transactions, and change: Embedded liberalism in the postwar economic order. *International Organization, 36*(2), 379–415. https://doi.org/10.1017/S0020818300018993.

Ruggie, J.G. (1997). *Globalization and the embedded liberalism compromise: The end of an era?* (MPIfG Working Paper 97/1). https://pure.mpg.de/pubman /item/item_1235631_6/component/file_2367702/mpifg_wp97_1.pdf? mode=download.

Rüland, J. (2012). The rise of "diminished multilateralism": East Asian and European forum shopping in global governance. *Asia Europe Journal: Studies on Common Policy Challenges, 9*(2–4), 255–70. https://doi.org/10.1007 /s10308-012-0311-9.

Sachs, W. (Ed.). (1992). *The development dictionary: A guide to knowledge and power*. Zed Books.

Sanders, L.M. (1997). Against deliberation. *Political Theory, 25*(3), 347–76. https:// doi.org/10.1177/0090591797025003002.

Saretzki, T. (1996). Wie unterscheiden sich Argumentieren und Verhandeln? Definitionsprobleme, funktionale Bezüge und strukturelle Differenzen von zwei verschiedenen Kommunikationsmodi. In V. von Prittwitz (Ed.), *Verhandeln und Argumentieren: Dialog, Interessen und Macht in der Umweltpolitik* (pp. 19–39). Leske + Budrich.

Saretzki, T. (2007). Argumentieren, Verhandeln und Strategie: Theoretische Referenzen, begriffliche Unterscheidungen und empirische Studien zu arguing und bargaining in der internationalen Politik. In P. Niesen & B. Herborth (Eds.), *Anarchie der kommunikativen Freiheit: Jürgen Habermas und die Theorie der internationalen Politik* (pp. 111–46). Suhrkamp.

Sassen, S. (1996). *Losing control? Sovereignty in the age of globalization*. Columbia University Press.

Schatzki, T.R. (2001). Introduction: Practice theory. In T.R. Schatzki, K. Knorr-Cetina, & E. von Savigny (Eds.), *The practice turn in contemporary theory* (pp. 10–23). Routledge.

Schatzki, T.R., Knorr-Cetina, K., & Savigny, E. von (Eds.). (2001). *The practice turn in contemporary theory*. Routledge.

Schelling, T.C. (1960). *The strategy of conflict*. Harvard University Press.

Scheufele, D. (1999). Framing as a theory of media effects. *Journal of Communication, 49*(4), 102–22. https://doi.org/10.1111/j.1460-2466.1999.tb02784.x.

Schimmelfennig, F. (1997). Rhetorisches Handeln in der internationalen Politik. *Zeitschrift für Internationale Beziehungen, 4*(2), 219–54. https://doi .org/10.1515/9783486788402-108.

Schimmelfennig, F. (2001). The community-trap: Liberal norms, rhetorical action, and the eastern enlargement of the European Union. *International Organization, 55*(1), 47–80. https://doi.org/10.1162/002081801551414.

Schimmelfennig, F. (2003). *The EU, NATO, and the integration of Europe: Rules and rhetoric.* Cambridge University Press.

Schirm, S.A. (2004). *Internationale Politische Ökonomie: Eine Einführung.* Nomos.

Scott, J. (2007). How the poor pay for the US trade deficit: And why it matters for the Doha Development Agenda. In D. Lee & R. Wilkinson (Eds.), *The WTO after Hong Kong: Progress in, and prospects for, the Doha Development Agenda* (pp. 97–118). Routledge.

Scott, J. (2008). The use and misuse of trade negotiation simulations. *Journal of World Trade, 42*(1), 87–103. https://doi.org/10.54648/TRAD2008003.

Scott, J. (2010). Developing countries in the ITO and GATT negotiations. *Journal of World Trade Law and Policy, 9*(1), 5–24. https://doi.org/10.1108/14770021011029582.

Scott, J., & Wilkinson, R. (2010). *What have the poorest countries to gain from the Doha Development Agenda (DDA)?* Manchester (BWPI working papers 132). https://www.research.manchester.ac.uk/portal/en/publications/what-have-the-poorest-countries-to-gain-from-the-doha-development-agenda-dda (35e3040b-4944-4b87-a29d-c9d60a2ba6f0).html.

Sell, S.K., & Prakash, A. (2004). Using ideas strategically: The contest between business and NGO networks in intellectual property rights. *International Studies Quarterly, 48*(1), 143–75. https://doi.org/10.1111/j.0020-8833.2004.00295.x.

Shaffer, G. (2005). Power, governance, and the WTO: A comparative institutional approach. In M. Barnett & R. Duvall (Eds.), *Power in global governance* (pp. 130–60) Cambridge University Press.

Shaffer, G. (2015). How the World Trade Organization shapes regulatory governance. *Regulation & Governance, 9*(1), 1–15. https://doi.org/10.1111/rego.12057.

Sikkink, K. (1993). The power of principled ideas: Human rights policies in the United States and Western Europe. In J. Goldstein & R.O. Keohane (Eds.), *Ideas and foreign policy: Beliefs, institutions, and political change* (pp. 139–70). Cornell University Press.

Simmons, B.A., Dobbin, F. & Garrett, G. (2006). Introduction: The international diffusion of liberalism. *International Organization, 60*(4), 781–810. https://doi.org/10.1017/S0020818306060267.

Slaughter, A.-M. (2004). *A new world order.* Princeton University Press.

Smith, A. (1776). *An inquiry into the nature and the causes of the wealth of nations.* W. Strahan and T. Cadell.

Sneyd, A. (2011). *Governing cotton: Globalization and poverty in Africa.* Palgrave Macmillan.

Snow, D.A., & Benford, R.D. (1988). Ideology, frame resonance, and participant mobilization. *International Social Movement Research, 1*(1), 197–219.

Soto, A. (2014). US farm bill may halt Brazil cotton retaliation … for now. *Chicago Tribune*, 6 February. http://articles.chicagotribune.com/2014-02-06 /news/sns-rt-brazil-usatrade-pix-20140206_1_u-s-cotton-subsidies-farm -bill-national-cotton-council.

Steffek, J. (2006). *Embedded liberalism and its critics*. Palgrave Macmillan.

Steinberg, R.H. (2002). In the shadow of law or power? Consensus-based bargaining and outcomes in the GATT/WTO. *International Organization, 56*(2), 339–74. https://doi.org/10.1162/002081802320005504.

Strange, M. (2014). *Writing global trade governance*. Routledge.

Strange, S. (1996). *The retreat of the state: The diffusion of power in the world economy*. Cambridge University Press.

Strauss, A.L. (1987). *Qualitative analysis for social scientists*. Cambridge University Press.

Strauss, A.L., & Corbin, J.M. (1998). *Basics of qualitative research: Techniques and procedures for developing grounded theory*. 2nd ed. Sage.

Strauss, A.L., & Corbin, J.M. (1990). *Basics of qualitative research: Grounded theory procedures and techniques*. Sage.

Toye, J. (1987). *Dilemmas of development: Reflections on the counter-revolution in development theory and policy*. Blackwell.

Trommer, S. (2011). After multilateralism: North–south development solidarity in resistance to the global trade agenda. Paper presented at the workshop Trade unions, free trade, and the problem of transnational solidarity. Centre for the Study of Social and Global Justice, University of Nottingham, 2–3 December 2011.

UK House of Commons. (2006). *The WTO Hong Kong ministerial and the Doha Development Agenda: Third report of session 2005–06*, Vol. II (House of Commons papers). H.M.S.O.

Ulbert, C., & Risse, T. (2005). Deliberately changing the discourse: What does make arguing effective? *Acta Politica, 40*(3), 351–67. https://doi.org/10.1057 /palgrave.ap.5500117.

Ulbert, C., Risse, T., & Müller, H. (2004). Arguing and bargaining in multilateral negotiations. Paper presented to the conference Empirical approaches to deliberative politics. European University Institute, Swiss Chair, Firenze, 21–2 May 2004.

UN. (1945). *Charter of the United Nations*. San Francisco.

UNCTAD. (2013). *UNCTAD Handbook of Statistics 2013*. (United Nations publications/UNCTAD, TD/STAT. 38). United Nations.

UNCTAD. (2014). *The United States Farm Bill of 2014 and its implications for cotton producers in low-income developing countries*. https://unctad.org/en /PublicationsLibrary/suc2014d3_en.pdf).

UNCTAD (2020). *UNCTADSTAT*. https://unctadstat.unctad.org/EN/Index
.html.

UN-OHRLLS. (2018). *List of least developed countries as of 13 December 2018.*

US Government Printing Office. (1964). Public papers of the president of the
United States, Harry S. Truman, 1949: Containing the public messages,
speeches, and statements of the president, January 1 to December 31, 1949.

USDA. (2005a). *USDA announces changes to export credit guarantee programs to
comply with WTO findings.* Washington, D.C. (USDA News Release 0238.05).

USDA. (2005b). USDA proposes legislative changes to cotton and export credit
programs to comply with WTO findings. Washington, D.C. (USDA News
Release 0242.05).

Vickers, B. (2009). "Reclaiming development" in multilateral trade: South Africa
and the Doha development agenda. In A. Narlikar & B. Vickers (Eds.),
Leadership and change in the multilateral trading system (pp. 149–80). Republic of
Letters.

Walton, R.E., & McKersie, R.B. (1965). *A behavioral theory of labour negotiations:
An analysis of a social interaction system.* McGraw-Hill.

Weaver, C. (2011). *Hypocrisy trap: The World Bank and the poverty of reform.* Princeton
University Press.

Weinhardt, C. (2020). Emerging powers in the world trading system: Contestation
of the developing country status and the reproduction of inequalities. *Global
Society, 34*(3), 388–408. https://doi.org/10.1080/13600826.2020.1739632.

Weinhardt, C., & Geck, A. (2019). Development. In K. Dingwerth & C. Weinhardt
(Eds.), *The language of world trade politics: Unpacking the terms of trade* (pp. 132–51).
Routledge.

Weinhardt, C., & Schöfer, T. (2022). Differential treatment for developing
countries in the WTO: The unmaking of the North–South distinction
in a multipolar world. *Third World Quarterly, 43*(1), 74–93. https://doi
.org/10.1080/01436597.2021.1992271.

Wenger, E. (1998). *Communities of practice: Learning, meaning, and identity.* Cambridge
University Press.

White, E., et al. (2021). US backing paves way for Nigeria's Okonjo-Iweala
to lead WTO. *Financial Times,* 5 February. https://www.ft.com/content
/5c50d594-0df3-4204-8325-0882303631bc.

White, L.J. (2015). *Executive leadership in international organisation: A case study
of WTO directors-general (1995–2013).* Thesis submitted to the University
of Manchester for the Degree of Doctor of Philosophy in the Faculty of
Humanities. University of Manchester. https://www.research.manchester
.ac.uk/portal/files/54572372/FULL_TEXT.PDF.

Wiener, A. (2007). Demokratischer Konstitutionalismus jenseits des Staates:
Perspektiven auf die Umstrittenheit von Normen. In P. Niesen, &
B. Herborth (Eds.), *Anarchie der kommunikativen Freiheit: Jürgen Habermas und
die Theorie der internationalen Politik* (pp. 173–98). Suhrkamp.

Wiener, A. (2014). *A theory of contestation*. Springer.

Wilkinson, R. (2006). *The WTO: Crisis and the governance of global trade*. Routledge.

Wilkinson, R. (2009). Language, power, and multilateral trade negotiations. *Review of International Political Economy, 16*(4), 597–619. https://doi.org/10.1080/09692290802587734.

Wilkinson, R. (2012). Of butchery and bicycles: The WTO and the "death" of the Doha Development Agenda. *The Political Quarterly, 83*(2), 395–401. https://doi.org/10.1111/j.1467-923X.2012.02272.x.

Wilkinson, R. (2017). Back to the future: "Retro" trade governance and the future of the multilateral order. *International Affairs, 93*(5), 1131–47. https://doi.org/10.1093/ia/iix158.

Wilkinson, R., Hannah, E., & Scott, J. (2014). The WTO in Bali: What MC9 means for the Doha Development Agenda and why it matters. *Third World Quarterly, 35*(6), 1032–50. https://doi.org/10.1080/01436597.2014.907726.

Wilkinson, R., Hannah, E., & Scott, J. (2016). The WTO in Nairobi: The demise of the Doha Development Agenda and the future of the multilateral trading system. *Global Policy, 7*(2), 247–55. https://doi.org/10.1111/1758-5899.12339.

Wilkinson, R., & Lee, D. (2007). The WTO after Hong Kong: Setting the scene for understanding the round. In D. Lee & R. Wilkinson (Eds.), *The WTO after Hong Kong: Progress in, and prospects for, the Doha Development Agenda* (pp. 3–25). Routledge.

Wilkinson, R., & Scott, J. (2008). Developing country participation in the GATT: A reassessment. *World Trade Review, 7*(3), 473–510. https://doi.org/10.1017/S1474745608003959.

Williams, M.S. (2000). The uneasy alliance of group representation and deliberative democracy. In W. Kymlicka (Ed.), *Citizenship in diverse societies.* (pp. 124–52). Oxford University Press.

Winslett, G. (2016). How regulations became the crux of trade politics. *Journal of World Trade, 50*(1), 47–70. https://doi.org/10.54648/TRAD2016005.

World Bank (2022a). *Commodity markets outlook: The impact of the war in the Ukraine on commodity markets*. Washington, D.C. https://openknowledge.worldbank.org/bitstream/handle/10986/37223/CMO-April-2022.pdf.

World Bank (2022b). *Research and outlook: Commodity Markets: "Pink sheet" data. Annual prices*. https://thedocs.worldbank.org/en/doc/5d903e848db1d1b83e0ec8f744e55570-0350012021/related/CMO-Historical-Data-Annual.xlsx.

WTO. (1994). *Agreement establishing the World Trade Organization*.

WTO. (2000a). *G/AG/NG/W/15: Committee on Agriculture, Special Session: proposal for comprehensive long-term agricultural trade reform. Submission from the United States*.

WTO. (2000b). *G/AG/NG/W/90: Committee on Agriculture, Special Session: EC comprehensive negotiating proposal*.

WTO. (2001a). *G/AG/NG/W/142: WTO African Group: Joint proposal on the negotiations on agriculture*.

WTO. (2001b). *WT/MIN(01)/DEC/1: Ministerial conference, fourth session, Doha, 9–14. November 2001: Ministerial declaration. Adopted on 14 November 2001.*

WTO. (2001c). *WT/MIN(01)/DEC/2: Ministerial conference, fourth session, Doha, 9 - 14 November 2001: Declaration on the TRIPS agreement and public health. Adopted on 14 November 2001.*

WTO. (2002a). *TN/MA/W/1: Negotiating Group on Market Access: Market access for non-agricultural products. Communication from the European Communities.*

WTO. (2002b). *TN/MA/W/5: Negotiating Group on Market Access: Market access for non-agricultural products. Contribution paper from Japan.*

WTO. (2002c). *TN/MA/W/7: Negotiating Group on Market Access: Market access for non-agricultural products. Contribution from Norway.*

WTO. (2002d). *TN/MA/W/8: Negotiating Group on Market Access: Market access for non-agricultural products. Communication from Singapore.*

WTO. (2002e). *WT/DS267/1: United States – Subsidies on upland cotton. Request for consultations by Brazil.*

WTO. (2002f). *TN/MA/W/9: Negotiating Group on Market Access: WTO non-agricultural market access. Communication from Canada.*

WTO. (2002g). *TN/MA/W/10: Negotiating Group on Market Access: Market access for non-agricultural products. Submission by India.*

WTO. (2002h). *TN/MA/M/3: Negotiating Group on Market Access: Minutes of the meeting held in Centre William Rappard on 12–13 September 2002. Chairman: Ambassador P-L. Girard (Switzerland).*

WTO. (2002i). *TN/MA/W/11: Negotiating Group on Market Access: Market access for non-agricultural products. Communication from the European Communities.*

WTO. (2002j). *TN/MA/W/12: Negotiating Group on Market Access: Market access for non-agricultural products. Contribution from Hong Kong, China.*

WTO. (2002k). *TN/MA/W/13: Negotiating Group on Market Access: Market access for non-agricultural products. Communication from Mexico.*

WTO. (2002l). *TN/MA/W/15: Negotiating Group on Market Access: Market access for non-agricultural products. Communication from Japan.*

WTO. (2002m). *TN/MA/W/16: Negotiating Group on Market Access: Market access for non-agricultural products. Communication from Switzerland.*

WTO. (2002n). *TN/MA/W/17: Negotiating Group on Market Access: Market access for non-agricultural products. The views of Chile.*

WTO. (2002o). *TN/MA/W/18: Negotiating Group on Market Access: Market access for non-agricultural products. Communication from the United States.*

WTO. (2002p). *TN/MA/W/19: Negotiating Group on Market Access: Market access for non-agricultural products. Submission by the separate customs territory of Taiwan, Penghu, Kinmen, and Matsu.*

WTO. (2002q). *TN/MA/W/20: Negotiating Group on Market Access: Market access for non-agricultural products. Proposal of the People's Republic of China.*

WTO. (2003a). *World Trade Report.* Geneva.

WTO. (2003b). *TN/MA/W/10/Add.1: Negotiating Group on Market Access: Market access for non-agricultural products. Second submission by India. Addendum.*

WTO. (2003c). *TN/MA/M/4: Negotiating Group on Market Access: Minutes of the meeting held in the Centre William Rappard on 4–5 November 2002.*

WTO. (2003d). *TN/MA/W/26: Negotiating Group on Market Access: Negotiating group on non-agricultural market access. Communication from Thailand.*

WTO. (2003e). *WT/GC/W/491: General Council: Singapore issues – the question of modalities. Communication from the European Communities.*

WTO. (2003f). *TN/MA/W/15/Add.2: Negotiating Group on Market Access: Market access for non-agricultural products. Japan's submission on "zero-for-zero" and "harmonization." Addendum.*

WTO. (2003g). *TN/MA/W/30: Negotiating Group on Market Access: Market access for non-agricultural products. Communication from Barbados, Jamaica, and Trinidad and Tobago.*

WTO. (2003h). *TN/MA/W/31: Negotiating Group on Market Access: Market access for non-agricultural products. Communication from Egypt, India, Indonesia, Kenya, Malaysia, Mauritius, Nigeria, Tanzania, Uganda, and Zimbabwe.*

WTO. (2003i). *TN/AG/GEN/4: WTO. Negotiations on agriculture. Poverty reduction: Sectoral initiative in favour of cotton. Joint proposal by Benin, Burkina Faso, Chad and Mali.*

WTO. (2003j). *TN/MA/W/35: Negotiating Group on Market Access: Draft elements of modalities for negotiations on non-agricultural products.*

WTO. (2003k). *TN/MA/W/37: Negotiating Group on Market Access: Market access for non-agricultural products. Communication from the United Arab Emirates.*

WTO. (2003l). *News item: Trade Negotiations Committee. Address by President Blaise Compaoré of Burkina Faso. On the cotton submission by West and Central African countries to the Trade Negotiations Committee of the World Trade Organization.* https://www.wto.org/english/news_e/news03_e/tnc_10june03_e.htm.

WTO. (2003m). *WT/GC/W/501: General Council: Comments on the EC communication (WG/GC/W/491) on the modalities for the Singapore issues. Communication from Bangladesh, Cuba, Egypt, India, Indonesia, Kenya, Malaysia, Nigeria, Pakistan, Venezuela, Zambia, and Zimbabwe.*

WTO. (2003n). *TN/MA/M/5: Negotiating Group on Market Access: Minutes of the meeting held in the Centre William Rappard on 2–3 December 2002. Chairman: Ambassador P-L. Girard (Switzerland).*

WTO. (2003o). *TN/MA/W/21/Add.1: Negotiating Group on Market Access: Market access for non-agricultural products. Communication from Mauritius. Addendum.*

WTO. (2003p). *TN/MA/M/6: Negotiating Group on Market Access: Minutes of the meeting held in the Centre William Rappard on 19–21 February 2003. Chairman: Ambassador P.-L. Girard (Switzerland).*

WTO. (2003q). *TN/AG/GEN/6: WTO. Negotiations on agriculture. Poverty reduction: Sectoral initiative in favour of cotton. Joint proposal by Benin, Burkina Faso, Chad, and Mali. Proposal on implementation modalities.*

WTO. (2003r). *TN/MA/W/40: Negotiating Group on Market Access: Market access for non-agricultural products. Joint statement by Ghana, Kenya, Madagascar, Mauritius, Nigeria, Rwanda, Tanzania, Tunisia, Uganda, Zambia, and Zimbabwe on draft elements of modalities for negotiations on market access for non-agricultural products.*

WTO. (2003s). *TN/MA/W/41: Negotiating Group on Market Access: Market access for non-agricultural products. Communication from Turkey.*

WTO. (2003t). *TN/MA/W/42: Negotiating Group on Market Access: Market access for non-agricultural products. Communication form South Africa.*

WTO. (2003u). *WT/GC/W/511: General Council: Draft decision concerning specific measures in favour of cotton with a view to poverty alleviation. Communication from Benin, Burkina Faso, Chad, and Mali.*

WTO. (2003v). *TN/MA/W/44: Negotiating Group on Market Access: Market access for non-agricultural products: Non-agricultural market access modalities. Joint communication from Canada, the European Communities, and the United States.*

WTO. (2003w). *WT/L/540 and Corr.1: Implementation of paragraph 6 of the Doha Declaration on the TRIPS Agreement and Public Health. Decision of the General Council of 30 August 2003.*

WTO. (2003x). *Summary of 10 September 2003: Day 1: Conference kicks off with "facilitators" named and cotton debated.* http://www.wto.org/english/thewto_e /minist_e/min03_e/min03_10sept_e.htm.

WTO. (2003y). *WT/MIN(03)/INF/14: Ministerial conference, fifth session, Cancún, 10–14 September 2003: List of representatives.*

WTO. (2003z). *JOB(03)/150/Rev.2: Preparations for the fifth session of the ministerial conference. Draft Cancún ministerial text. Second revision.*

WTO. (2003aa). *WT/GC/W/516: General Council: Poverty reduction: Sectoral initiative in favour of cotton. Wording of paragraph 27 of the revised draft Cancún ministerial text. Communication from Benin.*

WTO. (2003ab). *WT/GC/74: General Council: Statement by Benin on behalf of the four co-sponsors of the sectoral initiative in favour of cotton.*

WTO. (2003ac). *TN/MA/M/7: Negotiating Group on Market Access: Minutes of the meeting held in the Centre William Rappard on 14–16 April 2003. Chairman: Ambassador P-L. Girard (Switzerland).*

WTO. (2003ad). *TN/MA/M/8: Negotiating Group on Market Access: Minutes of the meeting held in the Centre William Rappard on 26–28 May 2003. Chairman: Ambassador P-L. Girard (Switzerland).*

WTO. (2003ae). *TN/MA/M/9: Negotiating Group on Market Access: Minutes of the meeting held in the Centre William Rappard on 9–11 July 2003. Chairman: Ambassador P-L. Girard (Switzerland).*

WTO. (2004a). *TN/MA/W/47: Negotiating Group on Market Access: Market access for non-agricultural products. Communication from Trinidad and Tobago on behalf of the ACP Group of States.*

WTO. (2004b). *WT/L/564: WTO African regional workshop on cotton. Cotonou, Republic of Benin – 23–24 March 2004. Summary conclusions.*

WTO. (2004c). *TN/MA/W/37/Add.1: Negotiating Group on Market Access: Market access for non-agricultural products. Proposal on a sectoral agreement for materials – the primary aluminum case. Communication from the United Arab Emirates. Addendum.*

WTO. (2004d). *WT/L/579: Doha work programme. Decision adopted by the General Council on 1 August 2004.*

WTO. (2004e). *TN/MA/M/13: Negotiating Group on Market Access: Minutes of the meeting held in the Centre William Rappard on 9–11 June 2004. Chairman: Ambassador S.h. Jóhannesson (Iceland).*

WTO. (2004f). *WT/DS267/R: United States – subsidies on upland cotton. Report of the panel.*

WTO. (2004g). *WT/L/587: WTO African regional workshop on cotton. Cotonou, Republic of Benin. 23–24 March 2004. Note by the Secretariat.*

WTO. (2004h). *WT/GC/83: Implementation of the development assistance aspects of the cotton-related decisions in the July package, first periodic report by the Director-General.*

WTO. (2005a). *TN/AG/SCC/R/1: Sub-Committee on Cotton: Summary report on the meeting of the Sub-Committee on Cotton held on 16 and 28 February 2005, Note by the secretariat.*

WTO. (2005b). *TN/MA/W/49: Negotiating Group on Market Access: Market access for non-agricultural products. Treatment of non-reciprocal preferences for Africa.*

WTO. (2005c). *WT/DS267/AB/R: United States – subsidies on upland cotton. Report of the Appellate Body.*

WTO. (2005d). *TN/AG/SCC/GEN/1: Sub-Committee on Cotton: Ouagadougou declaration on the cotton situation since the adoption of the July 2004 package. Communication from Burkina Faso.*

WTO. (2005e). *TN/MA/M/18: Negotiating Group on Market Access: Minutes of the meeting held in the Centre William Rappard on 14–18 March 2005. Chairman: Ambassador Jóhannesson (Iceland).*

WTO. (2005f). *WT/DSB/M/186: Dispute Settlement Body. 21. March 2005. Minutes of meeting.*

WTO. (2005g). *TN/MA/W/55: Negotiating Group on Market Access: Market access for non-agricultural products. How to create a critical mass sectoral initiative. Communication from Canada and the United States.*

WTO. (2005h). *TN/AG/SCC/R/2: Sub-Committee on Cotton: Summary report on the second meeting of the Sub-Committee on Cotton held on 22 March 2005. Note by the secretariat.*

WTO. (2005i). *TN/AG/SCC/GEN/2: Sub-Committee on Cotton: Proposed elements of modalities in connection with the sectoral initiative in favour of cotton. Communication from the African Group.*

WTO. (2005j). *TN/AG/SCC/1: Sub-Committee on Cotton: Work programme of the Sub-Committee on Cotton adopted on 22 March 2005.*

WTO. (2005k). *TN/AG/SCC/R/3: Sub-Committee on Cotton: Summary report on the third meeting of the Sub-Committee on Cotton held on 29 April 2005. Note by the secretariat.*

WTO. (2005l). *News item: WTO cotton subcommittee: Africans call for response to cotton proposal as attention turns to end-July farm paper.* https://www.wto.org/english/news_e/news05_e/cotton_22june05_e.htm.

WTO. (2005m). *TN/MA/W/58: Market access for non-agricultural products: Tariff liberalization in the chemicals sector.*

WTO. (2005n). *TN/AG/SCC/R/4: Sub-Committee on Cotton: Summary report on the fourth meeting of the Sub-Committee on Cotton held on 22 June 2005. Note by the secretariat.*

WTO. (2005o). *TN/AG/SCC/R/5: Sub-Committee on Cotton: Summary report on the fifth meeting of the Sub-Committee on Cotton held on 18 July 2005. Note by the secretariat.*

WTO. (2005p). *TN/AG/SCC/R/6: Sub-Committee on Cotton: Summary report on the sixth meeting of the Sub-Committee on Cotton held on 28 September 2005. Note by the secretariat.*

WTO. (2005q). *TN/AG/SCC/R/7: Sub-Committee on Cotton: Summary report on the seventh meeting of the Sub-Committee on Cotton held on 28 October 2005. Note by the secretariat.*

WTO. (2005r). *News item: WTO cotton sub-committee. Two cotton proposals for Hong Kong conference discussed.* https://www.wto.org/english/news_e/news05_e/cotton_18nov05_e.htm.

WTO. (2005s). *TN/MA/16: Negotiating Group on Market Access: Progress report by the chairman, Ambassador S.H. Jóhannesson, to the Trade Negotiations Committee.*

WTO. (2005t). *WT/L/641: Amendment of the TRIPS agreement. Decision of 6 December 2005.*

WTO. (2005u). *WT/MIN(05)/DEC: Ministerial conference, sixth session, Hong Kong, 13–18. December 2005: Doha work programme: Ministerial declaration. Adopted on 18 December 2005.*

WTO. (2006a). *TN/MA/W/8/Add.1: Negotiating Group on Market Access: Market access for non-agricultural products. Update on the negotiations on the sectoral tariff component. Communication from Singapore. Addendum.*

WTO. (2006b). *TN/AG/SCC/GEN/3: Sub-Committee on Cotton: Proposed elements of the reduction formula for domestic support for cotton. Communication from the co-sponsors of the sectoral initiative in favour of cotton.*

WTO. (2006c). *TN/AG/SCC/GEN/4: Sub-Committee on Cotton: Proposed modalities for cotton under the mandate of the Hong Kong ministerial decision. Communication from the co-sponsors of the sectoral initiative in favour of cotton.*

WTO. (2006d). *TN/AG/SCC/R/8: Sub-Committee on Cotton: Summary report on the eighth meeting of the Sub-Committee on Cotton held on 18 November 2005. Note by the secretariat.*

WTO. (2006e). *TN/AG/SCC/R/9: Sub-Committee on Cotton: Summary report on the ninth meeting of the Sub-Committee on Cotton held on 31 January 2006. Note by the secretariat.*

WTO. (2006f). *TN/MA/W/18/Add.13: Negotiating Group on Market Access: Market access for non-agricultural products. Progress report: Sectoral discussions on tariff elimination in the chemicals sectors. Addendum. Communication from the United States.*

WTO. (2006g). *TN/AG/SCC/W/5: Sub-Committee on Cotton: Implementation of the development assistance aspects of the cotton-related decisions in the 2004 July package. Item 2C: Coherence between trade and development aspects: Update on the development aspects of cotton. Tenth meeting of the Sub-Committee on Cotton (2 March 2006). Secretariat progress report.*

WTO. (2006h). *TN/MA/17: Negotiating Group on Market Access: Progress report by the chairman, Ambassador Don Stephenson, to the Trade Negotiations Committee.*

WTO. (2006i). *TN/MA/18: Negotiating Group on Market Access: Progress report by the chairman, Ambassador Don Stephenson, to the Trade Negotiations Committee.*

WTO. (2006j). *TN/MA/W/72: Negotiating Group on Market Access: Market access for non-agricultural products. Tariff liberalization in the chemicals sector. Communication from Canada, Norway, Singapore, Switzerland, the Separate Customs Territory of Taiwan, Penghu, Kinmen and Matsu, and the United States.*

WTO. (2006k). *TN/AG/W/3: Committee on Agriculture, Special Session Draft possible modalities on agriculture.*

WTO. (2006l). *TN/MA/W/80: Negotiating Group on Market Access: Towards NAMA modalities.*

WTO. (2006m). *TN/AG/SCC/R/11: Sub-Committee on Cotton: Summary report on the eleventh meeting of the Sub-Committee on Cotton held on 27 March 2006. Note by the secretariat.*

WTO. (2006n). *TN/AG/SCC/R/12: Sub-Committee on Cotton: Summary report on the twelfth meeting of the Sub-Committee on Cotton held on 28 April 2006. Note by the secretariat.*

WTO. (2007a). *TN/AG/SCC/W/7: Director-General's Consultative Framework Mechanism on Cotton. High-level session, 15–16 March 2007. Director-General's summary remarks.*

WTO. (2007b). *TN/AG/W/4 and Corr.1: Committee on Agriculture, Special Session Revised draft modalities for agriculture.*

WTO. (2007c). *TN/MA/W/91: Negotiating Group on Market Access: Market access for non-agricultural products. Elements of NAMA modalities that meet the ministerial directions. Communication from the ACP Group, the African Group, the NAMA-11 Group of Developing Countries, and Small and Vulnerable Economies.*

WTO. (2007d). *TN/MA/W/95: Negotiating Group on Market Access: Market access for non-agricultural products. Joint paper on revised draft modalities for non-agricultural market access (NAMA). Communication from Canada, the European Communities, Iceland, Japan, New Zealand, Norway, Switzerland, and the United States.*

WTO. (2007e). *TN/MA/W/97: Negotiating Group on Market Access: Market access for non-agricultural products. Sectoral negotiations in non-agricultural market access (NAMA). Communication from Canada; European Communities; Hong Kong, China; Iceland; Japan; Korea; New Zealand; Norway; Oman; the Separate Customs Territory of Taiwan, Penghu, Kinmen and Matsu; Singapore; Switzerland; Thailand; the United Arab Emirates; and the United States.*

WTO. (2007f). *TN/AG/SCC/W/9: Sub-Committee on Cotton: Implementation of the development assistance aspects of the cotton-related decisions in the 2004 July package and paragraph 12 of the Hong Kong ministerial declaration. Item 2C: Coherence between trade and development aspects: Update on the development aspects of cotton. Secretariat progress report.*

WTO. (2007g). *WT/DS267/RW: United States – subsidies on upland cotton. Recourse to Article 21.5 of the DSU by Brazil. Report of the panel.*

WTO. (2008a). *WT/DS267/AB/RW: United States – subsidies on upland cotton. Recourse to Article 21.5 of the DSU by Brazil. Report of the Appellate Body.*

WTO. (2008b). *TN/MA/W/103/Rev.2: Negotiating Group on Market Access: Draft modalities for non-agricultural market access. Third revision.*

WTO. (2008c). *JOB(08)/89: Negotiating Group on Market Access: Market access for non-agricultural products. NAMA-11 ministerial communiqué. 20 July 2008, Geneva. Communication from the NAMA-11 Group of Developing Countries.*

WTO. (2008d). *TN/MA/W/108: Negotiating Group on Market Access: Market access for non-agricultural products. Sectoral negotiations. Communication from the NAMA-11 Group of Developing Countries.*

WTO. (2008e). *TN/MA/W/109: Negotiating Group on Market Access: Market access for non-agricultural products. Communication from Argentina.*

WTO. (2008f). *TN/AG/W/4/Rev.4: Committee on Agriculture, Special Session Revised draft modalities for agriculture.*

WTO. (2008g). *TN/MA/W/103/Rev.3: Negotiating Group on Market Access: Fourth revision of draft modalities for non-agricultural market access.*

WTO. (2008h). *TN/AG/SCC/W/10: Sub-Committee on Cotton: Implementation of the development assistance aspects of the cotton-related decisions in the 2004 July package and paragraph 12 of the Hong Kong ministerial declaration. Item 2C – coherence between trade and development aspects: Update on the development aspects of cotton. Secretariat progress report.*

WTO. (2009a). *TN/AG/SCC/W/11: Sub-Committee on Cotton: Implementation of the development assistance aspects of the cotton-related decisions in the 2004 July package and paragraph 12 of the Hong Kong ministerial declaration. Item*

2C – *coherence between trade and development aspects: Update on the development aspects of cotton. Secretariat progress report.*

WTO. (2009b). *TN/AG/SCC/GEN/10: Sub-Committee on Cotton: Director-General's Consultative Framework Mechanism on Cotton. Communication from Burkina Faso.*

WTO. (2010a). *TN/MA/22: Negotiating Group on Market Access: Report by the chairman, Ambassador Luzius Wasescha, to the Trade Negotiations Committee for the purpose of the TNC stocktaking exercise.*

WTO. (2010b). *TN/AG/SCC/W/12: Sub-Committee on Cotton: Implementation of the development assistance aspects of the cotton-related decisions in the 2004 July package and paragraph 12 of the Hong Kong ministerial declaration. Item 2C – coherence between trade and development aspects: Update on the development aspects of cotton. Secretariat progress report.*

WTO. (2010c). *WT/DS267/45: United States – subsidies on upland cotton. Joint communication from Brazil and the United States.*

WTO. (2011a). *TN/C/14: Report by the Director-General on his consultations on NAMA sectoral negotiations.*

WTO. (2011b). *TN/MA/W/103/Rev.3/Add.1: Negotiating Group on Market Access: Textual report by the chairman, Ambassador Luzius Wasescha, on the state of play of the NAMA negotiations. Addendum.*

WTO. (2011c). *TN/AG/SCC/W/14: Sub-Committee on Cotton: Implementation of the development assistance aspects of the cotton-related decisions in the 2004 July package and paragraph 12 of the Hong Kong ministerial declaration. Item 2C – coherence between trade and development aspects: Update on the development aspects of cotton. Secretariat progress report.*

WTO. (2011d). *WT/MIN(11)/11: Ministerial conference, eighth session, Geneva, 15–17 December 2011: Chairman's concluding statement.*

WTO. (2012). *WT/MIN(11)/W/2: Ministerial conference, eighth session, Geneva, 15–17 December 2011: Elements for political guidance.*

WTO. (2013a). *TN/AG/GEN/33: WTO negotiations on agriculture. Communication from the co-sponsors of the sectoral initiative in favour of cotton. Draft decision on cotton.*

WTO. (2013b). *WT/MIN(13)/40: Ministerial conference, ninth session, Bali, 3–6 December 2013: Export competition. Ministerial decision of 7 December 2013.*

WTO. (2013c). *WT/MIN(13)/41: Ministerial conference, ninth session, Bali, 3–6 December 2013: Cotton. Ministerial decision of 7 December 2013.*

WTO. (2013d). *WT/MIN(13)/44: Ministerial conference, ninth session, Bali, 3–6 December 2013: Duty free and quota free (DFQF) market access for least-developed countries. Ministerial decision of 7 December 2013.*

WTO. (2014a). *WT/DS267/46: United States – subsidies on upland cotton. Notification of a mutually agreed solution.*

WTO. (2014b). *Dispute settlement: Dispute DS267. United States — subsidies on upland cotton,* 30 October. http://www.wto.org/english/tratop_e/dispu_e/cases_e/ds267_e.htm.

WTO. (2015a). *WT/MIN(15)/45: Ministerial conference, tenth session, Nairobi, 15–18 December 2015: Export competition. Ministerial decision of 19 December 2015.*

WTO. (2015b). *WT/MIN(15)/46: Ministerial conference, tenth session, Nairobi, 15–18 December 2015: Cotton. Ministerial decision of 19 December 2015.*

WTO (2017a). *TN/AG/GEN/46: WTO Negotiations on agriculture. Communication from the co-sponsors of the sectoral initiative in favor of cotton.*

WTO. (2017b). *News item: WTO and ITC launch cotton portal to enhance transparency and support development.* https://www.wto.org/english/news_e/news17_e/igo_11dec17_e.htm.

WTO. (2018). *JOB/AG/144: Sub-Committee on Cotton: The situation in cotton. Communication from the United States of America.*

WTO. (2019a). *Development: Geneva week: WTO organizes "Geneva weeks" for non-resident delegations.* https://www.wto.org/english/tratop_e/devel_e/genwk_e.htm.

WTO. (2019b). *WT/GC/W/765/Rev.2: The continued relevance of special and differential treatment in favor of developing members to promote development and ensure inclusiveness. Communication from China, India, South Africa, and the Bolivian Republic of Venezuela, Lao People's Democratic Republic, Plurinational State of Bolivia, Kenya, Cuba, Central African Republic, and Pakistan.*

WTO. (2019c). *TN/AG/GEN/49: Agricultural negotiations at the WTO. Communication by the co-sponsors of the sectoral initiative on cotton.*

WTO. (2019d). *TN/AG/GEN/49/Rev. 1: Agricultural negotiations at the WTO. Communication by the co-sponsors of the sectoral initiative on cotton. Revision.*

WTO. (2019e). *WT/GC/W/764/Rev.1: General Council, 9–11 December 2019: Draft General Council decision. Procedures to strengthen the negotiating function of the WTO. Revision*

WTO. (2019f). *News item: Agriculture meeting marks "turning point" as negotiations enter decisive stage, chair says.* https://www.wto.org/english/news_e/news19_e/agri_03dec19_e.htm.

WTO. (2020a). *WTO directory* (Data obtained from the WTO secretariat).

WTO. (2020b). *News item: DG Azevêdo announces he will step down on 31 August.* https://www.wto.org/english/news_e/news20_e/dgra_14may20_e.htm.

WTO. (2020c). *IP/C/W/669: Council for Trade-Related Aspects of Intellectual Property Rights: Waiver from certain provisions of the TRIPS agreement for the prevention, containment, and treatment of COVID-19. Communication from India and South Africa.*

WTO. (2021a). *Speeches: DG Okonjo-Iweala: WTO can deliver results if members "accept we can do things differently."* https://www.wto.org/english/news_e/spno_e/spno1_e.htm.

WTO. (2021b). *News item: General Council: DG Okonjo-Iweala underlines urgent need to address equitable access to vaccines.* https://www.wto.org/english/news_e/news21_e/gc_05may21_e.htm.

WTO. (2021c). *News item: General Council chair briefs members on work towards MC12 outcome document.* https://www.wto.org/english/news_e/news21_e/gc_07oct21_e.htm.

WTO. (2021d). *News item: Trade and development: "Development issues should be at the heart of work at the WTO" – DG Okonjo-Iweala.* https://www.wto.org/english/news_e/news21_e/devel_10nov21_e.htm.

WTO. (2022a). *Data portal.* https://timeseries.wto.org.

WTO. (2022b). *Ministerial conferences: Twelfth WTO ministerial conference.* Geneva. https://www.wto.org/english/thewto_e/minist_e/mc12_e/mc12_e.htm.

WTO. (2022c). *Doha Development Agenda: The Trade Negotiations Committee.* http://www.wto.org/english/tratop_e/dda_e/tnc_e.htm.

WTO. (2022d). *Trade-related technical assistance: Trainee programmes and internships.* http://www.wto.org/english/tratop_e/devel_e/train_e/trainee_programmes_e.htm#internship.

WTO. (2022e). *Understanding the WTO: The organization: Members and observers.* http://www.wto.org/english/thewto_e/whatis_e/tif_e/org6_e.htm.

WTO. (2022f). *Understanding the WTO: The organization: WTO organization chart.* https://www.wto.org/english/thewto_e/whatis_e/tif_e/org2_e.htm.

WTO. (2022g). *WTO "cotton days."* www.wto.org/cottondays.

WTO. (2022h). *WTO Director-General Ngozi Okonjo-Iweala.* https://www.wto.org/english/thewto_e/dg_e/dg_e.htm.

WTO. (2022i). *WT/GC/W/471: General Council: Preparatory process in Geneva and negotiating procedure at the ministerial conferences. Communication from Cuba, Dominican Republic, Egypt, Honduras, India, Indonesia, Jamaica, Kenya, Malaysia, Mauritius, Pakistan, Sri Lanka, Tanzania, Uganda, and Zimbabwe.*

WTO. (2022j). *News item: TRIPS Council hears initial reactions to Quad's outcome document on IP Covid-19 response.* https://www.wto.org/english/news_e/news22_e/trip_06may22_e.htm.

WTO. (2022k). *WT/MIN(22)/W/19: Ministerial conference, twelfth session, Geneva, 12–15 June 2022: Draft ministerial decision on agriculture.*

WTO. (2022l). *Speeches: DG Okonjo-Iweala: MC12 opening sessions: Opening remarks by the Director-General.* Geneva. https://www.wto.org/english/news_e/spno_e/spno26_e.htm.

WTO. (2022m). *WT/MIN(22)/30; WT/L/1141: Ministerial decision on the TRIPS agreement. Adopted on 17 June 2022.*

Young, I.M. (1996). Communication and the other: Beyond deliberative democracy. In S. Benhabib (Ed.), *Democracy and difference: Contesting the boundaries of the political* (pp. 120–35). Princeton University Press.

Young, I.M. (2001). Activist challenges to deliberative democracy. *Political Theory, 29*(5), 670–90.

Young, I.M. (2002). *Inclusion and democracy.* Oxford University Press.

Yu, P.K. (2024). The COVID-19 TRIPS waiver and the WTO ministerial decision. In J. Schovsbo (Ed.), *Intellectual Property Rights in times of crisis* (pp. 1–25). Edward Elgar.

Zangl, B., & Zürn, M. (1996). Argumentatives Handeln bei internationalen Verhandlungen: Moderate Anmerkungen zur post-realistischen Debatte. *Zeitschrift für Internationale Beziehungen, 3*(2), 341–66.

Ziai, A. (2004a). *Entwicklung als Ideologie? Das klassische Entwicklungsparadigma und die Post-Development-Kritik. Ein Beitrag zur Analyse des Entwicklungsdiskurses.* (Schriften des Deutschen Übersee-Instituts Hamburg, Nr. 61). DÜI.

Ziai, A. (2004b). Zur Ordnung und Transformation des Entwicklungsdiskurses. In S. Kollmann & K. Schödel (Eds.), *PostModerne De/Konstruktionen: Ethik, Politik und Kultur am Ende einer Epoche* (pp. 157–69). Lit Verlag.

Index